ALMOST HOME

The Story of Otto Gruenbaum,
Pianist and Ritchie Boy

By

Irene Wittig

Copyright 2022 Irene Wittig

ISBN 9798351702803

TABLE OF CONTENTS

AUTHOR'S NOTE……………………………………………..4

PREFACE ……………………………………………………….5

I — 1918 to 1942 ……………………………………..6

II —1942 t0 1945……………………………………………..24

III —18 November 1945……………………………………..45

IV —The Search for Answers……………………………….54

APPENDIX A - Otto's Letters……………………………….71

APPENDIX B - Official documents, records, and letters…………..129

APPENDIX C - Otto's life in music ………………………………152

APPENDIX D - Notes on the Ritchie Boys, IPW teams
                and interrogations………..…………………….177

APPENDIX E - Letters, documents, interviews etc. of family
                and friends…………………………………..270

APPENDIX F - Relevant information on Austria………………..324

AUTHOR'S NOTE

I was born during the war ten days after the liberation of Rome. World War II was always in the background, a setting against which morality, justice, kindness, loyalty, good luck and bad were discussed and measured. All my parents' and grandmother's friends were fellow Europeans displaced by war, most of them Jewish. A few were Concentration Camp survivors. Unlike immigrants who'd left Europe for a better life in the U.S., these immigrants had been forced to give up lives they'd loved. When they were together, they'd reminisce and listen to familiar songs, nostalgic for the worlds they'd once known, and loved, though they knew those worlds had been irredeemably broken. There was no going back. Yet they were resilient. With shared humor about their situations, they went on to build new lives. For Jews especially, humor had long been a weapon against the fates, a way to mock the absurdities of life. "*Oppressed people tend to be witty,*" Saul Bellow once said.

I listened to their stories and laughed at their jokes. I read about the war, watched movies about the war, and wondered if I'd have had the strength they had.

I took piano lessons at the New York College of Music, where Otto's old teacher from Vienna, Prof. Weschler, still taught and where Otto received his degree. My grandmother practiced with me, playing the left hand, while I played the right, something she probably had not done when Otto was a child and life was so different. Sadly, as much as I enjoyed playing, I did not have his talent.

Underneath it all, I missed the uncle I would never know.

As I had my mother's and grandmother's papers, as well as their memories, it was only natural for me to be the family historian. Some years ago I put these memories and relevant photographs into a family history book for my children and grandchildren, although the puzzle of Otto's death remained unanswered.

With the unending support and help of my husband, I have written this book as my way of paying tribute to my uncle.

I have not solved the puzzle of his death, but I have learned many things along the way—especially with the generous help of Dan Gross, Florian Trussing, Beverley Eddy, helpful archivists at the National Archives, the Library of Congress, the ever-expanding ability to do research online.

PREFACE

It was in Rome on the 5th of October 1945 that my mother saw her brother for the first time since she left Vienna seven years earlier. He looked older, and wore the same uniform as the GIs she'd been a translator for since Rome's liberation. Otto's curly brown hair was shorter than she remembered, but his voice was the same, and his soulful brown eyes filled with emotion as he held the niece he'd been waiting months to meet. Sixty years later, my mother still remembered everything about that one short day.

My grandmother kept the telegram we sent. She kept everything to do with Otto, but things get lost when you move, and when you die. So now I only have what's left. With those pieces of paper and my own research, plus memories of the stories I heard over the years, I will tell you about the uncle I never knew but came to love.

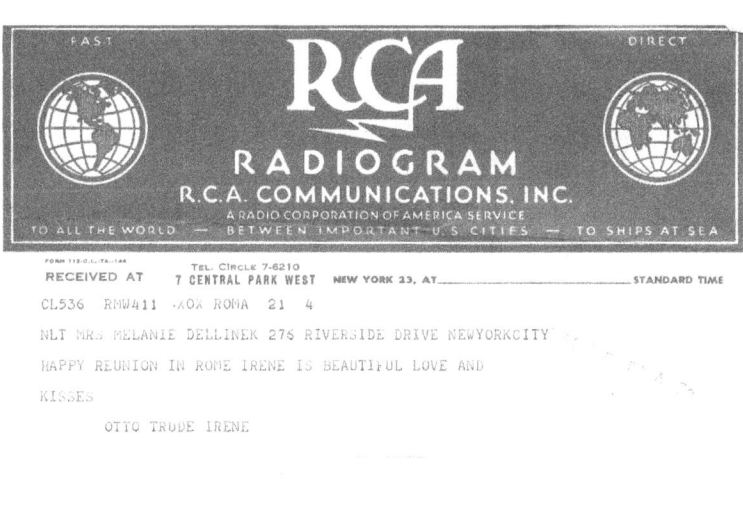

I

1918-1942

Otto was born Otto Karl Grünbaum on August 18, 1918 in Vienna, once the center of an empire whose archduke was, for two hundred and fifty years, the Holy Roman Emperor. At the time of Otto's birth, the multi-ethnic Austro-Hungarian Empire was still at war, but within months the Empire would be dead and Vienna transformed into the capitol of a small, landlocked republic called Austria. Yet, in many ways it would remain, despite its economic troubles, a city that valued culture, and *Lebenskunst*—the art of living and surviving changing rulers and times. The same songs would be sung, the same pastries eaten, the same wine drunk. With the Great War at an end, no one imagined another would come a mere two decades later.

Otto was named for his father Otto and his father's beloved younger brother Karl, who was a prisoner-of-war somewhere in the East at the time, and would not return home until 1922.

Otto was the second child of a Jewish father and a Catholic mother. His sister Trude had been born only seventeen months earlier..

Although aware of Austria's deep-seated anti-Semitism and Vienna's repeated election of its anti-Semitic mayor Karl Lueger, Otto's father was a proud Austrian, loyal to the Emperor who had bestowed civil rights on the Empire's Jewish population in the mid 19th century. Both Otto and his brother Karl served in the Imperial Army during the Great War.

During Kaiser Franz Josef's regime, Jews contributed enormously to Austrian culture, intellectual and business life, and even sports. By the 1930's, two-hundred thousand Jews lived in Vienna, and made up 45% of the city's university faculty and 51% of the city's doctors.

The post-war years saw Austria in financial turmoil. Companies were established, went under, and re-established. Resilience became a necessity. Otto's father left his uncle's well-established and renowned fashion business to found his own. Early bankruptcy was to be repeated later, but for some years, the Grünbaum were financially comfortable as Otto Grünbaum's fur and fashion store became noted for its elegance, even receiving mention in the respected Baedeker Travel Guide. Encouraged by his success, Otto Grünbaum soon opened a branch in the popular Czech spa town of Karlsbad, putting his brother Karl in charge.

Posters for the store in 1920 by artist Hans Neumann
(One is above; the second on the following page)

Both posters are now in Vienna's Museum of Applied Arts.

The Grünbaums and their friends loved their city and the cultural richness it offered them. Music more than anything was a symbol of that. Concerts and operas were attended regularly by young and old whether in box seats or standing-room. Opera singers were the rock stars of the period. It was in this period that young Otto and his sister Trude spent their early years. Finances and politics were not discussed at home. Otto and Trude remained unaware of the more challenging times their parents were soon to face.

*Otto's parents, Otto and Melanie Grünbaum
and their apartment in the Third District of Vienna (Ungargasse 39)*

Above: carriage ride to celebrate Otto's birthday
Below: a nursery school excursion with curly-haired Otto on far right of first row, and Trude behind him, with a large bow in her hair.

Otto and Trude

Otto was a lively, affectionate child that delighted everyone, His sister, Trude adored him unconditionally as did their cousins Emmy and Helly, seen in the photos below.

Otto and Trude attended the children's music conservatory from the age of six, where they were introduced to music and dancing.

When Trude began piano lessons, she noticed that her little brother was able to play all her pieces without lessons. They made a deal. Otto would practice for her and she would do his homework. This ruse lasted a year but was finally discovered when Trude's piano teacher asked to speak to her mother.

"Trude is not making any progress," she said. "You must make her practice more."

"But I do! She practices every day. I can hear her from my room…oh, I see."

After some discussion, and to the delight of both children, it was decided that Otto would take piano lessons and Trude would concentrate on her dancing. Otto learned so quickly that he was soon entertaining guests at family parties, replacing Trude, who had had the more tiresome job of winding up the phonograph.

Otto and Trude continued at the children's conservatory as they went on to high school (he to the Stubenbastei *Gymnasium,* and she to the Albertgasse *Gymnasium)* after which they were both accepted into the Vienna Music Conservatory—Otto for piano and conducting, and Trude for voice and dance.

Brother and sister were very close and shared optimistic, sunny, and fun-loving personalities. Trude was the more mischievous, but Otto was known for his stubbornness

Otto age 10

when it came to things he didn't like. As a child he refused to eat asparagus, no matter his mother's entreaties. In *Gymnasium*, he risked everything when—in his final *Matura* exam in biology—he was asked to describe what he knew about the lilac plant. "Nothing" he said calmly. "It doesn't interest me." After some discussion, he was allowed to retake the exam a month later. Again, he was asked what he knew about the lilac plant. "Nothing," he replied again. "It still does not interest me." Because his other grades were excellent, and his future as pianist looked so promising, he was allowed to graduate,

Both Otto and his sister were passionate about what they wanted to do with their lives. For Trude it was the theatre, for Otto the piano. Otto's exceptional gift for music was soon recognized and he began giving concerts when he was fourteen. When he appeared as an interlude pianist for Vienna State Opera's soprano Elizabeth Schumann, he so impressed her that he became her accompanist in all her concerts. Soon he even performed outside of Vienna. Bruno Walter, conductor of the Vienna Philharmonic, wrote a reference for him. His future looked bright.

As for other business owners in Europe and America at the time, the Grünbaums' financial challenges began to surface in the late 1920s, leading to bankruptcy in the 1930's and a move for the Grünbaum store from the well-respected address Am Kohlmarkt to Johannesgasse. It is because of these challenges that the father's gambling became an added burden for the family rather than a wished-for solution.

The 1930s also saw the beginning of political changes that would convulse the Grünbaums, their Jewish friends, their beloved city, and soon the whole world.

In 1932, Conservative Catholic Engelbert Dollfuss became Chancellor of Austria. Inspired by Mussolini's Italian Fascism, he opposed Austrian Nazism and resisted pressure from Germany's National Socialists as Hitler became chancellor of Germany in 1933. Despite the popularity of Socialist policies in Vienna, Dollfuss quickly appointed an anti-Socialist cabinet and banned both the Communist and the Austrian Nazi parties. In early 1933, he dissolved Parliament and assumed dictatorial powers.

Otto at age 15

Happy days—Otto in the country with his mother and sister in 1936

February 1934, events escalated into a brief but decisive civil-war in which Austro-Fascism won a bloody victory. Dollfuss immediately banned the Social Democratic Party and all labor unions; and in May, with a new constitution, and backed by the Catholic Church, he swept away the last remnants of democracy and the Austrian Republic.

In July 1934, under the influence of Nazi Germany, Austrian Nazis assassinated Dollfuss, but their plan to form a new government failed. The assassins were arrested and executed, and a less dictatorial Kurt von Schuschnigg became the new chancellor.

Although Otto and Trude had both been christened Protestants, as a compromise for their Jewish father and Catholic mother, religion never played a great part in their upbringing. Their friends were mostly but not exclusively Jewish, with some of their friends also being from religiously mixed families.

In her interview with the U.S. Holocaust Memorial Museum, Trude tells of the anti-Semitism she remembers experiencing in school, especially at the hands of Inge Seyss-Inquart, who sat next to her in class. Inge's father, later chancellor, was an unwavering anti-Semite who was convicted of war crimes in Nuremberg and executed. [Trude's complete interview is in Appendix E].

Otto and Trude's parents separated in 1935, and divorced in 1937. The cause was financial instability, and their mother Melanie soon married Josef Jellinek, also Jewish, who lived upstairs. Josef and his family had been close friends for many years. Otto's father appears to have encouraged the marriage as a way for Melanie to avoid poverty, and they remained on good terms even after the divorce.

Trude began working in the theatre in 1934 with the famous cabaret entertainer, Fritz Grünbaum. To avoid confusion, she took the stage name of Trude Hermann. Some of her fellow actors had come from Germany and told disturbing stories of what was happening there to Jews and dissidents. One of them had been held for a few months in Dachau, the first concentration camp set up by the Nazis. Trude feared those policies would soon spread to Austria. In 1937, she applied for a dancing engagement in Sudetenland, but once they learned her real surname they would not hire her. The same thing happened with a theatre in Linz. Her agent said it was unlikely that with her Jewish surname she would get any engagement in a German-speaking country and suggested she go to Italy. Now convinced that Nazi policies would soon spread to Austria, Trude accepted a contract to dance in a theatre in Milan. Other far-sighted Viennese had also begun leaving, emigrating to whatever country would give them a visa. One cousin and his wife left for Uruguay. A few managed to obtain work as domestics in England.

Unlike his sister, Otto was focused on his music, still found life pleasant, and thought "it can't happen here."

In February 1938, Dollfuss' successor Kurt Schuschnigg crossed the border to Germany hoping for a peaceful meeting with Hitler but encountered only threats. Thinking appeasement would prevent Germany's invasion, he agreed to a cascade of capitulations to the Nazi chancellor.

In March 11th, Schuschnigg warned Austrian citizens not to spill German blood by taking arms against the Wehrmacht. When he began talks with Social Democrats to win their support, there was a glimmer of hope that resistance was still possible, but a furious Hitler called for his resignation. With France and Britain unwilling to come to Austria's assistance, Schuschnigg resigned that very evening.

On March 12th, Schuschnigg was arrested and Seyss-Inquart was appointed chancellor.

On March 13th, Hitler and his forces entered Linz, his childhood home, and he announced that the Anschluss was complete. Austria was annexed to the greater German Reich and no longer existed as an independent republic. This was in direct violation of the Treaty-of-Saint-Germain-en-Laye of 1919, which prohibited such a union. Ecstatic at his achievement, Hitler and his forces marched into Vienna and were greeted with thundering enthusiasm.

Otto's father was in Switzerland on business and asked for asylum. He was denied. Fluent in French he secretly entered France and never returned to Vienna. His brother Karl remained in Vienna. With the help of his Catholic wife, who brought food every night, he and two other men survived by hiding in a coal cellar for more than two years.

Members of the Catholic side of Otto and Trude's family went along with the new regime, some more enthusiastically than others.

When Trude's year in Milan was completed, she called her mother, to tell her she was coming, but her mother warned her not to return. It was too dangerous. So Trude renewed her contract with the theatre in Milan.

"The German embassy came to the theater, took all our passports away because we were thirty girls from Vienna," Trude told her Holocaust Museum interviewer. *"They told us we had to go to the consulate and when we were there they said we had to go to vote on the torpedo boat "Wolf" which was in Genoa."*

She did not want to go but a sympathetic consul or attaché persuaded her to vote in the plebiscite to accept Hitler's Anschluss, despite her intention not to. He pointed out that she could not stop Hitler, but if she refused, he would have to stamp her passport with a "J" for "Jude" (Jew) . So she agreed, and without the "J," had at least a chance for safety.

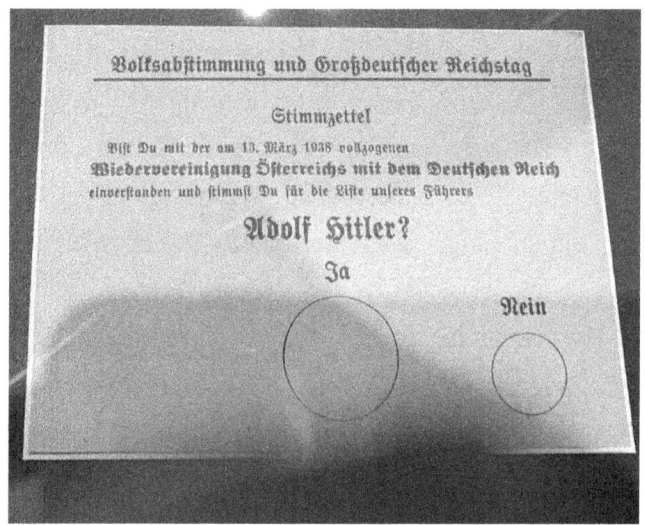

Otto, was still in Vienna when Hitler marched in and announced the Anschluss. A mass-hysteria of anti-Semitism gripped the country and Otto was expelled from the Vienna Conservatory.

"Overnight, Vienna became a city of terror," Otto said when interviewed by the Air Force Paper THE BEAM on October 13, 1943. *"Friends I had grown up with began to shun me. Everyone had to wear the Swastika to show they were friendly toward the occupying Germans. Naturally, I didn't. One night, I was walking along when two men stopped me and ordered me to go with them. They took me to a cellar where they had other people mopping and cleaning.*

"They told me to wait my turn to work. In the confusion I escaped. I realized then that if I stayed in Vienna, I probably would be shipped to a German concentration camp."

With no money to obtain an exit visa, Otto asked permission to enter The Eugène Ysaÿe Music Competition [now known as the Queen Elizabeth Competition] in Brussels in May 1938, and was granted a one-time travel permit from Vienna to Brussels and back.

"It was just an excuse to get out of Austria. I wanted to get to Paris, where I thought I would be safe."

When he reached Brussels the Belgians would not let him play because for them Otto was German. He stayed in Brussels for a month, hoping in vain that they would grant him an extension to his visa. He tried to go to France but could not obtain a visa, so —at his mother's suggestion—his sister wrote a letter from Italy saying she was very ill and he should come immediately. The Italian Consulate granted him a permit to enter Italy and he bought a ticket.

"When the train reached France, I got off and went to Paris and told the police I was a refugee. They told me I could stay a week. Then they extended it to two weeks, a month, two months. I stayed fourteen months. Every week or so I would have to go to the police for another extension."

Otto wasn't allowed to work. His father gave him what money he could, allowing Otto to continue his piano studies.

"Between that and being busy visiting officials, I had little time for other things," Otto said.

Through a Viennese friend now in New York, Otto became acquainted with a wealthy New York physician who had already financed the escape of fifty refugees to the United States. With the benefactor's affidavit that Otto would not need public support, and—according to his mother—a good word from famed violinist Fritz Kreisler, Otto was able to obtain a student visa. With that, and with money his father was able to give him, Otto booked a passage on the French ocean liner SS Champlain, sailing from LeHavre on August 11, 1939 just twenty-one days before Germany invaded Poland.

Otto's sister Trude, working in Italy, took a dancing engagement in Ethiopia and Eritrea. The troupe left by ship on 1 September 1939, the day Germany invaded Poland. Trude would spend the next few months on tour, before returning to Italy. For the next few years, she traveled frequently, dancing in various cities in Italy, but always with Rome as her home base.

Meanwhile, Otto's mother and her husband, Josef Jellinek, had left Vienna for Prague, moving on to Lyon after a year. There they were finally awarded a visa to the United States, traveling via Spain, Portugal, Casablanca and Cuba, and arriving In New

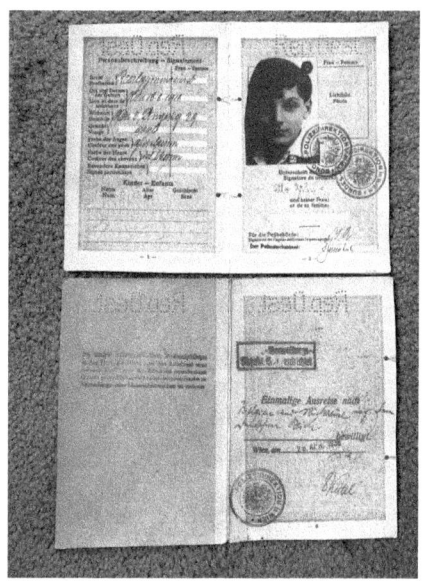

Otto's passport with a one-time exit permit to allow him to go to Belgium and return to the Reich

York City by ship in 1941. Many tears of joy were shed when Otto was reunited with his mother.

After his arrival in New York, Otto had rested a while on a farm but soon began to work and earn his own way by giving piano lessons. Thanks to the generosity of a distant relative then also living in New York, he was able to continue his own piano studies with the renowned pianist Arthur Schnabel. Soon Otto was playing on the concert stage, giving recitals at Carnegie Chamber Music Hall and Town Hall in New York, as well as on smaller stages and for various refugee groups. As an accompanist, he performed in Detroit, Buffalo, Philadelphia and other cities. He earned enough to be able to send money regularly to his father, until he lost contact with him in May 1941.

Otto's father left Paris when the Germans approached and went south to Nice, in Vichy France. At some point—probably in May, when he and his son lost contact—he was caught in Monaco with false papers, arrested and imprisoned for fourteen months by the French. He was lucky to escape the Gestapo. Old clients of his, Lord Henry and Caroline Paulet, the Marquess and Marchioness of Winchester, helped him get out of prison and hid him in their home for the duration of the war. [When he died at the age of 99 in 1962, Lord Henry was the oldest ever member of the House of Lords.]

In New York, Otto had not only been reunited with his mother, but also with friends from Vienna—most significantly, his best friend from school, Kurt Elias, and Susanne Hohenberg, a fellow pianist, whom he married in February 1942 with Kurt as best man.

Kurt, in remembrances he wrote when he was in his nineties, described Otto this way: "*a budding promising pianist who once even composed a song for me. He was a loving, soft-hearted gentle soul.*" He also mentioned musical evenings spent with them, and another friend, Peter Lynn, "*with Susi accompanying or all of us singing Lieder and parts of Opera (usually Mozart). Peter Lynn is and was a veritable encyclopedia of especially operatic music.*"

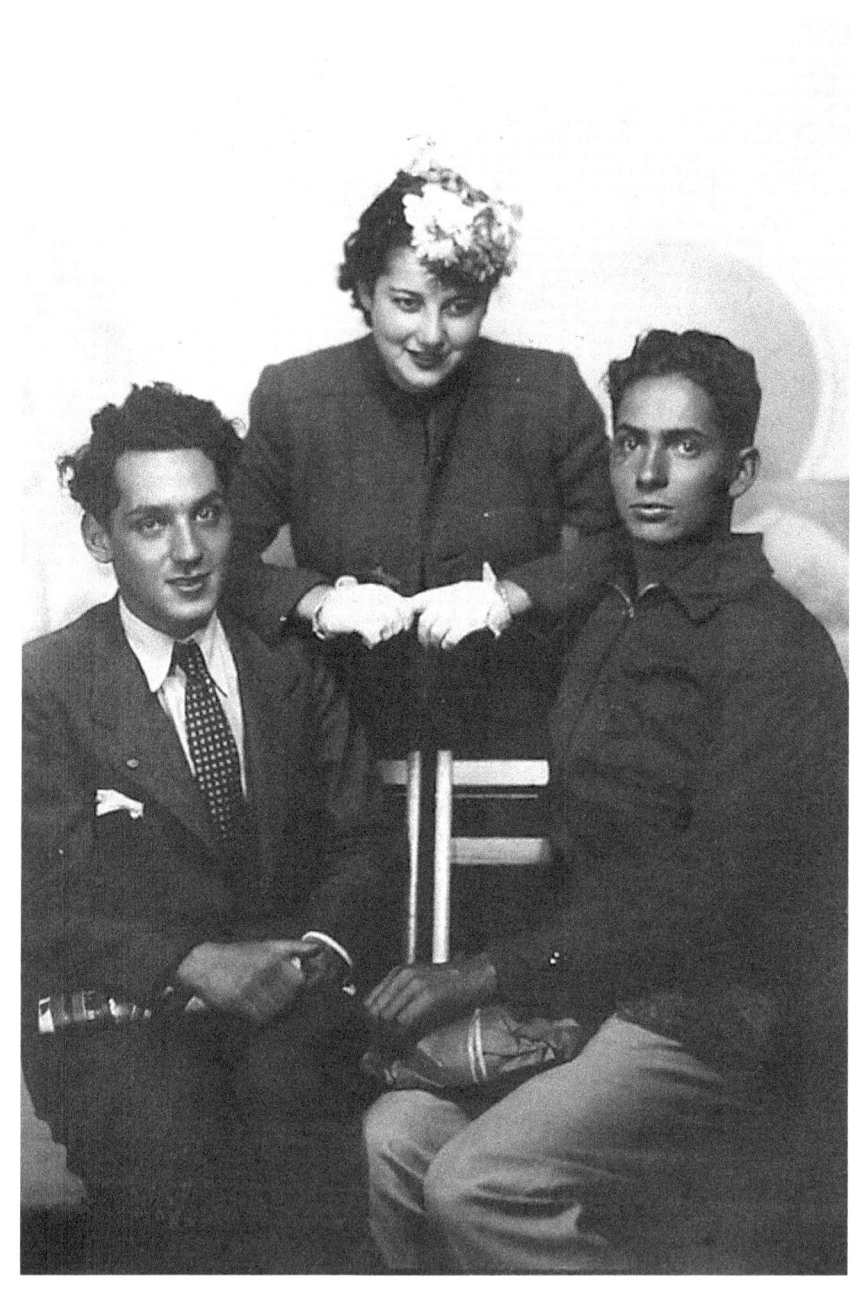

Otto and Susi's wedding day - with Otto on the left and Kurt on the right.

II

1942-1945

Once his student visa expired, Otto was given a choice between deportation or enlistment in the Army. The choice was easy, and on 12 October 1942 he was inducted into the U.S. Army in St. Louis as a private, and the spelling of his name was changed from Grünbaum to Gruenbaum.

After basic training, he was stationed in the Medical Detachment at Goldsboro, North Carolina, where he was assigned to duty as a ward boy, scrubbing floors, taking temperatures and pulses and making himself generally useful around the hospital ward.

In January 1943, he was transferred to Atlantic City where he served as a Lab Technician, but was also often called upon to play the piano at USO events. He was guest soloist when the Army Air Force Band performed at the Atlantic City Convention Hall.

On 25 March 1943, Otto became a naturalized citizen.

Four months later, he was promoted to the rank of T-5, or Technician Fifth Grade, equivalent to Corporal.

"I have no regrets," Otto told the Air Force paper THE BEAM in the October 1943 interview. "*It is too bad that I can't think of Vienna now with happiness. My feeling[s] there before I left had too much fear and rage and helplessness in them. Being a soldier in the American Army means much to me, probably more than to a lot of Americans.*" Hopeful about resuming his musical career after the war, he said, "*All my experiences will give me new impressions that can only be helpful to me later on.*"

THE BEAM published an official U.S. Army photo of Otto with the following caption:

> **An Undaunted Artist:** Cpl. Otto Gruenbaum, soldier-pianist stationed at the England General Hospital is an example to his comrades and civilians alike in courage and fortitude.

In June 1942, the U.S. Army established a Military Intelligence Training Camp (MITC) at Camp Ritchie in Maryland. Recognizing the urgent need for servicemen with language skills, a call was made to military camps around the country. Recent immigrants, academics and people who traveled or lived abroad and were fluent in German, French, Italian, Japanese and other languages, were pulled from their units and sent to Camp Ritchie without explanation. From the beginning, an air of secrecy was mandated for all its activities. Military and support personnel were told not to identify themselves, as being connected with intelligence—not even to their families. Independence was encouraged as much as teamwork. Many were born or had lived in other countries and understood the culture and thinking of the countries they would be fighting. A high number were German speaking. 19% were Germans or Austrian, and 19.7% were Jewish, most of them refugees. Their knowledge of the mindset of German soldiers was especially valuable.

Otto was transferred to Camp Ritchie in May of 1944 for eight weeks of intensive training. He was identified as SCSU (Service Command Service Unit) for promising soldiers with high scholastic records; and received specialized training as Interrogator of Prisoner of War (IPW). Training changed from one class to another as needs changed, but generally all classes included training in interrogation of enemy prisoners of war; identification and translation of documents; aerial photo identification; military intelligence interpreters; terrain intelligence; and signal intelligence.

In the student assessment logbooks, Otto was described as: "**Highly intelligent man, but slightly soft. German excellent. Lacks military bearing. Young and slightly immature. Average interrogations.**" Not a surprising description for someone who had never imagined he'd be drawn into war as a soldier.

Otto graduated in August 1944 as a member of Class 20 and was classified as German Linguist 1. In September 1944 he was promoted to T/3, or Staff Sergeant.

In all, 11,637 "Ritchie Boys" graduated (out of 15,253 originally enrolled), comprising 3,368 officers and 8,269 enlisted men. 80% served overseas. According to Brig. Gen. Conrad's official report, "**About 62% of all Combat Intelligence gathered in the European Theater of Operations, was the product of Military Intelligence Service Specialist Teams.**"

In September, Otto was released from Camp Ritchie and on 4 October 1944 he and his fellow Ritchie Boys embarked on the troopship USS New Amsterdam to Glasgow. He was promoted to Master Sergeant, and received additional training in England.

Otto was assigned to IPW (Interrogation Prisoner of War) Team 120. The Officer in Charge was Capt. Robert W. Andrae. Fellow team members were Wolf Goeltzer, Sol Neugeboren, and Joseph M. Kramer (not a Ritchie Boy).

In a report on IPW Team 120 I found at the National Archives in College Park, Maryland, were these notes:

"Initially attached to the Seventh U.S. Army 12 November 1944. Attached to the 14th Armored Division on 6 January 1945. Team worked half at the division cage, half at Combat Command level. One of the more unusual assignments was the preparation and delivery of propaganda broadcasts addressed to the 47th Volks-Grenadier Division along the Moder River Line. While at Steinfeld, much work was done in the study of the Siegried Line defenses.

At Bouxviller, Alsace, in January 1945, the Officer-in-Charge says that three members of his team innocently enough nearly caused the arrest of the entire team. "Three members of the team went up to a house to secure quarters. The men, feeling satisfied that they had been successful in obtaining quarters in a crowded town, returned to the Cage, The woman of the house, being so pleased that she had American soldiers who spoke German, told her friends that she had made quarters for American soldiers who spoke German as well as anyone. Friend told friend, and when the interrogators arrived at the house in the evening, they found three FFI men (French resistance forces, known as French Forces of the Interior), and two MPs waiting to arrest them as saboteurs. Finally the CIC of the team arrived, surprised to find his men with their hands up. After a brief explanation to the MPs, the interrogators were freed."

An example of novelty and surprise in capturing POWs was described as follows:

"One of the interrogators developed a novel means of capturing by-passed German soldiers albeit a rather uncertain method. In Wiesthal, Germany, an interrogator went into the woods blowing a whistle and yelling to the Germans to throw their weapons away and come out with their hands up. One morning's work in the woods netted him 48 POWs. In another instance, an interrogator was in column just outside a village in which battle was still raging. The interrogator, thinking to get out of the vehicle for a stretch and a better view of the battle, walked into an open field. The field was very unassuming in appearance—just a plain open field, with piles of manure scattered about. However, with the appearance of the interrogator in the field, these manure piles seemed to grow prisoners, for about a dozen German soldiers sprang up from behind the piles, with their hands up and very much frightened."

These reports were light moments in a time that the U.S. and the 14th Armored Division fought the German Panzer Corps to a standstill during the German Operation Nordwind.

One of several battles to halt the German advance was fought in the area of two small Alsatian towns known as the The Battle of Hatten-Rittershoffen., which Otto experienced. The battle was brutal and has been described as "An Alsatian Hellscape."

So much of what I have learned about the 14th Armored Division, and the Ritchie Boys' work is thanks to the internet, research at the National Archives in College Park, Md., correspondence with and presentations by other researchers such as Dan Gross, and books—especially Beverley Eddy's *Ritchie Boy Secrets*.

Contact with Otto during his time in Europe was only possible through one-page letters on small forms called V-Mail. [A sample is shown in Appendix A.] My grandmother diligently marked the dates she received them. He was unable to correspond with his sister Trude as she was in enemy territory, and I never had the chance to read letters he wrote his father, his wife or his friends. I have transcribed and included all the letters from Otto that I have in my possession in APPENDIX A, with added points of explanation to some of them. In the letters to his mother—except for a long letter written at war's end, it is clear that Otto was trying his best not to worry her. The tone was often light and even humorous, as one can see in the following excerpts yet I know that every letter that arrived was received with utmost seriousness. Her hands trembled every time a new one arrived, she told me, and she would sit at the kitchen table, where the light was brightest, and write the date she received it on the top, and read the letter again and again. Then she'd look out the window at Riverside Park and the Hudson River and whisper, *Stay safe, dear boy.*

From somewhere in England on 23 October 1944, Otto wrote, "*I realize what I owe to my famous military ancestry* [his mother's father had been an officer in the Imperial Austro-Hungarian Army] —*but as you know my way of fighting is rather talking than shooting.*" This gift of talking would serve him well in trying to win the trust of prisoners he would interrogate as a Ritchie Boy.

On 26 November, in an unidentified village in Alsace that had very recently still been occupied by the Germans, a piano had been found in a stable *"and I played for hours, the boys all sitting around requesting their favorites."*

A month later, on 22 December, still from Alsace: "*Now I hope to get letters from Papa and Trude very soon, that would be a wonderful Christmas present. I wrote already a few letters directly to Papa and sent him 1000Fr—I'm sure he'll need money very badly. We have not been paid for some time—but right here I have no possibility of spending anything; a great advantage of actually 'campaigning'.*"

On 17 January 1945, in what would be shown to be a real understatement, Otto wrote, "*You probably read about us a lot in the newspapers—it doesn't go too easy right now. But now as the Russian offensive started, I'm sure it can't take much longer anymore.*"

On 20 January, Otto wrote that he'd heard from his father but still not from his sister. He had mentioned in earlier letters that it was very cold, and in this letter he mentions a massive snowfall and one can sense his fatigue. "*It's hard to fight a war in a time like that—I think for the time being I have to leave that to my friend Marshall Zhukov* [one of the Soviets most important Generals]. *We'll meet soon, I hope, even if he has to take the longer part of the way to get to this meeting. The civilians look with slight worry upon invaders in their houses, but I convinced them that we are very civilized people and wouldn't take or use anything of their property unless we need it. Well, there are certain things we need very badly. On the other hand, we liberate and defend them, don't we?"*

In her interview with the Holocaust Museum, Trude said *"My brother told me that the Germans always thought when he interviewed someone that he was also the one who passes judgment which was not the case. He was only the interpreter. And he said the Germans, if you have a uniform, think you're a general. You have so much to say, which he didn't."*

On 25 January Otto wrote: *"By now we know all the stories of the Alsatians by heart—yet we listen patiently to all their troubles."*

Alsace-Lorraine, once German and then French had been re-annexed by Hitler, and over 100,000 of its men forced against their will to fight for the Wehrmacht, while others fought for the French. This complicated and often tragic situation is explored more fully in Appendix F.

On 28 January, Otto wrote, *"it snows almost continuously and the streets are very difficult for any kind of traffic. Hard to fight a war, so again we turn the business over to Joe [Stalin]—he likes this kind of weather."*

Then on 6 March: *"Yesterday, we were filmed and photographed to our great surprise—just while we were on the job. So don't be surprised if you recognize in one of the rugged soldiers you see in the Newsreel your own son—or if you see my picture in LIFE (or somewhere) busily studying the maps. Naturally a lot of people tried to get in the pictures, standing behind us and our victims. Yes, that's the way to become famous!"*

With the help of an archivist in the Still Picture Department at the National Archives in College Park, Maryland, I found a photograph of Otto at work.

On the back was this description: *A German prisoner of war who surrendered as a result of propaganda broadcasts, gives information to an interrogator of the 14th Armored Div., U.S. Seventh Army, Ringendorf Area, France. 3/5/45.*

On 27 March, Otto wrote that he was finally going to Paris. "*It will be just wonderful—3 nights and 2 days time. My very nice Major fixed me up and got the pass for me faster than I ever thought. Of course, there was no way of informing Papa about my coming so it will be complete surprise to him. That will be a great reunion after 6 years—and then of course Paris and all the music, art and books—*"

In many of his letters, Otto expressed his longing to hear from his sister, but that would not be possible until the war was over.

On 18 May 1945, ten days after the war in Europe ended, Otto gets the chance to write his mother a long letter in which he can say things he was unable to say before. She did not receive this letter until June 11th.

The complete letter follows, and is also in Appendix A.

"My dear Mama, I am sure you will be happy to read a typewritten letter for a change. Today I will try to tell you a few things which I couldn't say in war times because of security regulations, but today im tiefsten Frieden [in deepest peace] it isn't so important anymore.

Well, when I left NYC on the 4th of October I found myself on the big NEW AMSTERDAM, the greatest Dutch boat. About 9000 people were on board, so I heard, and went all alone by ourselves without any protection. The only protection was our speed and a few guns on board of the ship. It took us 9 days to cross the ocean; at first we went straight East till we came near to the Azores. Not far from the Spanish coast we turned North and went up between Ireland and England to reach GLASGOW. We did not go into GLASGOW itself but we stayed in one of the suburbs and left the same night with the train heading SOUTH. We came to a Replacement Depot near BIRMINGHAM. As you remember, we stayed there almost 3 weeks. It was very hard to get passes to BIRMINGHAM, but most of the boys went anyway, as there were certain means and ways to get there.

One nice day one group of Ritchie people were sent to London and we took the plane to PARIS, which really was a wonderful experience. It was quite a big plane flying very smoothly and I never had any air-sickness, but watched with great pleasure the lovely bird's view. We stayed 2 days outside of PARIS and then a few teams were selected to go to the 7th Army.

We took off in trucks, and after one day's traveling we arrived in VITEL (where you get the water from.) The next day we continued to EPINAL, where the 7th Army Headquarters were at the time.

In EPINAL I had my first experiences with Prisoners and did a few interrogations, which were not too interesting compared with all the following ones. After 5 days, our team (6 men) were assigned to the 14th Armored Div., a new outfit with no battle experience at that time. The team was split in two parts; 3 men stayed in Div HQ and myself and 2 men went to the Combat Command "a", which is the equivalent to a Regiment in an Armored Division.

At first we had no "peep" [jeep] of our own and were depending on other people continuously. It was cold and raining continuously when we joined CC"A" near ST. Die in France/ Our first campaign was across the VOSGES mountains south of Strassbourg to go to Schlettstadt on the way to Colmar. The first campaign took 14 days, but never got as far as Schlettstadt, which was captured 2 months later by somebody else. In these 2 weeks, we had about 150 prisoners and luckily enough a brilliant reputation.

My first prisoner told me the exact position of some German artillery, our artillery fired at this point and 2 days later, when we passed this particular point in our advance you could see clearly that the position was correct and the German gun had been hit. Another fellow on the very first days, gave us some position of mines on the road, and we got a lot of credit for our work. All our reports were handwritten at the time because our typewriter had not as yet arrived; we got the equipment after the first campaign together with our "peep".

After that we had a rest period in a little village West of STRASSBOURG. Our next move was through the HAGENAU forest straight north to WEISSENBURG [now known as WISSEMBOURG] *, the border city between*

ALSACE and GERMANY, and up to the Siegfried line just behind the German border. This was from the 14th to the 24th December. At that time our division did not break the Siegfried line, in fact we didn't even try because by the time we got there, our troops were already tired and the Germans were still very strong in the line with a lot of fire power. That was the first time that we felt the German artillery and we had many noisy nights with a lot of shelling in our immediate neighborhood.

In WEISSENBURG we interrogated a lot of soldiers and civilians, all about the Siegfried line which was very helpful two months later, when we actually went through the line in the last big offensive.

After this campaign we traveled around in ALSACE for two weeks. If I say "we" I mean the Headquarters Co. consisting of the Staff and Radio men, Kitchen supplies etc. all in Halftracks or "peeps." Nobody is marching in our army. At that time the German counter offensive had started in the Ardennes and a similar attack was expected in Alsace every day.

It started when the Germans on the 31 December sent over two American planes bearing the Allied star, a sign of recognition for Allied planes, vehicles and equipment. Seeing the familiar sight of our own planes, nobody worried till suddenly these "friendly" planes started dropping bombs. Three very good friends of mine were amongst the victims and from now on every plane was looked at with greatest suspicion. This happened south of WEISSENBURG. [according to Army records, the date was 30 December.]

On the 11th of January we arrived in a little village by the name of KUHLENDORF, near Hagenau, north west of Strassbourg. While our troops were fighting a cruel defensive battle in RITTERSHOFEN and HATTEN, we really had a rough time in KUHLENDORF. Every day seemed like a month, so crowded it was with experiences; and now, as I am slowly forgetting most of the other places, every little incidence of KUHLENDORF is still fresh in my memory. Our own little farm house was hit several times by artillery, the next house was hit by aerial bombing. To go outside to the latrine was a Heldentat [an act of heroism], and to stand in line for food was more of a crawling there on your belly than a walking. There I had to do interrogations in cellars, or under most unpleasant conditions.

On the 21st of January we staged our great strategic retreat, rear guarding the retreat of the entire 7th Army in this sector. We went to a place called WIWISHEIM without any excitements. Here I did a lot of other things, amongst them I had to do some house searching which made me a very feared man in the village. In that time I visited STRASSBOURG twice.

On the 4th of March we left and went in line on the MODER River near PFAFFENHOFEN and ÜBERBACH. This was the most glorious time of my five broadcasts to the German lines. Only 300 yards away from the Germans we put up our loudspeaker [on] what was left of the roof of a farm house, and I delivered my speech, interrupted by machine gun fire. About 15 deserters were the success of our speech. My lieutenant produced the speech in English and I made a very dramatic German translation. . The Germans who did not follow my advice to surrender were sorry about their decision on the 18th of March, our D-Day for the last big offensive of the 7th Army.

[According to Austrian researcher Florian Trussing, it was unusual for a Ritchie Boy to also have done propaganda broadcasts, as they were usually done by the soldiers trained psychological warfare at Camp Sharpe, about whom both he and Beverley Eddy have written in their books, respectively" Die Psychokrieger ads Camp Sharpe: Österreicher als Kampfpropagandisten der US-Armee im Zweiten Weltkrieg *and* Camp Sharpe's "Psycho Boys": from Gettysburg to Germany.*]*

Soldier holding a loudspeaker used for broadcasts.
The public address system was powered by a generator carried in a weapons carrier. Germans were told of the futility of further resistance and encouraged to surrender.
NARA photograph

Again we went through the Hagenau Forest to WEISSENBURG, which we reached this time already after two days, passing by in a hurry KUHLENDORF and RITTERSHOFFEN, which both naturally are completely destroyed. Our troops fought for three days in STEINFELD, a strong point of the Siegfried Line and in the night of the 23rd of March we passed through a burning, completely destroyed STEINFELD between the famous Dragon's Teeth and all the Siegfried Bunker and fortifications.

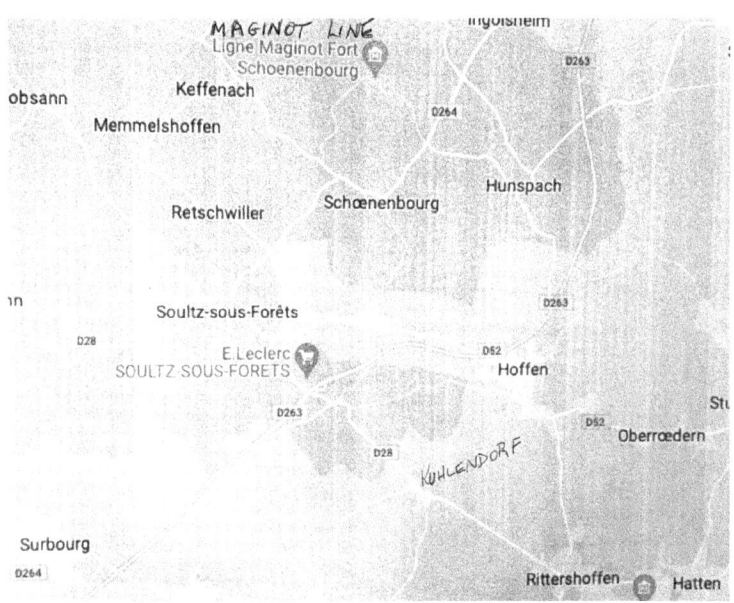

Map of the Alsace area where IPW120 served in the winter of 1944-45. At the top is the Maginot Line. On the bottom left is Surbourg, where Otto's team mates were killed. On the lower right are Ritterhoffen and Hatten where the fiercest battle took place. On the road between Rittershoffen and Soultz-sur-Forêts is Kuhlendorf which Otto writes about.

At that time we captured hundreds and thousands of prisoners. Otto's letter continues. *At first we very seldom had officers, but in the meanwhile I had already all ranks including a general, whom I interrogated.*

Then came my visit to PARIS and coming back I crossed the RHINE at LUDWIGSHAFEN and MANNHEIM - there is little left of either of the cities - before that I passed though SPEYER which is in good shape, no bombing. Then to DARMSTADT, ASCHAFFENBURG, HANAU, and north of BAMBERG I finally found my company. We passed through the lovely BAD BRÜCKENAU and on the 10th of April our Division achieved its greatest advance of almost 30 miles in a day in reaching NEUSTADT. We continued in direction BAYREUTH, which we never reached, but we went south toward NUREMBERG, and reached HERSBRUCK on the 18th of April. Before that I passed through COBURG which is in perfect condition; our bombers missed that one.

Otto with his father in Paris

In HERSBRUCK we lived in the SS Concentration Camp I wrote you about, and

we had the unpleasant experience of a surprise attack of the Germans, just on our little town, but fortunately enough it was repulsed after two hours of fighting. Then we went down to the DANUBE, which we crossed at INGOLSTADT, and went right on to cross the ISAR at MOOSBURG and then we finally came to this place, one hour from MUNICH, where we awaited the final VICTORY. This division captured about 45,000 prisoners in all the campaigns, most of them naturally in the last phase of the war.

So, this was a long letter! Next time about some of my interrogation experiences.

1000 kisses, all my best, lots of love, your Otto.

I just received your letter of 2 May. Many thanks!

Otto's letter about the Hersbruck Concentration camp is missing, but I learned that Hersbruck was a subcamp of the Flossenburg Concentration Camp, established in May 1944 to force prisoners to construct a series of tunnels in the nearby mountains to hold an underground airplane engine plant for BMW. The camp consisted of fifteen overcrowded prisoner barracks. Treatment was brutal, and as the number of prisoners increased from 1,900 to 6,000, the chance of surviving fell to 50%. 4000 prisoners perished there, most of them Hungarian.

Otto mentioned that he'd been assigned to a Command Combat A, which was equivalent to a regimental level. Enemy information obtained at this level was generally of especially great importance because of its highly tactical nature. IPW teams realized the importance of reporting their findings as soon as possible so that they could be disseminated. Teams with armored units made use of the radio, while other teams relied heavily on the telephone. When neither was available, delivery by motor transport became essential—something that was complicated by the fact that some team members were inexperienced drivers. Otto's letters indicate that he learned to drive and enjoyed it, though he promised his mother he was careful.

Interrogators found it very helpful in breaking the ice with prisoners to be familiar with German geography, history, economics and culture, as well as regional differences and rivalries. An enemy soldier's *Soldbuch* provided the first important information about him as it was a combination pay-book and army service records with assignments, promotions, present rank, supply records, hospitalizations etc. listed. Interrogators were especially successful in obtaining tactical information if they had a well-rounded knowledge of the German Army organization, uniforms, insignia, tactics, military map symbols, abbreviations and military slang. Prisoners would then feel free to provide information they thought the interrogator already possessed.

Civilians who were interrogated often provided important tactical information as well.

Notes were not taken in sight of the prisoners so that they would talk more freely without fear that they were providing crucial information.

I do not have, nor have ever seen, the letter in which Otto describes his interrogation experiences. There must have been one or more such letters because I remember my grandmother talking about how he'd reported that the Russians complained that Americans were too soft on the Germans, and there were even arguments. He also mentioned an East German girlfriend of one of the Americans that he did not trust.

There are other letters Otto referenced that are also missing that might have filled in information about Trude's experiences during the war. By the time I realized how many letters were missing, it was too late to ask my mother about them. Although my mother told many stories, it is clear that there were things she did not want to talk about.

Photo Otto took of his sister and niece in Rome

In her interview with the United States Holocaust Museum, she talked about the day Otto came to see her in Rome in October 1945. [She incorrectly said it was September].

"He was stationed with the third Army in Schongau, Germany." She hadn't seen him since 1937. *"Eight years. A lot of time."*

The interviewer asked if Otto had told her what he'd done and seen.

"He told me he saw concentration camps. He said everyone they interviewed never heard of Nazis. Nobody was ever a Nazi."

The interviewer asked what Otto's feelings were towards the Germans.

"Well, he was not enthusiastic about the Germans. He didn't feel any hatred, I think. That was not in his character. All he wanted was to go back to America, resume his career as a musician. He didn't think he could be a pianist anymore because three years of not practicing the piano daily makes your fingers stiff, but he wanted to go into conducting because he had the qualifications to be a conductor. But music was his life."

The interviewer asked Trude what she thought her brother would say was the most dramatic time of his life during the war.

"I don't know. He had a lot of dramatic experiences in Germany when he was a soldier because he told me that one there was a terrible bombardment. He said, 'I was hungry. I was going into the kitchen and everybody said don't be crazy. You're not going out when the bombs are firing' and he said 'Yes, I'm going out.' And he went out of the barracks where they were staying and into the next one where the kitchen is and the barracks where they were staying was bombed and he was the only survivor."

That was 20 December 1944. And three friends who were killed were his fellow IPW120 team members and friends—Capt. Robert Andrae, M/Sgt. Wolf Goeltzer and T/5 Joseph Kramer.

On 6 January 1945, their positions were filled by 1st Lt. Gerhardt Schueler, 2nd Lt. Frank David, S/Sgt Lucas Reid, and T/4 Frank Lehnen.

Otto with 1st Lt. Schueler. *Otto and work*

The following description of the 14th Armored Division's campaigns is part of the U.S. Holocaust Memorial Museum's collections:

The 14th Armored Division joined the Allied invasion of western Europe in October 1944, when it landed in Marseille in southern France. By early 1945, the "Liberators" had advanced as far as Alsace-Lorraine, provinces that had been incorporated into Germany after France's defeat in 1940. In March and April, the 14th penetrated the Rhineland and moved into Bavaria. By war's end, the division had reached the Danube River.

As the 14th advanced into southern Germany, it uncovered several subcamps of the Dachau concentration camp. Operating near the towns of Ampfing andMühldorf the unit discovered four large munitions plants built underground, some 15,000 tons of high explosive, and three large forced-labor camps, housing thousands of Polish and Soviet civilian workers. The 14th also liberated two other camps nearby, one holding 1,500 Jewish prisoners and the other filled with Jewish female inmates. The unit reported that of the 1,500 prisoners in the first camp, only 900 could walk, and that the lime pits were filled with the corpses of inmates.

The 14th Armored Division was recognized as a liberating unit by the US Army's Center of Military History and the United States Holocaust Memorial Museum in 1991.

Casualty figures for the 14th Armored Division, European theater of operations:
Total battle casualties: 2,690
Total deaths in battle: 566

Although lacking a nickname during the war, the 14th became known as the "Liberators" soon afterward to signify its accomplishments in liberating hundreds of thousands of forced and slave laborers, concentration camp prisoners, and Allied prisoners of war in 1945.

This was their insignia - in red, yellow and blue

A more detailed description with photographs can be found online at https://military-historian.squarespace.com/blog/2020/10/20/an-alsatian-hellscape-the-battle-of-hatten-rittershoffen?rq=battle%20of%20hatten-rittershoffen

https://14thad.org/history/history_of_the_14th.pdf provides the full text of a book about the 14th Armored Division in World War II. Chapter IX has another detailed description of the battle with references to Kuhlendorf and the CCA Headquarters there. The days in Kuhlendorf were Otto's toughest.

III

18 November 1945

On the 9th of October 1945, Otto wrote his mother.

My dear Mama,
I surprised Papa quite much in coming to Paris directly from Rome. I'll stay here for one day as my plane is leaving not before tomorrow and I have a chance to tell Papa all about Trude. As soon as I get to Schongau, I'll write to you a more detailed letter about Trude. Everything is fine in Paris and Papa is living quite well right now.

All my best - 1000 kisses
Your Otto

It is the only letter I have until a letter he wrote on 16 November which begins:

My dear Mama,
Many thanks for your letter of 1 Nov. Don't worry about my Bergtouren [mountain walks] ich geb schon Acht [I'm careful], and I don't do difficult things, just gemütliche Aufstiege [easy ascents]. And don't worry about my jeep-tours either, I am a very careful driver, never taking chances, and I go fast only on excellent, wide roads. It's much safe to ride with me from most of the other soldiers, who are sometimes very careless.

Yet, on 18 November 1945, Otto left his quarters in Schongau and did not return.

I have no record of how or when Otto's wife or mother were first notified that he was missing—whether it was in person, as one often saw in films, or by telegram or letter. The earliest correspondence I had until recently was dated Schongau, Bayern [Bavaria], 3 January 1946 and was not received by my grandmother until 6 February 1946.

Dear Mrs. Jellinek,

The team on which your son Otto worked is quite small in comparison to other army units, consequently we grow to know one another very well. Otto commanded the respect of every one of us from the first day of his assignment because of the great amount of tolerance he had for his fellows' whims and by reason of his standards of clean living.

During the beginning of the Bavarian winter, all our thoughts turned toward American ways and customs and we grew more and more homesick for our loved ones there; at that time Otto proved to us how much we had grown to depend on him. He felt as lonely as any of we boys, yet he outdid himself playing the piano and, with his playing, he tried to alleviate our mental ills. He played long hours for our amusement and was always very willing to lend a sympathetic ear to hear our personal problems.

His thoughtfulness evidenced itself toward the prisoners with whom we work. Otto very unselfishly instigated an education program for them which helps to clear their thoughts thereby providing more fertile fields which the seeds of democracy can take root. He sponsored discussion groups for them and worked hard editing a library of some contemporary authors in order to elicit interest from their tired, confused minds.

Otto's love for the outdoors was a tremendous thing. On free days he was out of his bed early and eager to seek out new peaks and views in the surrounding countryside. In fact, this is what happened on the weekend of November 18. Otto had made a casual remark Saturday evening about wishing to find a new peak the next morning if the weather permitted. When the breakfast table was assembled, it was discovered that your son had set off alone about three hours earlier. Every effort is being and has been made to discover his whereabouts and, you may rest assured, that some answer will result from this search.

We shall be very glad to answer any further questions you may have, Mrs. Jellinek, and we shall notify you immediately concerning any developments in this problem.

Lt. Ernest F. Hauser
Hq XX Corps, G-2
Section CIE #10,
APO 340 c/o Pm New York

One can only imagine the emotions this letter aroused in my grandmother: gratitude to the lieutenant for his compassion and kindness; terror that the length of time that had already elapsed since Otto's disappearance could only mean that something terrible had happened to him; and grief—grief that she couldn't allow herself to feel, not yet, not while there was still hope. My grandmother held on to the hope that her beloved son was being held by the Russians, as his uncle Karl had been after World War I, and would be released one day. This last shred of hope ended when the Russians released the last of their prisoners of war in 1955.

The next document in my files, chronologically, is this letter written to my grandfather:

HEADQUARTERS
UNITED STATES FORCES
EUROPEAN THEATER
AG CASUALTY BRANCH

16 May 1946

Mr. Gruenbaum,
10 rue Pasquier
Paris 8

Dear Mr. Gruenbaum,

It is with the deepest regret that I am writing to you in reply to your letter of 6 March 1946 requesting more information about the disappearance of your son <u>M/Sgt Otto Gruenbaum 32527211.</u> Missing since 18 November 1945. Knowing how keenly his loss is felt by the members of his immediate family, I am taking the liberty of explaining the circumstances attending his death in the hope that despite its sadness, the news will be of some comfort to you.

M/Sgt Otto Gruenbaum departed Schongau, Germany on 18 November 1945. He planned to go mountain climbing and never came back. An intensive investigation has been conducted in view to obtain all information about your son's fate. I regret to inform you that the results of the searches concluded to his accidental death. His body was found in Mittenwald, Germany with fractured skull and multiple lacerations.

You may be certain that a Chaplain of his own faith officiated in his burial. He was buried on 22 April 1946 at a United States Military Cemetery. The exact location of his grave is U.S. Military Cemetery St Avold, France, Plot NN, Row 10, Grave 109.

I know this tragedy has brought you an almost insurmountable burden of grief and can well imagine your sorrow and bitter disappointment in this disheartening news you received.

I extend my heartfelt sympathy and express the hope that the Almighty who saw fit to take your loved one will also give you the courage to bear your loss bravely.

> *Sincerely yours,*
> *ROBERT A. BOWEN*
> *2nd Lt. AGD*
> *Asst. Adjutant General*

As religion had not been a part of our family's daily life, my grandfather would probably not have found this especially comforting. My mother and I arrived in Paris from Rome shortly afterwards, and before my grandfather had a chance to tell my mother, she noticed and read the letter. The shock of learning of her brother's death in this way left her unable to speak for several days.

In July 1946, my grandfather received a handwritten letter. I have transcribed it and the question marks indicate words that were illegible:

Dear Mr. Gruenbaum,

I wish first to explain the long lapse of time between your letter of 23 May 46 and my answer, I received your letter after some delay on the eve of my departure for the U.S. I was never settled long enough during the long trip home to give you a proper reply.

While I never knew your son personally, I am possibly possessed with more information surrounding his death than anyone else. I first recall the broadcast requesting information concerning him as being received from

AFN Munich. These were in the latter part of November and first part of December, the year of 1945.

Now follows the circumstances by which I became connected with the recovery of his body and the places en route to point of death and description of locality.

On a night early in April I received a call from a detachment of men who were stationed in Mittenwald, Bavaria stating that a German forester had reported that he had located the body of an American soldier in the mountains near Mittenwald. I ascertained that the soldier had died some month previous and that the body had been preserved only by the snow.

Early the next morning, I with seven men, met the forester and proceeded, under his guidance, to again locate and recover the body. The route we took from Mittenwald to the Lautersee and to a point midway between Lautersee and Fenchen See. This point may be recognized by borders that lie on each side of road as it leaves a small meadow. At this point we left the Jeep and proceeded into the woods where we hit a foot trail which led along the edge of the woods and then turned south into the mountains. After 30 minutes of hard walking and climbing we came upon the body of your son, Otto.

His body was located about two feet off the trail. It was at the base of a rockslide which extended steeply upwards for perhaps 150 feet and there ended at the base of a perpendicular cliff. Snow was about fifty feet above the body. The position of the body was with head nearest the trail, legs extended directly toward the cliff, left leg over right leg and ??? Compound ??? And body lying on back.

It is not my belief that he suffered from his fall. There was nothing to indicate he had ever moved. The position in which the body was lying was such that a man in even semi-consciousness would have changed, the head being much lower than the hips. The arms being in a very awkward position over head indicates he did not move them. The medical examiner, basing his opinion on certain broken bones in the head, expressed to me, unofficially, that death was instantaneous.

I found in the snow at the peak of the slide his glove, one glove only, and hat. There was nothing to indicate that he was the victim of a crime. I do not know whether he fell from the cliff to the slide, and then rolled to the bottom, or merely fell from the top of the slide. My belief is that his death was instantaneous and resulted from an accidental fall.

It is possible that you can visit the place, I suggest that you go first to the local police in Mittenwald to the S-2 Office of 2DBn, 47th inf, who from their informal files should be able to give you the name of the forester who first discovered the body. He could be your guide.

Please permit me to express my sorrow and deepest sympathies to you, his mother and his wife. From conversations with those who knew him, I know he was loved and respected by them all. Please feel free to call on me at any time for any or formation or service I may be able to give in your further the place of his death. I'm sorry I cannot now be able to return and photograph the spot.

Yours respectfully,
Milton R. LeRoy
Lt. Milton R.LeRoy, Jr
Rte 3, Ninety Six, S.C.

Although Lt. Bowen and Lt. Roy's assessments were that Otto's death was an accident and there was no sign of a crime, my grandmother always felt there were too many unanswered questions to be convinced that their assessment was correct. I don't know personally how Otto's widow Susanne felt, but I can only imagine she felt the same.

.   Then on 14 November 1946, Edward F. Witsell, Major General, The Adjutant General of the Army sent Susanne the following letter:

Dear Mrs. Gruenbaum:

I am referring to the letter of 5 June 1946, from this office, which confirmed the death of your husband, Master Sergeant Otto K. Gruenbaum on 18 November 1945 in the European Area.
A report has been received that your husband's death was due to a fractured skill and multiple lacerations. The report further disclosed that his death occurred in line of duty and was not due to his own misconduct.
You have my heartfelt sympathy in your bereavement.

To Otto's mother, this assessment was an indication that the Army did not consider Otto's death an accident after all.

Otto's death was a wound that never healed, not only because he was a deeply loved son, brother, husband, friend, but because he had so much promise that would never be fulfilled.

When the Army closed the cemetery in France where Otto had been buried, Otto's wife and mother decided to have his remains transferred to the military cemetery in Farmingdale, New York on Long Island, so they could visit. And we visited often. And every time, we would remark on that fact that that even at his young age of twenty-seven he was one of the older young men buried there. We weren't the only ones to have suffered terrible loss.

It took me many years to fully understand what Otto's loss meant to my family. Loss often feels like a hole where someone used to be but is no more. And yet, to me Otto was and always has been as much a presence as a loss. We thought of him, talked about him, had pictures of him. In many ways I thought I knew him. As I grew older, I began to understand the deep sadness my grandmother and my mother felt as they thought of all he could have achieved, of all the joys he'd missed. Every major change or event made them reflect on what he would have thought. When President Kennedy —a symbol of such youth and hope—was assassinated, my grandmother was so grief-stricken, it was as if Otto had died again.

It took me even longer to realize that *our* lives would have been different had Otto lived. Ours was a very small family in New York—just my sister, parents and grandmother. Had Otto lived, I thought, there would have been cousins, my grandmother would have been happy, my mother would have been pulled into a world of music again. Otto would have been a conductor. In New York, I assumed, but, of course, the future isn't decided by our wishes. Things might have turned out very differently from anything I'd imagined.

This sketch of Otto hung in my grandmother's living room, then my mother's, and now in mine:

IV

The Search for Answers

In the 1950s Trude and her mother tried to get information from the Army, regarding not only Otto's death, but also his service. They were told that his records were classified and would remain so indefinitely. Although they knew that he'd been part of the CIC, the Counterintelligence Corps, the story of the Ritchie Boys and their invaluable contributions was not known until decades later.

In 1977 we tried again to obtain records but with little success.

In April 1992, I contacted the National Personnel Records Center in St. Louis, Missouri, hoping that by then Otto's records would have been declassified. The Center informed me that my uncle's record was not in their files. On 12 July 1973, there had been a fire, and if his record was there, it would have been in the area that suffered the most damage and may have been destroyed. They suggested writing to Veteran's Affairs.

Instead, I wrote Frank R. Wolf, who was our Congressman at the time. I explained the situation and asked if he could help us obtain the information we were seeking. He answered that he'd made an inquiry on our behalf to the National Personnel Records Center.

In their response to him, they mentioned my earlier request, explained about the fire again, and said that there were alternate record sources that often contain information which can be used to reconstruct some service record data lost in the fire. But not everything. A portion of Otto's records had been sent to the Department of Veterans Affairs (DVA), for use in adjudicating the DVA claim filed by Otto's next of kin. They had contacted the DVA for copies of all available records, copies of which they enclosed. Some of the photocopies were of poor quality but were the best they had.

Rep. Wolf had also written the DVA and the DVA sent copies that pertained to Otto's death. There was no information on where Otto served and when, and what his duties were.

Here, in chronological order, is what we received from Veteran Affairs.

1. An official **REPORT OF INVESTIGATION**, dated January 1946, filled out by 1st Lt. Ernest Hauser, HQs XX Corps, Tutsing, Germany. (The same Lt. Hauser who had written such a kind letter to my grandmother at the time.) A copy was later received by the Record Verification Section on 15 Oct. 1946, and that is the one I have a copy of. It states: *Gruenbaum left his quarters early the morning 18th November 45 to climb mountains, vicinity Garmisch Germany. Still missing.*

The report further states that Otto was within the territorial limits indicated by the authorization to be absent; was not under the influence of drugs; was exercising reasonable care; was not violating any civil, moral, or military law; was not missing due to gross carelessness or negligence; was mentally sound. *These items as near to similar items on original report as available record and memory permit. Original report was submitted by undersigned while serving in the G-2 section, Hq XX Corps from 20 December 45 to 26 January 46.*

Attached was a description [shown below] of the search for Otto, with stamps indicating when it was received by three different offices. The report signed by Lt. Hauser, was then approved by C.A. Mixon, Captain, AGD, Assistant Adjutant General, HQ US Forces, European Theater in order to approve burial in France.

OTTO GRUENBAUM, Master Sergeant, working in a CIC Detachment (Counter-Intelligence Corps) general vicinity of Garmisch went for a hike in the mountains (vicinity Garmisch) by himself early one Sunday morning, November 1945. This is the last time he was seen by anybody. Information received from his colleagues indicate that he was contented and happily married, was about to be redeployed to the States (the week following his disappearance), was an ardent hiker and was well able to take care of himself.

Upon being missed, continuous searches were conducted the following two weeks by air and ground forces. The German Forestry Police combed the mountainous area, US troops searched the surrounding areas and liaison planes flew over all the areas he could possibly have travelled into. Large posters carrying his picture and description were distributed throughout the area.

The latter part of the month as assistant S-2, XX Corps, conducted an investigation. The early part of January another investigation was conducted by the undersigned officer—results of both as to determining the whereabouts of the Enlisted Man were negative.

The information as determined by the two investigations was compiled and reported to higher Headquarters at that time. Who finally decided that the subject Enlisted Man is dead is not known by this officer.

2. Copy of the letter sent to Otto's father in Paris on 16 May, 1946 and signed by 2nd Lt. Bowen, stating that Otto's death had been accidental. [The complete letter was included in Chapter III].

3. Copy of handwritten letter sent by Lt. LeRoy to Otto's father in July 1946 describing how Otto's body had been found and in what condition, with the conclusion that death had been accidental. [This complete letter was also included in Chapter III.]

4. A letter dated 8 October 1946 from the War Department, signed by E.E. Ewing, Adjutant General. [NOTE: death was now considered *in the line of duty.*]

Held by the War Department that this report will be accepted as the final report of investigation, without exhibits and testimonies, due to the lack of witnesses. Master Sergeant Otto K. Gruenbaum, 32,527,211, death occurred on 18 November 1945, result of a fractured skull and multiple lacerations, in line of duty and not the result of his own misconduct, BY THE ORDER OF THE SECRETARY OF WAR.

5. An official War Department form:

The individual named in this report of death is held by the War Dept to have been in a missing status from 18 November 1945 until such absence was terminated on 28 May 1946, when evidence considered sufficient to establish the fact of death was received by the Secretary of War from a commander in the European Area.

6. On 14 November 1946, Otto's widow received a letter referring to a letter of 5 June 1946 [which I do not have] which confirms Otto's death on 18 November 1945 and that it occurred in the line of duty and was not due to his own misconduct. It expressed heartfelt sympathy and is signed Edward F. Witsell, Major General, the Adjutant General of the Army.

Lt. Hauser's report of investigation stated *Gruenbaum left his quarters early the morning 18th November 45 to climb mountains, vicinity Garmisch Germany,* whereas his letter to Otto's mother specifies he left Schongau. The more detailed report describing steps taken, and signed by Capt. Mixon states *GRUENBAUM, Master Sergeant, working in a CIC Detachment (Counter-Intelligence Corps) general vicinity of Garmisch went for a hike in the mountains (vicinity Garmisch).*

Not mentioned in any of these documents is what Otto's mother, sister, and friend believed was the reason for Otto's excursion.

Trude, in her interview with the Holocaust Museum said *"On the 18th of November, he told one of his friends that he was going to see Richard Strauss in Garmisch-Patenkirchen and he left early in the morning and was never seen again."*

Otto's friend Kurt, in his late-in-life reminiscences, wrote that Otto *"attempted to visit Richard Strauss and was killed."*

Otto, as a classical musician, was a great admirer of Richard Strauss, and must have learned that he was apprehended by American soldiers at his Garmisch-Patenkirchen estate. The lieutenant in charge of apprehending him was also a musician and allowed him to stay.

Although Strauss had been criticized for continuing to conduct under the Nazi regime, he managed to protect his Jewish daughter-in-law, and at the end of the war wrote: *"The most terrible period of human history is at an end, the twelve year reign of bestiality, ignorance and anti-culture under the greatest criminals, during which Germany's 2000 years of cultural evolution met its doom"*

Otto must have heard Strauss was in Garmisch, as he was stationed in Bavaria then. I don't know if or how often they met, and none of the letters I have mention a meeting—yet, his mother, sister and friend thought that on 18 November 1945, Otto might have been going to say good-bye, which also implies he had met him at least once before.

Yet, according to my research, Strauss and his family left Garmisch for Switzerland in October, a whole month earlier. Wouldn't Otto have known? And if he hadn't known and had gone to Garmisch in vain, wouldn't he have turned around and gone back to Schongau? Why go on to Mittenwald? But more important is that Schongau is 50 to 60 km from Garmisch. Should we conclude from Capt. Mixon's statement that Schongau was considered general vicinity Garmisch? They are both a part of Upper Bavaria (Oberbayern) but today are not considered to be in the same district.

Based on the above mentioned documents, and the distances involved, we were left to think that if Otto left Schongau on foot, as was stated repeatedly, it would have taken him ten to eleven hours to walk one way to Garmisch and another 4 to 5 hours to Mittenwald, even longer to the path between the two lakes where his body was found. Round trip would have meant walking at least thirty hours, which is clearly impossible to do in one day. To go for two days, he would have had to ask permission. If he drove part way, why wasn't an abandoned Jeep found?

Why, after two weeks of intensive searching, by air and ground forces, was Otto or Otto's body not found? According to historical records of weather conditions on the Zugspitze, there was no precipitation between 15 and 25 November 1945. As Mittenwald is only 21km from the Zugspitze, it is unlikely Otto's body was covered with snow at the time of the search. Heavy snows did not occur until the next February.

Exactly when Otto died would have been impossible to ascertain months later when his body was found. His death might not have been the day he disappeared. It could have been the next day or a week later. Lt. LeRoy found traces of a landslide, but there was no way to know when that landslide occurred. Did it catch Otto unprepared? He was not found buried by one. If it was earlier, it might have made the ground dangerous to walk. Wouldn't Otto, an experienced hiker by then, have understood that? Or had it happened after, therefore not the cause of Otto's disappearance? Had anyone ever asked those questions? .

Why was Otto's death referred to as an accident in Lt. Bowen's report of 16 May 1946, but later always referred to as death in the line of duty and not a result of his own misconduct?

Now, these many years later, thanks to Beverley Eddy's research, and information she found on HonorStates.org, I learned that Otto was awarded a Purple Heart, indicating that his death had not been an accident. "*During his service in World War II, Army Master Sergeant Gruenbaum experienced a critical situation which ultimately resulted in loss of life on November 18,1945. Recorded circumstances attributed to: Died in Service. Incident location: Germany.*"

I was unable to find any information on whether any other American soldiers had died after the end of the war under similar unexplained circumstances.

It was with these unanswered questions in mind that, in May of 2022, my husband and I took a trip to Alsace and the Bavarian Alps to visit some of the places Otto had been. We started in Alsace, in the lovely border town of Wissembourg, and explored the area from there.

Wissembourg

I was especially interested in what I might find out about the terrible Hatten-Rittershoffen battle and the village of Kuhlendorf, which Otto had described as the site of his most difficult days.

I had read about a small museum in Hatten that I thought might provide information on the battle, but found that much of the exhibit was dedicated to the Malgré-Nous, the Alsatians who had been forced to fight for the Reich and died in Russia or in captivity.

A monument in memory of the Hatten-Rittershoffen Battle of January 1945

100,000 Alsatians and 30,000 Mosellans [people from Lorraine] were forced into service of the Reich, under threat that their relatives would be deported should they consider fleeing or deserting. Many were sent to fight in Russia. Some went over to join the Russian Red Army but many were captured and held in Tambov, a Russian POW camp. It is estimated that 30,000 were killed in action, 10,000 still unaccounted for. Between 5,000 and 10,000 of those that were prisoners of war died in captivity, most of them at Tambov. The last to return came as late as 1955. 40,000 of the Malgré-Nous were invalids after the war. Those that returned were often seen less as victims than as collaborators or traitors, leaving them feeling marginalized and betrayed.

German propaganda poster promising Alsatians fame and honor

A cross and sign in memory of the 40,000 Malgré-Nous who died or were missing

Kuhlendorf is now a peaceful and pretty village of half-timbered houses common to Alsace. It has even been awarded the coveted title of *Village Fleuri*,

Our next important destination was the beautiful town of Mittenwald in the Bavarian Alps. There we followed Lt. LeRoy's geographical description to try and locate the area where Otto's body was found.

This map shows the area Lt. LeRoy described in his letter. The first route he took, which we followed also, was the path marked in green (No. 828) that leads from Lautersee to Ferchen See. Above it, in blue, is the route 872 which we also walked. A portion of it becomes the lower No. 871 and is at the base of the Ferchen See Wande [also known as Wände] described as a cliff i.e. a high steep perpendicular slope overlooking the water.

I do not have the sketch that Lt. LeRoy mentions in his letter, but this location fits his description completely and I believe that Otto was on the upper route No. 871 and fell or was thrown off the cliff down to the lower No. 871.

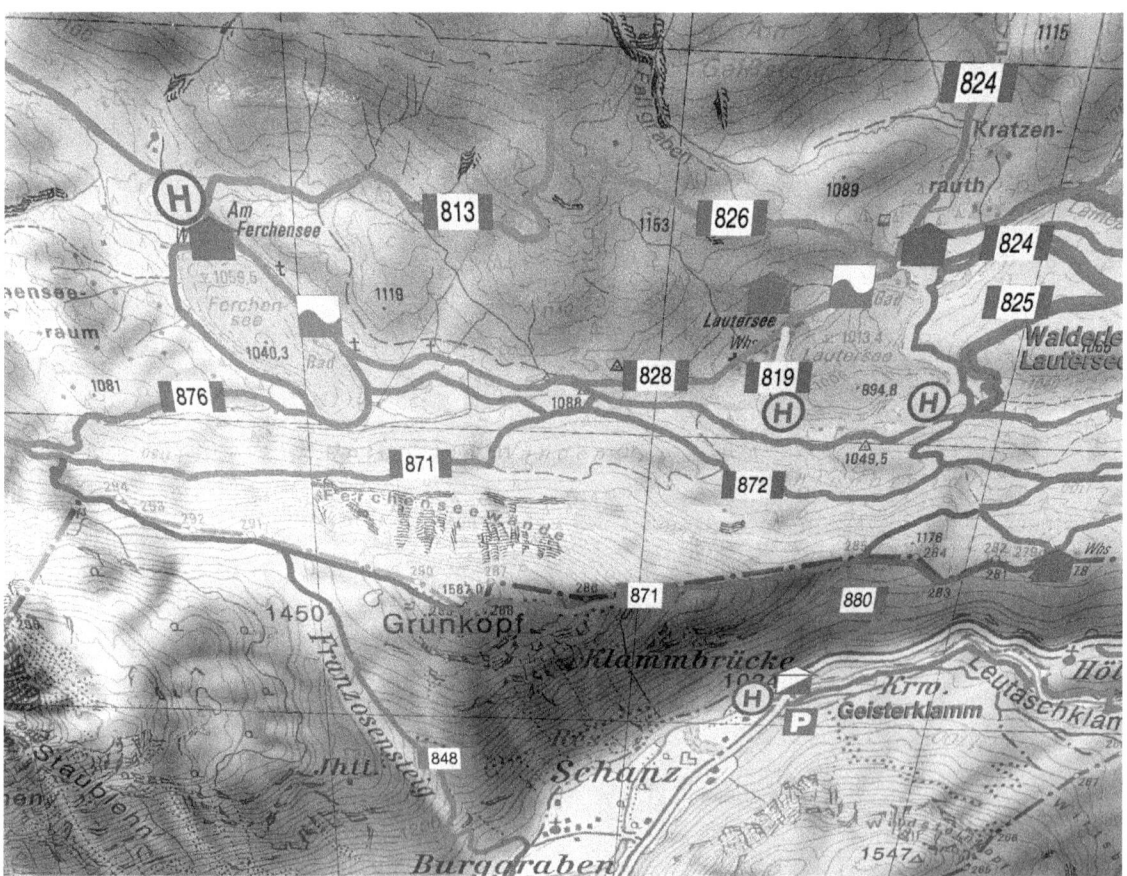

In a description meant for hikers, Route No. 871 is described as *Überwiegend schmalz Steig, oft steil angelegt, kann abstürzgefährliche Passagen aufweisen, Trittsicherheit und Ausdauer erforderlich* —translated as *Predominantly narrow climb, often steep, can have passages where there is a risk of falling, sure-footedness and stamina are required.*

View of the cliff from the lower path

In my mother's interview with the Holocaust Museum she said, Otto " *was not a mountain climber. He liked to take a walk in the woods but not in the mountains. He never did that before.*" Army documents refer to him as an avid hiker but not mountain climber.

In his last letter to his mother, Otto reassured her that he was being careful, taking only morning walks, nothing risky. I don't believe that he would have taken a walk that was that demanding, that risky, that far from his base, and alone, a week before he was to return home.

Upon advice of the College Park NARA archivists, before we left for Germany, I contacted the National Archives in St.Louis to request Otto's death records, in the hope that they would have information I did not yet have. After some months, I received a pack of records, many of which were copies of documents I already had, but also included many that regarded his burial first in France, and later the transfer of his remains to the national cemetery in Farmingdale, New York. Reading the description of Otto's body and the small number of items he had with him, I was struck by how difficult it must have been and still is for servicemen, medical personnel and embalmers who time and again have to identify, embalm, inter and sometimes re-inter the damaged bodies of so many young men.

On 12 March 1947, Otto's widow Susanne wrote "*I received a letter from your office over two months ago saying that my husband's belongings would be sent to me. A week later I received a small box with a few coins of German money and a notebook which were taken from his pockets when he was found in the mountains. Nothing came since. I know that he had bought a number of books and music in Europe, and he had also written some music; therefore, I would be very happy to get the rest of his belongings, and especially his own notes and writings, if they still exist.*"

P.U. Maxey, Lt. Col, QMC, Effects Quartermaster responded on 24 March 1947: "*Dear Mrs. Gruenbaum: ...A check of our records and European Theater Area records, now in custody of this Bureau, fails to reveal any information relative to the property about which you inquire. You may be assured that in the even any additional property is received here at a later date, it will be forwarded to you promptly.*"

Books can be replaced but it is sad to think there was music Otto wrote that has gone unplayed and unheard.

I did, however, receive one document that provided information we never had before. In a NON-BATTLE CASUALTY REORT issued on 13 December 1945, which I don't believe Otto's wife or mother received, was the news that Otto "**hitch-hiked from Schongau, Germany, where he was stationed, to Garmisch and has not returned.**"

This statement is in contrast to all the other reports I have stating that Otto left his quarters to climb mountains.

Rather than answering questions, this new piece of information only added more.

Was Otto on his way to see Richard Strauss after all, even though Lt. Hauser's letter said Otto had gone for a walk?

From whom did Otto hitch a ride? The safest and most likely would have been from a fellow GI, but I found no mention of a GI reporting where he'd dropped Otto off. Would Otto, in uniform, have risked asking a lift from a local, a stranger in a country whose soldiers had just been the enemy? And if it was a local with no ill intentions toward Americans, wouldn't the man (or woman) have answered the call for information since posters were widely distributed?

If Otto intended to visit Strauss in Garmisch but did not find him, why would he have gone on to Mittenwald? Garmisch has many hiking possibilities. In fact, so does Schongau.

My mother and grandmother often spoke about the arguments Otto said the interrogators had with the Russians; and about the mysterious East German girl he did not like. There must have been a lot of Germans still in thrall of Nazi ideology and anti-Semitism. Such mindsets did not vanish overnight and anti-American sentiment was still strong among many Germans.

In the end, no matter the circumstances of Otto's death, the simple fact remains that after surviving the Anschluss, persecution, and the horrors of war, if he hadn't left the base on 18 November, he would have been on his way home a week later. His mother had already decorated her apartment with *Welcome Home* banners.

Countless families have suffered tragedies greater than ours. I know that loss of hope and promise happens at every moment, in every corner of the world—yet it has always been the words *almost home* that have made Otto's death so unbearably sad.

PLEASE NOTE: My website **https://all-that-lingers.com** offers a variety of articles, photographs, and links to videos and audios on the Historical, Cultural and Gastronomic Vienna of pre-war, wartime and post-war Vienna, as well a list of recommended books. I hope you will take a look.

APPENDIX A

OTTO'S LETTERS

The following are the letters that I have in my possession. Except for one, they were all written to Otto's mother, my grandmother.

They are presented chronologically, starting with 16 October 1944 and running through 16 November 1945.

Except for the long one after the war, the letters were all written on small V-Mail forms and most of them were handwritten. The people most frequently mentioned in the letters are:

Mama—Otto's mother, Melanie (known as Melli or Mela) Jellinek,
Papa—Otto's father, Otto Grünbaum,
Susi—Susanne, Otto's wife, also a pianist from Vienna
Jo—Otto's mother's second husband, Josef Jellinek, also referred to as Ingi, short for *Ingenieur* (engineer).
Trude—Otto's sister and my mother.
Mrs. Weschler--Otto's piano teacher in Vienna and who emigrated to New York and taught at the New York College of Music.

Please note, I have not italicized the letters as I did in the preceding narrative, so as to make them easier to read.

When I have multiple question marks ???? It means I could not read Otto's handwriting.

Letter to Otto Grünbaum dated 16 October 1944 from his mother Melanie (Melli) Jellinek. She did not speak English until she arrived in the U.S. and mostly learned it from listening to the radio. I do not know who Mr. Knapp is.

October 16, 44
My dearest Otto,

      It is sad for me to be without news from you, particularly spoiled getting a letter every day from you. Expect your words with impatience. I hope you are all right, cheerful and in good spirits.
      We are all well. In the next day Susi and we are going to have lunch with Mr. Knapp. Jo spoke on the phone with him and his first question was: Where is Otto? He asks for your address and will write to you. Mrs. Weschler often calls too and inquires after you. I am always thinking of you, my dear boy. Remain in good health, God protect you, and many many kisses and love,

    Yours,

    Mother

Best regards and wishes, Ingi

*Letter from Otto to his mother, dated 23 October and received 31 October 1944.
"famous military ancestry" refers to Melanie's father who was an officer in the Austro-Hungarian Imperial army. This letter was written from somewhere in England.*

T/3 #32527211 APO 1110 Postmaster NY NY

23 Oct
My dear Mama, dear Ingi!

Many thanks for your dear letter from the 5th Oct.
I hope too I will come back very soon – but with those decorations I will take it easy – of course I realize what I owe to my famous military ancestry – but as you know my way of fighting is rather talking than shooting.
Yesterday I heard another concert in town – we are now in the regular European concert season, with many things happening everyday. It's getting pretty cold now and the nights get longer – and the nights are here really dark. Besides I am still leading my lazy life – I wonder for how long. By the way, I met some Viennese refugees here in town. They have an Austrian club – like everywhere else.

    Many kisses and much love,

    your Otto

Letter from Otto to his mother dated 27 October 1944, received in New York 6 November 1944.
Otto had a full head of dark, curly hair. In France collaborators had their heads shaved.

APO11110NY

27 Oct
My dear Mama –

After having been exposed to a real army haircut – I look like a collaborationist. It has the big advantage that I am now completely relieved from combing or fixing my hair. And all this to celebrate my 2nd anniversary in the armed forces. At this occasion I send in my special military invention to "Ike": our army duffel bags (containing all our properties) should have the opening at the bottom because everything you are looking for is always at the bottom! I'm sure it will be accepted. How are you all? I'm not as yet washing my own laundry – I found some English people doing that.

Best regards and many kisses,

Your Otto

Letter from Otto to his mother dated 6 November 1944, received in New York on 17 November 1944

APO11110 NY

6 Nov
My dear Mama,

I heard that some letters were returned to the sender stating that my APO number does not exist anymore. I hope it did not happen to you. Anyway, we get our new APO very soon and I will inform you immediately. It was just a temporary number so this error is possible.
Besides that I am feeling fine and I am very curious about further developments.

Best regards to Ingi.

Many 1000 kisses,

Your Otto

Letter from Otto to his mother dated 18 November 1944, received in New York 6 December 1944

Hq 7th Army G2 Sect IPW APO 446 NY

18 Nov – France
My dear Mama –

We just moved into a nice little house and are discussing the matter, whether it is convenient for 3 people to sleep in one bed. Considering all details, I think it is better for me to sleep on the floor, especially when we have not such a masterly composed bed roll as I have. An ingenious product made from blankets, handkerchiefs, and anything else I can lay my hands on. We are still in our little French town and are leading a quiet life. From very far we can hear the sound of the big guns, but it does not disturb our delicious dinner. Thank God France is not as cold as N.Y. as we haven't got too many fireplaces here.

Best regards to Ingi –

Many kisses and much love,

Otto

Letter from Otto to his mother dated 26 November 1944, received in New York 13 December 1944

Hq CC "A" 14th Armored Div IPW120 APO446 NY
26 Nov – France

My dear Mama –

Every day new surroundings, new people, and new impressions. Last night in a stable of a pretty well shot up French town, we found a piano and I played for hours, the boys all sitting around requesting their favorites. Right now we are in a big empty house – the "Boches" [French slang for the Germans] left yesterday and everybody is looking for wine, and of course, for souvenirs. We had a lot of rations and pretty soon we will prepare a great meal; and on the wall the German menu for this week is still hanging – the tables show signs of an interrupted meal. It adds to the atmosphere a lot. The reception by the civilians is brilliant and they all threw schnapps and wine at the soldiers when the first ones came in.

All my best and many 1000 kisses,

Your Otto

Letter from Otto to his mother dated 1 December 1944, received in New York 13 December 1944

Hq CC "A" 14th Armored Div, IPW120 APO446 NY
1 Dec – France

My dear Mama –

Right now in a nice warm room with piano, we are really having a good time. It's nice now, not raining and not too cold. I played some waltzes for the people – everybody started to dance. They are all so happy to be liberated and are only too glad to welcome the Yankees in their homes. My French is a great advantage – I can talk to the people and listen to their stories about the terrible Nazis – everybody has plenty of experiences to tell. Today was an easy day – but sometimes we really have a lot of work to do; yet it's always interesting. I only wish I could get some mail; how long do my letters take to reach you?
Anyhow, this war will be over very soon, and I'll be back as the great "victor" and hero, bragging about the hardships others had.

Best regards to Ingi –

1000 kisses and much love,

Your Otto

Letter from Otto to his mother dated 3 December 1944, received in New York 13 December 1944 (Mrs. Weschler was his piano teacher in Vienna, Mr. Leon was his sponsor in the U.S. and married to Otto's cousin)

HQ Ca CC "A" 14th Armored Div. IPW 120, APO 446NY

3 Dec – France
My dear Mama –

A really idyllic Sunday in a little French village. We cook our own meals, all four standing in the kitchen and suggesting our ideas. In one room is an old piano – never quiet as continuously somebody tries to produce something on it. We have a burning stove and it is very warm here. Not much to do right now, as we are awaiting some changes. But don't worry, very soon we 'll have our Headquarters in Vienna or Berlin. Everyday, people tell us how glad they are that we chased the Germans out of here – so we don't feel bad taking advantage of this hospitality to the fullest extent, we "liberators". I wrote a lot of Christmas cards – (Weschler, Leon etc) I hope they all arrive in time –

Much love, 1000 kisses,

Your Otto

Photocopy of V-Mail Letter from Otto to his mother dated 20 December 1944, received in New York 5 January 1945

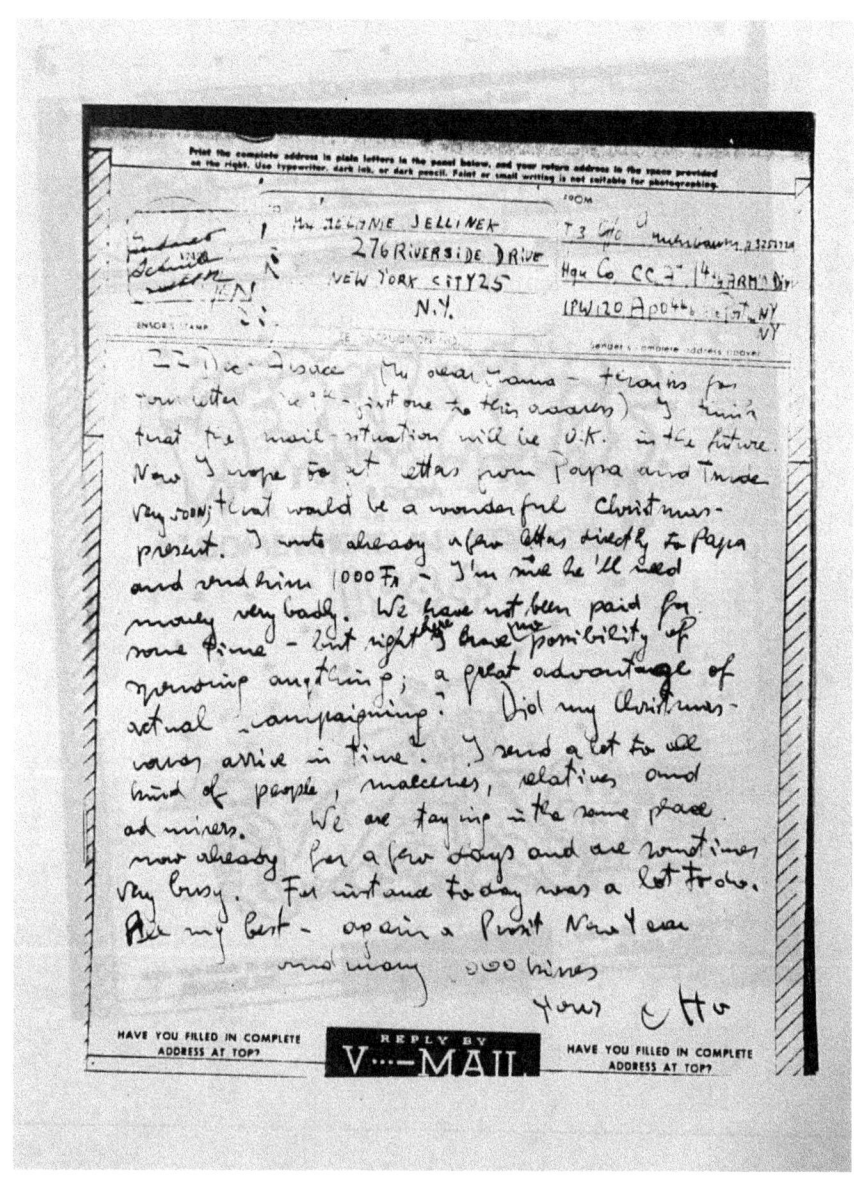

(I think Otto is referring to his cousin Edith. Risa is his mother's sister. The Collins are friends from Vienna living in the same building as his mother at 276 Riverside Drive, New York

HQ Ca CC "A" 14th Armored Div. IPW 120, APO 446NY

20 Dec, Alsace
My dear Mama –

Finally I got 3 of the old letters (4,6,7) – many thanks. I hope the rest will arrive eventually. Your English is really excellent and I have to admire it every time. It's too late now for Aunt Risa, and Edith – but I don't think I would have managed to see them anyhow. I was too far away from London. Poor Edith – all alone now. Everything is OK over here. I think we are before an easy period.
Give my regards to Ingi, and all friends like Collins, etc.

Many 1000 kisses,

Much love,

Your Otto

Letter from Otto to his mother dated 22 Dec 1944, received in New York 5 Jan 1945 (Otto's father was in France, and his sister, Trude, in Italy)
"Prosit" is equivalent to "cheers" and in this case means "Here's to the New Year."

HQ Ca CC "A" 14th Armored Div. IPW 120, APO 446, NY

22 Dec – Alsace
My dear Mama –

Thanks for your letter (Dec 9th – first to this address). I think that the mail situation will be OK in the future. Now I hope to get letters from Papa and Trude very soon. That would be a wonderful Christmas present. I wrote already a few letters directly to Papa and sent him 1000Fr – I'm sure he'll need money very badly. We have not been paid for some time – but right here I have no possibility of spending anything; a great advantage of actually "campaigning". Did my Christmas cards arrive in time? I sent a lot to all kinds of people, ?????, relatives and admirers. We are staying in the same place now already for a few days and are sometimes very busy. For instance, today was a lot to do.

All my best – again a Prosit New Year

And many 1000 kisses.

Your Otto

Photocopy of Otto's V-Mail Christmas card to his mother

Letter from Otto to his mother dated 1 Jan 1945, received in New York 22 Jan 1945

Hq CC "A" 14th Armored Div IPW120 APO 446NY

1 Jan 45 – Alsace
My dear Mama –

Prosit! I hope you had a nice New Year's Eve celebration. In our case it was rather quiet – today an Alsacien gave us a bottle of champagne, for some coming celebrations. Driving through a village we found all people on the street throwing apples in our cars and making quite some "holladria" [merry noise]. Our field kitchen prepared a turkey dinner "superfine"! Evening celebrations are not so easy – no civilian is allowed on the street and it is mighty dark. We had some snow too, but not enough for good skiing – so you don't have to send me my "Bretteln" [boards] as yet
In the meanwhile no further news from Papa.

All my best again – best regards to Ingi.

Many 1000 kisses,

Your Otto

Letter from Otto to his mother dated 10 Jan, received in New York 22 Jan 1945

Hq CC "A" 14th Armored Div IPW120 APO 446 NY

10 Jan – in Alsace
My dear Mama –

I'm a few days without mail from you; it probably will come all together at the same time. I am feeling fine, set up in another tiny little village, with people speaking a terrible language in between German, French and switzer-dütsch [Swiss-German] or something, Every village seems to have a different dialect. It's getting warmer and we have some more snow now,. Tonight there will me a movie for the company in some barn [Scheune] but I'm afraid it will be too cold for that – I have now a sleeping sack in which I can button up myself completely with blankets inside to keep warm. We have Schnee-Schuhe [snow shoes] too – so I don't have to worry about the winter. The first day we arrive in a new place we "bury" the people immediately with presents of chocolate, soup and chewing gum – in exchange we get wood to make a fire and warm water to wash.

All my best and much love and kisses,

Your Otto

Letter from Otto to his mother dated 17 Jan, received in New York 29 Jan 1945

Hq CC "A" 14th Armored Div IPW120 APO 446NY

17 Jan – Alsace
My dear Mama –

I just received your New Year's telegram – thanks very much. You see that telegrams are slower even than letters- but lately there was a slow down in letters too.
You probably read about us a lot in the newspapers – it doesn't go too easy right now. But now as the Russian offensive started, I'm sure it can't take much longer anymore. It isn't too cold out here fortunately enough and the many hills have a very romantic look. Too bad you can't go around on pleasure walks but that isn't customary around here.
How was your New Year's Eve? Big party?
Best regards to all friends.

Many 1000 kisses,

Your Otto

Letter from Otto to his mother dated 20 Jan 1945, received in New York 5 Feb 1945 . (Marshall Zhukov was the most important and successful Russian general in World War II, responsible for the successful defense of Moscow, Stalingrad, and Leningrad, pushing the German forces back to Germany. He led the final attack on Berlin.)

Hq CC "A" 14th Armored Div IPW120 APO 446NY

20 Jan – Alsace
My dear Mama,

No mail from the USA but 2 letters from Papa. He is fine – living alone, even cooking for himself as restaurants are too expensive. Today is big snowfall, it comes down en masse. We are together with the medics in a nice warm room, taking it easy. It's hard to fight a war in a time like that – I think for the time being I have to leave that to my friend Marshall Zhukov. We'll meet soon, I hope, even if he has to take the longer part of the way to get to this meeting. The civilians look with slight worry upon invaders in their houses, but I convinced them that we are very civilized people and wouldn't take or use anything of their property unless we need it. Well – there are certain things we need very badly. On the other hand we liberate and defend them, don't we? I wrote again to Trude – I hope one day, I'll really get some answer; would be wonderful.

All my best – and many 1000 kisses,

Your Otto

Letter from Otto to his mother dated 24 Jan 1945, received in New York 5 Feb 1945 ("Joe" refers to Stalin)

Hq CC "A" 14th Armored Div IPW120 APO 446NY

24 Jan - Alsace
My dear Mama -

Many thanks for your V-mail (17) of Dec 31; as you see the mail service is a bit slower right now, but such delays are bound to happen every once in a while.
I receive regular mail from Papa now – only for the first letter from Trude, I am still waiting. Life is easy now, and I am just coming back from a movie – given for us in some railroad station. Yesterday we had the thrilling experience of a shower, and our teeth were checked up. For you see, we are well taken care of.
I wonder where "Joe" is going to be, by the time you get this letter?

All my best to Ingi – and many kisses for you

Always your Otto

Letter from Otto to his mother dated 25 Jan 1945, received in New York 6 Feb 1945 (100th and Riverside is where Otto's mother lived)

Hq CC "A" 14th Armored Div IPW120 APO 446NY

25 Jan – Alsace
My dear Mama, dear Ingi –

I just received letter No. 20, Jan 11th.
Today one of my friends received a parcel sent to the same old address where all your packages were sent too, so there is definite hope that they will arrive very soon.
My life continues to be not too heroic – but that might change of course and we hope to meet Comrade ……..sky ?? in the near future.
By now we know all the stories of the Alsatians by heart – yet we listen patiently to all their troubles. Gratefully, they offer us warm rooms and force us to drink their terrible schnapps.(I always succeed in spilling the abominable stuff secretly in some corner – I am definitely not a drinker) – but you cannot insult your hosts. It's all white here – and pretty cold, naturally not as cold as on the famous corner 100th and Riverside!

All my best and much love,

Otto

Letter from Otto to his mother dated 26 Jan 1945, received in New York 5 Feb 1945

Hq CC "A" 14th Armored Div IPW120 APO 446NY

26 Jan Alsace
My dear Mama –

Many thanks for your 21st letter, Jan 15. I didn't get the letter as yet where you write to me about Trude; I am so anxious to get it! The reports I have are all together a bit confusing , but as long as she is well now, I am satisfied, I hope I can see the little Irene soon. I'm extremely proud to be an uncle. She must be very happy with the ????
Papa had a very hard time for about 1 year – 2 months he had to spend in prison in Monaco, as he was caught with false papers, but otherwise he was so lucky to escape the Gestapo and to hide himself successfully! He will move to Paris – and I hope soon I'll be able to visit him there.
The end of all the troubles is in sight – it's getting better every day!

All my love and 1000 kisses

Your Otto

Letter from Otto to his mother dated 28 Jan 1945, received in New York 15 Feb. 1945 (Again "Joe" refers to Stalin)

Hq CC "A" 14th Armored Div IPW120 APO 446NY

Jan 28 in Alsace
My dear Mama –

I just received letter No 1 of Oct 23 – written by Ingi – which somehow took a much longer trip than all the others. Thanks just the same! I had great pleasure reading about the parcels and their content – well, one day they will arrive too!
I received mail from Papa – he sends you his best regards – he is well and about to move to Paris.
About myself: everything is all right; it snows almost continuously and the streets are very difficult for any kind of traffic. Hard to fight a war, so again we turn the business over to Joe – he likes this kind of weather.

All my best and many 1000 kisses

Your Otto

Letter from Otto to his mother dated 1 Feb 1945, received in New York 14 Feb 1945. (Otto had not seen his father since 1939, and had not seen his sister Trude since 1937, when he was only nineteen and Trude, twenty, went to Italy. Unfortunately, I don't know what terrible things he is referring to when he mentions Trude).

Hq CC "A" 14th Armored Div IPW120 APO 446NY

1 Feb Alsace
My dear Mama –

Many thanks for the 2 V-mail no 14 Jan 10 and Jan 5th. In the meanwhile I had heard about Trude and the terrible things that happened to her. Poor Truderl – but I am sure she feels better having her little Irene. I would love to see both as soon as possible.
Papa is moving to Paris and I am about to send him some money; unfortunately I can't do it by money order and I have to take a chance with simple letters. As soon as I find out his Paris address I let you know. He heard about Trude through the Red Cross.
Out here there isn't much new, except that it's raining instead of snowing and the roads are like big lakes. But it's warm, what we don't mind at all. By the time you get this letter, the war must be almost over – you might not read about the 14th armored division rolling into Berlin – but somebody else will call in and it's all right with us too!

All my best and many 1000 kisses

Your Otto

Letter from Otto to his mother dated 3 Feb 1945, received in New York 16 Feb 1945

Hq CC "A" 14th Armored Div IPW120 APO 446NY
3 Feb in Alsace
My dear Mama –

It's almost spring here. Very pleasantly warm and of course a terrific Quatsch.[muddy mess]
We met a few friends from Ritchie and exchanged experiences of our famous trade, celebrating the event with some vin blanc.
Our host killed a rabbit especially for us and the 3rd man on my team – fortunately enough a professional cook, will prepare the same for a brilliant Sunday dinner. So you see, life is really "rugged"! In the meanwhile everybody is betting for the end of the war. We had a bottle of champagne saved for this very occasion.

Best regards to Ingi,

all my best and 1000 kisses

Your Otto

Letter from Otto to his mother dated 11 Feb 1945, received in New York 23 Feb 1945

Hq CC "A" 14th Armored Div IPW120 APO 446NY

11 Feb in Alsace
My dear Mama –

Again we are deep in mud, but having perfect Schnee-schuhe [snow shoes] we don't mind it too much,
We are still living a pretty easy life and I am getting to be so well known in town, that I'll be soon "Ehrenbürger" [honorary citizen] or something.
Our "Grandma" prepared for us a Gugelhupf [an Austrian bundt cake]bfor Sunday, but unfortunately the raisins were missing. C'est la guerre! Yesterday the band visited our village and gave a little concert. All the civilians were standing around and the Yanks became extremely popular. Everybody delights in the Tschin-da-ra-ta-bum-bum and thinks it's the best part of the war.

Best regards to Ingi

Much love and 1000 kisses

Your Otto

Letter from Otto to his mother dated 13 Feb 1945, received in New York 24 Feb 1945
"Oberleutnant" is the equivalent of an American Lieutenant Colonel

Hq CC "A" 14th Armored Div IPW120 APO 446NY

13 Feb Alsace
My dear Mama –

Today happed the most sensational, as I received my first package! Many, many, thanks – it's really perfect choice. I am almost afraid that Runmdstadt ??? might have captured it, and I saw already German soldiers eating my chocolate, and some Oberleutnant using my flashlight – but finally it arrived safely. It is complete according to contents: 3 Flashlights – I am especially happy about because you need it every day and they are hard to get. Brillo, handkerchiefs, and 2 boxes of excellent chocolate. I started right in – so I wasn't like the soldier who wrote home: I received the candies, the one I had was very good! This happens in Barracks where many soldiers are together and every box is immediately raided – but here one had more privacy in opening packages.
I think all the other parcels will now arrive too, as the "la glace est rompue" [the glass is broken] – It continues to be very warm and I was riding around in our "jeep" quite much lately.

Many thanks again!

And all my best and many kisses

Your Otto

Letter from Otto to his mother dated 15 Feb.1945, received in New York 28 Feb. 1945 (Lord Henry Paulet, became Marquess in 1924. His second wife was Caroline. He was the longest living member of the House of Lords, when he died at the age of 99 in 1962)

Hq CC "A" 14th Armored Div IPW120 APO 446NY

15 Feb in Alsace
My dear Mama:

I received Letter No. 8 (Nov.13) slightly delayed. The chocolate disappeared completely in the meanwhile – and everybody admired my tiny little flashlight. I even tried out the nail files – quite amazing, isn't it? – Yesterday I spent all day in the jeep riding in beautiful sunshine all through the country. It's warm like spring!
I received a letter from Papa – still from Nice (he must be in Paris by now) – and he asked me to write a letter of thanks to his saviors – the Marquis and Marchioness of Winchester, Monte Carlo. Oh la,la,la,la! I did that in my most beautiful Shakespeare-English and in my most beautiful handwriting. They helped Papa out of prison and afterwards in hiding. They are old clients of his.
Everything is fine on our front and life is easy.

All my best and 1000 kisses

Your Otto

Letter from Otto to his mother dated 17 Feb. 1945, received in New York 28 Feb. 1945

Hq CC "A" 14th Armored Div IPW120 APO 446NY

17 Feb. in Alsace
My dear Mama –

many thanks for your letter from the 3rd. Don't worry, it's still warm and pleasant around here. Tonight we are going to have movies in an empty warehouse and then, we linguists, go again to our friend the Bürgermeister [mayor] bringing along a bottle of wine. My lt. [lieutenant] might become a father today or tomorrow so it's a good reason to celebrate. You see, it's a rough war!

No news in the meanwhile from Papa or Trude. I would like so much to hear from her already! The(???) paid us a visit again – marching through the town and the war really seems to be very far away. At night we hear the news over the radio – and so we are well informed about our Russian allies.

All my best and many kisses

Yours Otto

Letter from Otto to his mother dated 20 Feb.1945. Receipt date not marked.

Hq CC "A" 14th Armored Div IPW120 APO 446NY

20 Feb.
My dear Mama –

our peaceful existence continues to be very pleasant. We are by now known by everybody in town and spent most of our evenings with the Bürgermeister [mayor] and his piano. Yesterday, I had to play for our Major and after a repeat performance of the Blue Danube he melted away completely.
Otherwise we don't overwork and busy ourselves mainly with helping all the other people out with the language and driving around with our jeep on all kinds of "missions" The headlines are occupied by McArthur and Komiens (???) and for us there are just a few lines – but we are not jealous, we give the others a chance too. How is the homefront?

All my best and many 1000 kisses

Yours Otto

Letter from Otto to his mother dated 26 Feb. 1945, received in New York 8 March 1945

Hq CC "A" 14th Armored Div IPW120 APO 446NY

26 Feb.
My dear Mama –

the news are little slow and even from Papa I didn't hear anything whether he is in Paris or not.
Last night for the first time I was invited to a brilliant dinner – 5 courses- poulet, hors d'oeuvres and wine. In exchange we brought to the mayor (our hosts) a box with coffee (we got it from our kitchen) which is here of the utmost value.
Life is still peaceful in our little village and while the rest of the Co. is engaged in all kinds of training, manoeuvres, we take it easy and run around with the "Tashen livre" [paperback] interpreting. I am our doctor's right hand man, when he examines the sick civilians here and of course the greatest help to my souvenir hunting colleagues.

All my best to Ingi –

Many 1000 kisses

Your Otto

Letter from Otto to his mother dated 28 Feb. 1945, received in New York 10 March 1945

Hq CC "A" 14th Armored Div IPW120 APO 446NY

28 Feb
My dear Mama –

many thanks for your dear letter of the 12th. I hope mail service is better now and you get all my letters in time. There are always some delays. From Papa I didn't hear anything as yet and I still don't know whether he arrived already in Paris or not. The packages are still "on the way".
It's very warm and sunny right now and it's quiet all over. My musical activities (???) and I have a concert engagement to the "front" tomorrow; 2 old Ritchie-friends will take me in their jeep. I might have an appearance to night ???
Otherwise I am always helping out in civilian affairs – they all come to us with their troubles.
We "liberated" a radio – but most unfortunately it doesn't work; yet we always hear the news in ??? to the Weihnachtsbericht [Christmas report] at a civilian house every night.

All my best and many 1000 kisses

Your Otto

Letter from Otto to his mother dated 4 March 1945, received in New York 13 March 45 (FFI stands for French Forces of the Interior, which is what DeGaulle called the Resistance)

Hq CC "A" 14th Armored Div IPW120 APO 446NY

4 March
My dear Mama –

we had another dinner invitation at the FFI chief, with many regrets and tears we left the place. Now, here, we enjoy the most unusual pleasure of having a mess hall (dining room), as a rule after getting the food from the Goulashkanone, most of the Company ate somewhere out in the open, which was not too pleasant. By the way, we never did it. We just walked into the next house and friendly smiling we sat down at the table and enjoyed our meal. Usually after talking to the amazed people in our Hochdeutsch, [high German] they provided some wine in true French manner.
What is the opinion in NY about the war? Here one doesn't dare to be too optimistic about an early end. We'll find out.

All my best and many kisses

Your Otto

Letter from Otto to his mother dated 6 March 1945, received in New York 15 March 45

Hq CC "A" 14th Armored Div IPW120 APO 446NY

6 March
My dear Mama –

many thanks for your V-mail of Feb 16th. I am glad everybody is well. Yesterday we were filmed and fotographed, to our great surprise – just while we were on the job. So don't be surprised if you recognize in one of the rugged soldiers you see in the Newsreel your own son – or if you see my picture in Life (or somewhere) busily studying the maps. Naturally a lot of people tried to get in the pictures, standing behind us and our victims. Yes, that's the way to become famous! Otherwise, we are busy again, and in a very interesting way too.
I might get a pass to Paris in a few weeks!

Best regards to Ingi

Many 1000 kisses,

much love,

Your Otto

Letter from Otto to his mother dated 10 March 1945, received in New York 19 March 45

Hq CC "A" 14th Armored Div IPW120 APO 446NY

10 March
My dear Mama –

Tonight I had again a concert evening and I played for 2 "Stabsärzte" [staff doctors] and a few other officers in some other town with a piano. The civilian hosts contributed apple and coffee cake and it was quite a pleasant evening.
I got news from Papa from Paris. He is fine and sends you his best regards. He is looking for a job in his old line, but most of his former associates left for the USA. I sent him again some money and so I hope he will be able to manage. We are still watching the others fighting – but they seem to do all right! (even without us).

All my best and 1000 kisses

Your Otto

Letter from Otto to his mother dated 12 March 1945, received in New York 21 March 45

Hq CC "A" 14th Armored Div IPW120 APO 446NY

12 March
My dear Mama –

I was very happy about your last letter (Feb 28) and I can imagine how glad you were to get the fotos of Trude and Irene. I would love to see one of those pictures too one day. I'm sure soon you will hear again personally from her and so will I. One has to be patient nowadays. I wrote to Papa about it right away. Otherwise everything is going along all right; one of my teammates is a Krefelder; just a few days ago he was "liberated". I wonder when we will be liberated? The Russians have to hurry up a bit. We are still together with the medics in our room, and the armbruestiger [?] of doctor and German speaking people brings us a lot of customers. Everybody in town feels some pain somewhere. They all get the same pills and are satisfied and grateful – for aspirins we get apples and for bandages fresh eggs. As we had a professional cook in our midst, we have most delightful snack suppers.

All my best and 1000 kisses,

Your Otto

Letter from Otto to his mother dated 14 March 1945, received in New York 24 March 45

Hq CC "A" 14th Armored Div IPW120 APO 446NY

14 March
My dear Mama -

here too in this little village I discovered a piano and we had a nice concert evening tonight; one of my colleagues has a beautiful baritone voice and we improvised along for a few hours.
It's already quite warm, and lately sunny and spring like. We are fairly busy, and I continued my (???) activities too. Mail is a little slower in the last days, but this is nothing too unusual.
From Paris too, it takes a long time for a letter to arrive, longer than from the States.
I hope everything is OK at home.

Best regards to Ingi

Many 1000 kisses

Your Otto

Letter from Otto to his step-father, Josef Jellinek, dated 16 March 1945, received in New York 26 March 1945

H CC "A" 14th Armored Div IPW120 APO 446NY

16 March
Dear Ingi –

today finally arrived your Xmas parcel with all the books. Thank you very much – now I really will have enough to read for some time. And my colleagues will be happy too, because reading material is scarce and our paper "Stars and Stripes" is usually read from cover to cover by everybody. It took quite a long time, but actually very few things get lost and in time I'll get everything.

We have now most beautiful spring weather, a much better time to fight a war. If everything goes all right I think I have a chance to get a promotion soon even before we get to Berlin.

Alsace is still nice and friendly, but they hope that the war will soon move away and (???) in the Reich. We all hope that.

All my best –many kisses to Mama

Yours,

Otto

Letter from Otto to his mother dated 20 March 1945, received in New York 30 March 45

Hq CC "A" 14th Armored Div IPW120 APO 446NY

20 March
My dear Mama –

we are back again to our lustiges Zigeunerleben! [merry gypsy life] In the last two days I was awfully busy, work coming in from all sides, and I hardly had a second to relax. Tomorrow is the official beginning of spring and it is pleasantly warm. This fact makes the Wanderleben [roaming life] more agreeable. You probably read the newspapers and you know that many Alsatian children are happy again to get "chocolat" and "cigarettes pour Papa" – they really missed it now for 2 months! I wrote you already that I received the parcel with the books and was very glad about it. Since then there was no mail, as our service stopped for a few days. I am afraid my Paris trip has to be postponed for the time being. Soon I'll make up for it!

All my best and 1000 kisses

Your Otto

Letter from Otto to his mother dated 27 March 1945, received in New York 9 April 1945

Hq CC "A" 14th Armored Div IPW120 APO 446NY

27 March – in Germany
My dear Mama –

you can imagine how happy and how excited I am to tell you that I am about to go to Paris! It will be just wonderful – 3 nights and 2 days time. My very nice Major fixed me up and got the pass for me faster than I ever thought. Of course, there was no way of informing Papa about my coming so it will be a complete surprise to him. That will be a great reunion after 6 years – and then of course Paris and all the music, art and books – tomorrow morning I'll leave and I think I'll be there late in the afternoon. Otherwise everything is fine – spring is coming slowly and all the fighting can't take too long anymore.

All my best and 1000 kisses

Your Otto

PLEASE NOTE: Letters written in the period 28 March through 17 May 1945 are missing.

Letter from Otto to his mother, dated 18 May 1945, and received in New York 11 June 1945

18 May in Bavaria

My dear Mama,

    I am sure you will be happy to read a typewritten letter for a change. Today I will try to tell you a few things which I couldn't say in war times because of security regulations, but today im tiefsten Frieden (in deepest peace) it isn't so important anymore.

    Well, when I left NYC on the 4th of October I found myself on the big NEW AMSTERDAM, the greatest Dutch boat. About 9000 people were on board, so I heard, and went all alone by ourselves without any protection. The only protection was our speed and a few guns on board of the ship. It took us 9 days to cross the ocean; at first we went straight East till we came near to the Azores. Not far from the Spanish coast we turned North and went up between Ireland and England to reach GLASGOW. We did not go into GLASGOW itself but we stayed in one of the suburbs and left the same night with the train heading SOUTH. We came to a Replacement Depot near BIRMINGHAM. As you remember, we stayed there almost 3 weeks. It was very hard to get passes to BIRMINGHAM, but most of the boys went anyway, as there were certain means and ways to get there.

    One nice day one group of Ritchie people were sent to London and we took the plane to PARIS, which really was a wonderful experience. It was quite a big plane flying very smoothly and I never had any air-sickness, but watched with great pleasure the lovely bird's view. We stayed 2 days outside of PARIS and then a few teams were selected to go to the 7th Army.

    We took off in trucks, and after one day's traveling we arrived in VITEL (where you get the water from.) The next day we continued to EPINAL, where the 7th Army Headquarters were at the time.

    In EPINAL I had my first experiences with Prisoners and did a few interrogations, which were not too interesting compared with all the following ones. After 5 days, our team (6 men) were assigned to the 14th Armored Div., a new outfit with no battle experience at that time. The team was split in two parts; 3 men stayed in Div HQ and myself and 2 men went to the Combat Command "a", which is the equivalent to a Regiment in an Armored Division.

At first we had no "peep" (=jeep) of our own and were depending on other people continuously. It was cold and raining continuously when we joined CC"A" near ST. Die in France/ Our first campaign was across the VOGES mountains south of Strassbourg to go to Schlettstadt on the way to Colmar. The first campaign took 14 days, but never got as far as Schlettstadt, which was captured 2 months later by somebody else. In there 2 weeks, we had about 250 prisoners, which was captured 2 months later, by somebody else. In these two weeks we had about 150 prisoners and luckily enough a brilliant reputation.

My first prisoner told me the exact position of some German artillery, our artillery fired at this point and 2 days later, when we passed this particular point in our advance you could see clearly that the position was correct and the German gun had been hit. Another fellow on the very first days, gave us some position of mines on the road, and we got a lot of credit for our work. All our reports were handwritten at the time because our typewriter had not as yet arrived; we got the equipment after the first campaign together with our "peep".

After that we had a rest period in a little village West of STRASSBOURG. Our next move was through the HAGENAU forest straight north to WEISSENBURG, the border city between ALSACE and GERMANY, and up to the Siegfried line just behind the German border. This was from the 14th to the 24th December. At that time our division did not break the Siegfried line, in fact we didn't even try because by the time we got there, our troops were already tired and the Germans were still very strong in the line with a lot of fire power. That was the first time that we felt the German artillery and we had many noisy nights with a lot of shelling in our immediate neighborhood.

In WEISSENBURG we interrogated a lot of soldiers and civilians, all about the Siegfried line which was very helpful two months later, when we actually went through the line in the last big offensive.

After this campaign we traveled around in ALSACE for two weeks. If I say "we" I mean the Headquarters Co. consisting of the Staff and Radio men, Kitchen supplies etc. all in Half tracks or "peeps." Nobody is marching in our army. At that time the German counter offensive had started in the Ardennes and a similar attack was expected in Alsace every day.

It started when the Germans on the 31 December sent over two American planes bearing the Allied star, a sign of recognition for Allied planes, vehicles and equipment. Seeing the familiar sight of our own planes, nobody worried till suddenly these "friendly" planes started dropping bombs. Three very good friends of mine were amongst the victims and from now on every plane was looked at with greatest suspicion. This happened south of WEISSENBURG.

On the 11th of January we arrived in a little village by the name of KUHLENDORF, near Hagenau, north west of Strassbourg. While our troops were fighting a cruel defensive battle in RITTERSHOFEN and HATTEN, we really had a rough time in KUHLENDORF.

Every day seemed like a month, so crowded it was with experiences; and now, as I am slowly forgetting most of the other places, every little incidence of KUHLENDORF is still fresh in my memory. Our own little farm house was hit several times by artillery, the next house was hit by aerial bombing. To go outside to the latrine was a Heldentat [an act of heroism], and to stand in line for food was more of a crawling there on your belly than a walking. There I had to do interrogations in cellars, or under most unpleasant conditions.

On the 21st of January we staged our great strategic retreat, rear guarding the retreat of the entire 7th Army in this sector. We went to a place called WIWISHEIM without any excitements. Here I did a lot of other things, amongst them I had to do some house searching which made me a very feared man in the village. In that time I visited STRASSBOURG twice.

On the 4th of March we left and went in line on the MODER River near PFAFFENHOFEN and ÜBERBACH. This was the most glorious time of my five broadcasts to the German lines. Only 300 yards away from the Germans we put up our loudspeaker [on] what was left of the roof of a farm house, and I delivered my speech, interrupted by machine gun fire. About 15 deserters were the success of our speech. My lieutenant produced the speech in English and I made a very dramatic German translation.

All the Germans who did not follow my advice to surrender were sorry about their decision on the 18th of March, our D-Day for the last big offensive of the 7th Army. Again we went through the Hagenau Forest to WEISSENBURG, which we reached this time already after two days, passing by in a hurry KUHLENDORF and RITTERSHOFFEN, which both naturally are completely destroyed. Our troops fought for three days in STEINFELD, a strong point of the Siegfried Line and in the night of the 23rd of March we passed through a burning, completely destroyed STEINFELD between the famous Dragon's Teeth and all the Siegfried Bunker and fortifications.

At that time we captured hundreds and thousands of prisoners. At first we very seldom had officers, but in the meanwhile I had already all ranks including a general, whom I interrogated.

Then came my visit to PARIS, and coming back I crossed the RHINE at LUDWIGSHAFEN and MANNHEIM - there is little left of either of the cities - before that I passed though SPEYER which is in good shape, no bombing. Then to DARMSTADT, ASCHAFFENBURG, HANAU, and north of BAMBERG I finally found my company. We passed through the lovely BAD BRÜCKENAU and on the 10th of April our Division achieved its greatest advance of almost 30 miles in a day in reaching NEUSTADT. We continued in direction BAYREUTH, which we never reached, but we went south toward NUREMBERG, and reached HERSBRUCK on the 18th of April. Before that I passed through COBURG which is in perfect condition; our bombers missed that one. In HERSBRUCK we lived in the SS Concentration Camp I wrote you about, and we had the unpleasant experience of a surprise attack of the Germans, just on our little town, but fortunately enough it was repulsed after two hours of fighting. Then we went down to the DANUBE, which we crossed at INGOLSTADT, and went right on to cross the ISAR at MOOSBURG and then we finally came to this place, one hour from MUNICH, where we awaited the final VICTORY. This division captured about 45,000 prisoners in all the campaigns, most of them naturally in the last phase of the war.

So, this was a long letter! Next time about some of my interrogation experiences.

1000 kisses, all my best, lots of love,

your Otto.

I just received your letter of 2 May. Many thanks!

Letter from Otto to his mother dated 23 May 1945, received in New York 1 June 1945

Hq CC "A" 14th Armored Div IPW120 APO 446NY

23 May, Erding near Munich
My dear Mama –

many thanks for your letter from the 13 May. The mail service is now really functioning most brilliantly and goes a lot faster than in war times.
So Trude went to Naples for a month, that's fine ! I wish I could visit her. You never know, everything is possible and maybe one day I get a pass to go to Rome. But up till now I can't even get letter from Rome. I am waiting to get to a larger place and then I will put in an application for Trude to come to the USA. I don't think there should be too much difficulty in obtaining a visa for her.
It seems that I am going to stay here for a little while and that we are going to continue to work in the PW camp here. This Camp probably will exist for quite some time, because it takes time till all will be examined and discharged; and many naturally won't be discharged for a long time, if at all.
I listen frequently to the various radio stations. There is no Radio Wien as yet; it seems to be kaput, only Radio Graz is very well heard from here. Besides the red sender Berlin. The Russians have the entire male population clean out the streets and repair the roads and bridges.

Froehliche Pfingsten – all my best

And 1000 kisses, yours, Otto

(NOTE: Pfingsten is the German term for Pentecost, and is a way to celebrate spring. I don't know whether Otto had the chance to apply for a visa for my mother,, but she told me she was unable to get one because she was unmarried and had an illegitimate child.)

Letter from Otto to his mother dated 21 June 1945, received in New York 3 July 1945 (Emmy is Otto's first cousin, whose husband owned a hotel in the Adirondacks that my grandmother liked to visit. Emmy and her husband escaped from Vienna via England. Emmy's sister Helly was a euthanasia victim, gassed by the Nazis.
Strobl, Bad Gastein and Bad Ischl were popular Austrian resorts the family used to go to in the summer)

Hq CC "A" 14th Armored Div IPW120 APO 446 NY

Erding, 21 June
My dear Mama –

thanks a lot for your letter 11 June. Mail Service is fine now and I am getting the package very shortly.

Now it really starts to get hot, but not to compare with the Hundstage [dog days] in NYC. Maybe we go to Austria soon, it is quite possible, but my hopes for a furlough or pass to Paris are for the time being out of the question. I have to be patient and await further developments. Maybe I spend the summer in Strobl or Bad Gastein – it's all possible. In Ischl I would miss the familiar faces on the Esplanade, and I wonder who is going to sit in Café Bazar? I hope you enjoy your summer with Emmy.

Letter from Otto to his mother dated 3 July 1945, received in New York 11 July 1945 Holding one's thumbs in Austria s equivalent to crossing one's fingers. Otto combined he two.

Hq CC "A" 14th Armored Div IPW120 APO 446 NY

Erding, 3 July
My dear Mama –

yesterday I received your wonderful package and thank you very much for it. Really all very excellent things – am glad to have the socks and handkerchiefs, now I really have a set of them, and the chocolate as usual is of the finest quality. Thanks so much for the wonderful music too, you know that this remains my chief pleasure. Especially now when I don't have a piano at my disposal. So I can continue to study some music and keep in close contact with my original profession.

It must be awfully hot over there, here it is rather cold than hot, with very frequent rains and very seldom one goes without a blouse or jacket on the streets, Yes, we very often have a fire burning in our office barracks in Camp. I finally saw München and I was very glad to make the trip. It must have been a very pretty and modern city one day, but today the Altstadt is completely destroyed and only a few houses in the outer sections of the city are still in good shape. I took my picture on the ruins of the Braune Haus, visited the Feldherrnhalle and the famous Bier Keller, now the chief attractions of Munich., There are still a lot of people living there and even broken down houses are inhabited as most people prefer to sleep in their own cellar than to wonder around as refugees in other overcrowded towns and villages. But as far as I heard most other cities are much worse off than Munich, and I remember Darmstadt and Mannheim to be a lot more destroyed. If everything goes all right I will get a pass to Paris on the 18th July but I am almost afraid that I will be transferred sooner. The whole division is slowly but surely being dissolved and distributed amongst other outfits. So there is a strong possibility that I will be called back to headquarters for reassignment shortly. Let's cross our thumbs [hold our thumbs in Austria is equivalent to crossing one's fingers] maybe I still make it, I would go to the Red Cross and try to do something for Trude, or at least find out what I could do for her. So let's hope I get it without trouble.

Now, all the best, thanks again and many 1000 kisses, Your Otto

Letter from Otto to his mother dated 7 July 1945
Emmerl is the nickname for Otto's cousin Emmy.

Hq CC "A" 14th Armored Div IPW120 APO 446 NY

7 July
My dearest Mama,

Thank you very much for your last two letters (24 and 29). I am so glad you get some mail from Trude almost regularly now. I'm still waiting for the first letter. I wrote Papa about the various packages you sent him, soon I hope I will see him personally. It is still not hot at all here, and I pity all the sweating New Yorkers. I read that the Salzburg festivals will take place again in August – so maybe I'll have a chance of going there on a pass. But I can't quite imagine how it should be done, with all this confusion all over.

Give my best regards to Emmerl when you see her.

All my best and many 1000 kisses

Yours Otto

Letter from Otto to his mother dated 14 July 1945, received in New York 21 July 1945

Hq CC "A" 14th Armored Div IPW120 APO 446 NY

Erding, 14 July
My dear Mama,

so on Monday the 16th I start my trip to Paris! You can imagine how happy I am about it. I almost had a chance to go by plane but it did not work out. Most probably when I come back, I won't come back to Erding anymore, because they will move out of here very soon. All our SS prisoners will be sent to Dachau and most of the others are discharged so something now will happen.
The weather is beautiful now and I hope it continues like that in France too.
Best regards to Ingi – have a nice vacation!
Much love,1000 kisses, Your Otto

Letter from Otto to his mother dated 15 July 1945

Hq CC "A" 14th Armored Div IPW120 APO 446 NY

Erding, 15 July
My dear Mama –

thank you very much for your letter of the 6 July. From tomorrow I'm going to Wasserburg and Tuesday morning I go on my trip to Luxembourg by truck and then with the train to Paris.
Today is first really hot day, and I hope the weather stays as nice.
When I come back I might have to run after my unit like last time, when they crossed the Rhine in the meanwhile. The Camp won't last too long here anymore.
Best of luck for your vacation.

All my best and many 1000 kisses

Yours Otto

Letter from Otto to his mother dated 4 August 1945 -received at Emmy and Walter's "Hollywood Hills Hotel" in Old Forge NY.
The "terrible consul" might refer to Trude's attempt to get a visa.

Hq CC "A" 14th Armored Div IPW120 APO 446 NY

4 Aug., Erding
My dear Mama –

the Camp is closing up and for the next time we probably go either to Burghausen, which is on the Inn river, right at the Austrian border, or to Wasserburg, where our headquarters are. There is not too much to do and this will be only a temporary occupation.
Any news from Trude, or from other people? I am curious how everything will work out with the terrible Consul.

Give all my best to Ingi

All my best and 1000 kisses

Your Otto

Letter from Otto to his mother dated 9 August 1945, received at Emmy and Walter's "Hollywood Hills Hotel" in Old Forge NY.

Hq CC "A" 14th Armored Div IPW120 APO 446 NY

Erding, 9 Aug
My dear Mama,

Thank you very much for the beautiful package I received today. Now I really have a large supply of socks and underwear and you don't have to worry about it for a long time. Thanks so much for the pineapple and the cheese. I always prefer it to candy. We get quite a lot of candy here, but good juices and cheese are very rare. Today we finally moved to Wasserburg, but had to come back again as we couldn't move all our things in one load. Wasserburg is a charming little town at the Inn river, situated in a lovely valley. There is no sign of any war around there, nothing has been destroyed. The town is jammed with soldiers and it wasn't easy to find quarters. But we found them on the outskirts of the town in a settlement of modern little houses and now we are gut untergebracht. [well lodged]
Our work will be mostly investigative work. It will mean a lot of driving around in the country. We don't mind that at all, in fact it is more pleasant than always to sit around in an office.
How long this will last is very indefinite, but I think we will stay here as long as we remain with the Division.
How is your Sommerfrische? [summer vacation] How is Emmy and Walter? Too bad that you have no car. It would make things a lot easier.

All my love and many kisses,

your Otto

Letter from Otto to his mother dated 12 August 1945 received at Emmy and Walter's "Hollywood Hills Hotel" in Old Forge NY.

Hq CC "A" 14th Armored Div IPW120 APO 446 NY

Erding,
12 August

My dear Mama –

many thanks for your letter from the 1st of August. I am glad Collins are joining you out there, you will have nice company; give them my best regards. It's too good to believe that the war should be over in a few days! Maybe when you get this letter there is already "tiefster Frieden!" [deepest peace] It doesn't change my situation right now; I think I will stay as the Polizei minister von Wasserburg for a little while. But there is no danger of overwork at all! Anyhow, it won't be too long before we all come back then! We – the ones from the former Camp – come back here to Erding for the midday, and Franks, our cook, as a special treat, tries some Salzburger Nockerln as a celebration.

All my best and 1000 kisses

Your Otto

Letter from Otto to his mother dated 17 Aug. 1945, received in New York 28 Aug. 45 Peter Lynn and Martin Herz were Otto's friends. Kurt is Kurt Elias, a doctor, and Otto's best friend. Kurt's mother had remained in Vienna.

Hq CC "A" 14th Armored Div IPW120 APO 446 NY

Wasserburg, 17 Aug
My dear Mama,

Mail was very slow this week and today is a holiday, so I suppose I won't get anything this week anymore. In the meanwhile everything is deep in peace and everybody is thinking of going home even more than before.

Our division changed a lot, all the men with low points were transferred to other units, and instead we got high pointers and so when in 3-4 weeks the division is going home, all these boys will be really going home for good. So when you read that the 14th AD will arrive, don't think that it means me, because I will have to wait till all the men with over 85 points reached home. Afterwards, we probably will be transferred o one of the occupational units.

From Peter I hear that my old friend Martin Herz and some others are in Vienna and so I believe that Kurti must have heard of his mother already. Otherwise there are no connections whatsoever with the Russian occupied territory. The Salzburg Festivals opened, but of course there are only very few tickets available: 25 for the whole 3rd army! But it doesn't matter it isn't the same this year anyhow, just a weak imitation of the glorious past.

How long will you stay in Old Forge? Don't go too early, you know how hot it is in NY. Here is continues to be rather cool, and really we hardly had any hot days during the summer at all.

All my best to Ingi and Emmy.

Much love and 1000 kisses, Your Otto

Letter from Otto to his mother dated 27 Aug 1945, received in New York 5 Sept. 45 (Arthur Schnabel, famous classical pianist, was Otto's piano teacher in New York)

Wasserburg, 27 Aug
My dear Mama,

The mail situation is worse than ever. Everything around here is closing up and the boys leave on Friday for Marseille already, so there is quite some excitement.
In my new job everything will be better then, as far as the mail is concerned and I hope I still get all the many letters I am missing now.
Sad to see all the fellows going home, but very few of my friends are amongst them, because they are all low pointers too. But I think it won't take too long in my case either. In March or April the latest and I will board the ship back too.
Yesterday I took a nice ride to Munich and then to Solln where I visited Schnabel's nephew and found him to be all right in a house which had not been touched by all the bombings. They were very glad to see me and he immediately wrote a letter to his uncle in America, which I mailed for him. It was a very nice trip which I did alone for myself. I am an experienced driver already and enjoy it very much. Saturday we report to Freising, but I am afraid we will have to give up our peep there, but there will be other opportunities for trips, I think.
My team mate is Frankie, who originally comes from Krefeld, and one officer who is Hamburger, started a trip together to their home towns and I am very curious whether they got as far as that. They were not able to get an official permission so they tried it anyway. It's English territory and so I wonder whether they will succeed.
The weather is fine now, not hot, but very beautiful and one really can enjoy Wasserburg, which is one of the prettiest towns in this section.

No news from Paris either and nothing from Italy.

Best regards to Ingi

Much love and 1000 kisses,

Your Otto

Letter from Otto to his mother dated 28 Aug 1945, received in New York 7 Oct 45
I was the baby and had been very ill, in a coma for three days, and saved by penicillin that my mother begged off an American medic.

Third Army Int.Center, G-2, APO 403 NY

Wasserburg, 28 Aug.
My dear Mama,

Thank you very much for your letter from 5 Aug, which I finally received today, together with some other letters that were by mistake sent to another outfit. But this is not all and I am sure there are still a few letters somewhere and take their time to come up here.

Now, on Saturday we move to Freising, and my address will probably be G-2 Army Int Center APOI 403 but there yet might be some changes.
I'm quite glad about the change, it was not pleasant to see here all the boys going home while I still have to stay here. But of course I realize they really deserved it, some of them are already since 3 years overseas. With some luck I will make it too in a few months.
I received a letter from Papa too, and he took a 2 weeks vacation and so can now take care of some other, little businesses, besides taking a rest.
There is a slight chance that from Friesing they will send me to Bad Schwalbach our headquarters, which I would enjoy a lot, mainly because I would meet a lot of friends there, amongst them Peter.
What do you hear from Trude? Any news about the baby? I hope she is all right in the meanwhile.

All my best,

Much love and 1000 kisses, Your Otto

Letter from Otto to his mother dated 9 Oct. 1945

Third Army Int.Center, G-2, APO 403 NY

9 Oct – Paris
My dear Mama,

I surprised Papa quite much in coming to Paris directly from Rome. I'll stay here for one day as my plane is leaving not before tomorrow and I have a chance to tell Papa all about Trude. As soon as I get to Schongau, I'll write to you a more detailed letter about Trude. Everything is fine in Paris and Papa is living quite well right now.

All my best – 1000 kisses

Your Otto

NOTE: *Unfortunately, the September letters are missing, as well as letters describing Otto's visits to Paris and Rome, and along with them so many things I would like to have known.*

Letter from Otto to his mother, dated 16 Nov. 1945 was handwritten and was received in New York 29 Nov. 1945 - eleven days after his disappearance.

16 Nov., München

My dear Mama,

    Many thanks for your letter of the 1 Nov. Don't worry about my *Bergtouren* [mountain walk]) *ich geb schon Acht* [I'm careful], and I don't go any more on afternoons, but in the morning, and I don't do difficult things, just *gemütliche Aufstiege* [easy climbs] And don't worry about my jeep-tours either, I am a very careful driver, never taking chances, and I go fast only on excellent, wide roads. It's much safer to ride with me from most of the other soldiers, who are sometimes very careless.

    Right now I am in Munich - because of my Linz trip last Monday, I have the day off and went to München to buy some books for me, because over the weekend all stores are closed.

    You don't find much, because you have no idea how many libraries have been destroyed, but I still find a few interesting things.

    I only have an open jeep, and so driving *ist ein kaltes Vergnügen, aber gesund an der frischen Luft*. [a cold pleasure, but healthy in the fresh air].

    We belong now to the XX Corps because the "Screening Center" has been dissolved, but that won't make too much difference in our work. I don't know as yet the new address so continue to write the same as before. I told you that we have a piano in the house and so I frequently play for my colleagues, however mostly "light classical" music.

I hope the change won't delay my departure for the USA!

    Auf bald [see you soon] - viele 1000 Küss*e* (many thousand kisses*)*

        your Otto

NOTE: *This is the last letter that I have and is probably the last letter Otto wrote.*

AMERICAN RED CROSS   29./XI 45

16 Nov - München   Air

My dear Mama,

many thanks for your letter of the 1 Nov.

Don't worry about my Bergtouren — ich geh' schon adit (?) and I don't go any more on afternoons, but in the morning and I don't do difficult things, just gemütliche Aufstiege. And don't worry about my jeep-tours either, I am a very careful driver, never taking chances and I go fast only on excellent, wide Roads. It's much safer to ride

APPENDIX B

OFFICIAL DOCUMENTS, RECORDS, AND LETTERS

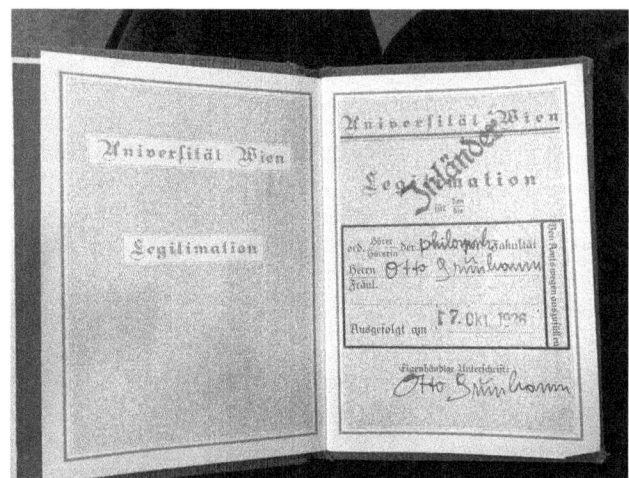

University ID

Passport with a one-time permit to exit Austria and return

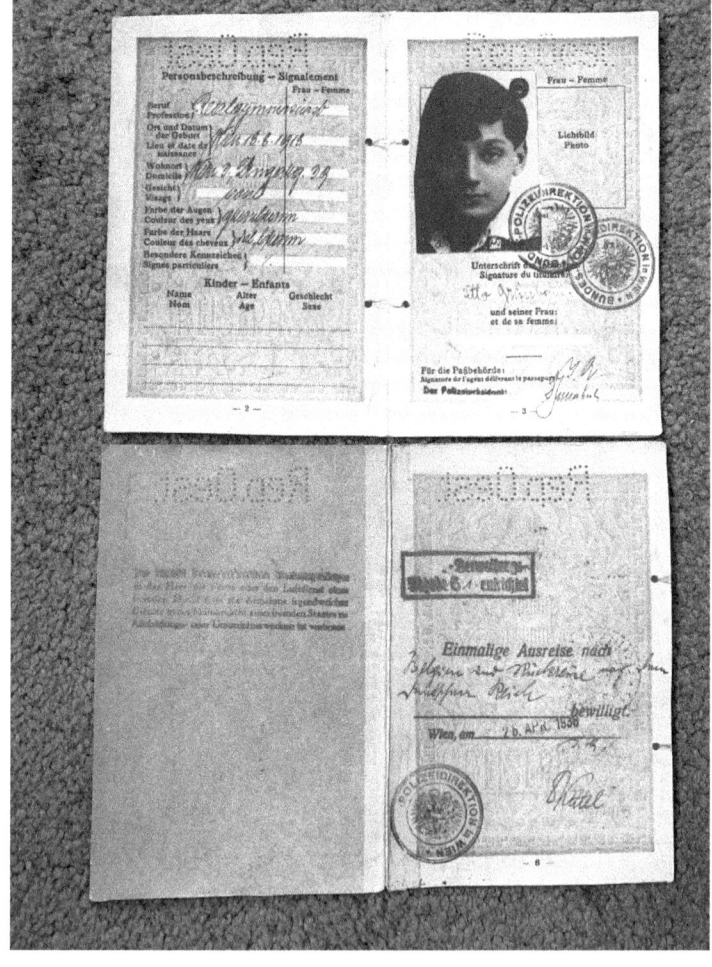

ADDRESS OFFICIAL COMMUNICATIONS TO
THE SECRETARY OF STATE
WASHINGTON, D. C.

Visa Form IVRC-4

DEPARTMENT OF STATE
WASHINGTON

August 20, 1942

In reply refer to
VD 811.111 GRUENBAUM, Otto
IVRC Docket No. 6726

Mr. Otto K. Gruenbaum,
   638 West End Avenue,
     New York, New York.

NOTICE OF HEARING

Case: GRUENBAUM, Otto K.

    Take notice that this case is assigned to hearing before an Interdepartmental Visa Review Committee at Temporary Building U, Twelfth Street and Constitution Avenue NW., Washington, D.C. The calendar will be called promptly at 1:30 p.m. on August 28, 1942 and you will be expected to answer the call at that time and be prepared to make any statement you may deem appropriate in connection with this case.

    If because of compelling reasons you are unable to appear on the above date, you should inform the Review Committee by registered letter, telegraph, or telephone, at least three days prior to the hearing date, giving the reasons for such inability to appear in order that appropriate consideration may be given thereto.

    Only persons who have submitted B or C and IVRC-1 forms and the attorneys of such persons, if any, are entitled to appear at the hearing.

                                    Secretary of Interdepartmental
                                        Visa Review Committee

LIST OR MANIFEST OF ALIEN PASSENGERS FOR THE UNITED STATES

List 4

S.S. "CHAMPLAIN" Passengers sailing from Le Havre (France), August 1st, 1939

No.	Head-Tax Status	Family name	Given name	Age Yrs./Mos.	Sex	Married	Calling or occupation	Able to read	Nationality	Race or people	Place of birth Country	City or town	Immigration Visa etc.	Issued Place	Date	Last permanent residence Country	City or town
1		WIENER	Bela	33	M	M	Mechanic	Y Hungarian	Y Hungary	Hebrew	Jugosla.	Orsosda	QIV 69	Budapest	Jul/3/39	Hungary	Budapest
2		AGUDO-INVERNON	Amaleto	27	M	M	Manufacturer	Y Spanish	Y Spain	Spanish	Spain	Valladolid				Pto/Rico	San Juan
3		LOPEZ y BARENA	Luisa	42	F	M	H/wife	Y "	Y "	"	"	Valdemoro				"	"
4	EXEMPT	ORSKY-PALLAVICINI	Helmuth	44	M	S	None	Y German-Engl. French	Y Czechoslovakia	Slovak	France	St Avold	T.C.	Nice	7/27/39	Czechoslovakia	Prague
5		LOMBROSO	Cesare	23	M	S	Student	Y Italian	Y Italy	Italian North	Italy	Rome	NI 8	Genoa	Jul/10/39	Italy	Genoa
6	EXEMPT	MILONA	Coula	20	F	S	None	Y Greek	Y Greece	Greek	Greece	Zante	T.C. 859	Paris	Aug/8/39	Greece	Athens
7	EXEMPT	PERRILLIAT	John	35	M	M	Jeweler	Y French Spanish	Y Mexico	French	Mexico	Mexico City				Mexico	Mexico City
8		REINBOLD	Hanoch	21	M	M	Merchant	Y German French Engl.	Y Poland	Hebrew	Poland	Nowy Sacz	QIV 6445	Antwerp	Apr/27/39	Belgium	Antwerp
9	QT.	SILBERBERG	Louis	20	M	S	"	Y English	Y U.S.A.	Naturalized	Father's Papers		Passport Nr. 536470				
10		SILBENBERG	Pauline	53	F	M	H/wife	Y Polish	Y Poland	Hebrew	Holland	Hague	NQIV 6	Antwerp	Aug/4/39	Belgium	Antwerp
11		FRANK	Helmuth	17	M	S	None	Y German	Y Germany	"	Germany	Rhens	QIV 1928		Jul/17/39	Luxembourg	Walferdange
12		SCHWARZSCHILD	Fritz	42	M	M	Insurance Agent	Y "	Y "	"	"	Frankfort on Main	QIV 4952	Paris	Aug/2/39	France	Paris
13		SCHWARZSCHILD	Rahel	45	F	M	H/wife	Y "	Y "	"	Danzig	Soppert	QIV 4953	"	"	"	"
14	UNDER 16	SCHWARZSCHILD	Stefan	15	M	S	Student	Y "	Y "	"	Germany	Frankfort on Main	QIV 4954	"	"	"	"
15	UNDER 16	SCHWARZSCHILD	Heinz	13	M	S	"	Y "	Y "	"	"	Wiesbaden	QIV 4955	"	"	"	"
16		GRUNBAUM	Otto	21	M	S	"	Y "	Y	German Hebrew		Vienna	NI 2148		Aug/5/39		
17	EXEMPT	LAMBERT-ZUCKERMANN	Leo	31	M	M	"	Y "	Y			Dublin	NI V12		Aug/5/39		Enghien les Bains
18		MARSHACK	Bertha	20	F	M	None	Y Russian	Y "	"		St Petersburg	NQIV 43		Aug/7/39		Boulogne s/Seine
19	EXEMPT	KLAGSBURGE	Maurice A.	31	M	M	Manufacturer	Y French	Y France	French	France	St Amand	NI 767		Aug/8/39	"	Orval

4

THE BEAM

VOL. III. No. 8.   ATLANTIC CITY, N. J., SATURDAY, OCTOBER 9, 1943   Free Distribution

THE COMING WEEK—
TONIGHT—Dance, 8 PM, Midtown USO.
Dance, 8 PM, Arcade USO.
SUNDAY—Coffee Time, all morning all three USOs.
Afternoon Tea, Arcade USO.
Movie, 3:30 PM, Midtown USO; 5 to 9 PM, Arcade USO.
Movie, 8:30 PM, Midtown USO.
MONDAY—Puzzle Night, Arcade USO.
Clay Modeling, 8 PM, Downtown USO.
(Continued on Page 7)

Soldier Pianist Fled from Nazis' Terror in Vienna

Working with test tubes and chemicals in England General Hospital's laboratory here is a quiet, dreamy-eyed youth of 25 who has lived through more of war's terror and turmoil than many a man facing shellfire on the battlefield.

Five years ago in his native Vienna, Otto Gruenbaum was an earnest young piano student who, according to at least one authority, faced a promising future on the concert stage.

Life Was Pleasant

The rising star of Adolf Hitler over Europe meant little to him. Politics was outside his interests. Life was pleasant in Vienna. Hitler was extending his power over other countries, but Austria had the "It-can't-happen-here" attitude.

Today, his life uprooted, that boy wears the uniform of an American soldier, a corporal's stripes on his sleeves. With the confidence of youth, he is living a new life in a different land. His thick, wavy hair is graying at the temples. He is a naturalized American citizen, is married, and, for the time being, is a soldier first and artist afterward. His brief career on the American concert stage is ended.

Helped By Luck

Like many another fugitive from Hitler's iron rule, Cpl. Gruenbaum had to connive and lie and cheat to

Varied Training Planned to Aid Wounded Men

That martial air that Atlantic City has begun to assume once again is the unfolding of the U. S. Army Medical Department's comprehensive reconditioning program that soon will be sending thousands of sick and wounded soldiers back to military duty, restored to physical and mental health.

The Army is just getting under

NEW AND OLD "C.O.'s"

The MEDS of England General Hospital have a new commanding officer in 2nd. Lt. Meyer Sockel, left, who succeeds 1st. Lt. John W. Bishop. (U. S. Army Official Photo)

Legal Worries To be Handled At Station Here

Legal worries that may burden the minds of some of the men passing through AAF Redistribution Station No. 1 will be dispelled by services offered by the legal assistance department of the Judge Advocate's Office.

Major James E. Bush, station judge advocate in charge of this unit, explained that a network of connections between his office and other similar Army offices, in addition to legal assistance societies set up by municipal bar associations throughout the country, facilitate the work of ironing out a soldier's legal problems.

Free of Worry

Freedom from such worries is considered important to soldiers arriving from overseas for reassignment. Here, they will undergo tests of various natures to determine how their aptitudes, training, and combat experiences may best be applied to the tasks of the AAF. Freedom from worry, it is believed, will be a soldier in a better frame of mind for the period of his examination for his new assignment.

AN UNDAUNTED ARTIST

Cpl. Otto Gruenbaum, soldier-pianist stationed at the England General Hospital, is an example to his comrades and civilians alike in courage and fortitude. Cpl. Gruenbaum was a piano student in Vienna when the Nazis seized Austria. He ultimately made his way to the United States, became a citizen and is now in the army.
(U. S. Army official photo)

Soldier Pianist Fled From Nazis in Vienna

(Continued from Page 1)

Paris, when he never knew from week to week if he was to be allowed to stay there. His early studies were at the Vienna Conservatory of Music, later at the Paris Conservatory of Music, and, in New York, under Arthur Schnabel, one of the world's most famous pianists.

In Vienna Cpl. Gruenbaum gave an audition for Bruno Walter, now conductor of the New York Philharmonic Orchestra. He brought with him to America a letter in which the famous conductor expressed appreciation of his talent and predicted "a good future" for him in the music world.

Cpl. Gruenbaum gave a concert last Sunday for a capacity audience of wounded-soldier patients in the theater on the top floor of the hospital officials, I had little time for other things."

The chance, or luck, to which Cpl. Gruenbaum owes his escape to America came when, through a Viennese friend in New York, he gained the acquaintanceship of a wealthy New York physician, who, according to the young musician, has financed the escape of 50 refugees to America.

Before he could leave for the United States, Cpl. Gruenbaum needed the affidavit which his friend sent him stating that he would not need public support. With that, and with money supplied by his father, then in Nice, he booked passage for this country and sailed from Le Havre on August 11, 1939, 21 days before the German army invaded Poland and France's entry into the war.

SERIAL NUMBER	1. NAME (Print)	ORDER NUMBER
3162	Otto Karl Gruenbaum	39 A

2. ADDRESS (Print) 301 W. 89 St. ~~638 West End Ave.~~ N.Y., N.Y., N.Y.

3. TELEPHONE: SC 4-9797
4. AGE IN YEARS: 22 — DATE OF BIRTH: Aug. 18, 1918
5. PLACE OF BIRTH: Vienna, Austria
6. COUNTRY OF CITIZENSHIP: Austria
7. NAME OF PERSON WHO WILL ALWAYS KNOW YOUR ADDRESS: Mrs. Melanie Jellinek
8. RELATIONSHIP OF THAT PERSON: Mother
9. ADDRESS OF THAT PERSON: 276 Riverside Drive, N.Y., N.Y., N.Y.
10. EMPLOYER'S NAME: Unemployed

I AFFIRM THAT I HAVE VERIFIED ABOVE ANSWERS AND THAT THEY ARE TRUE.

Otto Karl Gruenbaum
(Registrant's signature)

REGISTRATION CARD
D. S. S. Form 1

Note below that race is marked as "J" for Jewish, although he was only half-Jewish, was christened Protestant and did not practice any religion

YEAR OF BIRTH	18	18
RACE AND CITIZENSHIP	J	White, not yet a citizen
EDUCATION	4	4 years of high school
CIVILIAN OCCUPATION	024	Musicians and teachers of music
MARITAL STATUS	6	Single, without dependents
COMPONENT OF THE ARMY	7	Selectees (Enlisted Men)
CARD NUMBER	#	#
BOX NUMBER	0526	0526
FILM REEL NUMBER	2.190	2.190

GRUENBAUM, Otto K.   Tec 5   (# 3)

Highly intelligent man, but slightly soft. German excellent. Lacks military bearing. Young and slightly immature. Average interrogations.

(IPW)(~~ITT~~)(~~ITA~~)(~~ITY~~)(~~CIC~~)/Team   120   28 May 1945
                                       (Number)   (Date)

DECLASSIFIED
Authority NND 745001

SUBJECT: Team Status Report for the Month of ___May 1945___.

TO : Hq Military Intelligence Service, European T of Opns, US Army, APO 887.

1. Personnel of Team:

Name	Rank	ASN	Branch	Unit with Which On Duty *
GERHARDT A. SCHUELER	1st Lt	O-1638458	AC	Div Hq
FRANK H. DAVID	2nd Lt	O-1587838	QMC	CCB
Otto K. Gruenbaum	M/Sgt	32527211		Div Hq
Lucas F. Ried	S/Sgt	37015165		CCB
Frank J. Lehnen	Tec 4	38460604		Div Hq
Sol(NMI) Neugeboren	Tec 5	32524474		CCB

* If other than that shown in paragraph 2, below.

2. Team attached to ___Hqs 7th Army___ for duty with ___14th Arm'd Div___
                     (Army, Corps, Division)

per par __1__, SO __F6__, dated __6 Jan 1945__, Hq __MIS ETOUSA__.

3. Registration numbers of all team motor vehicles and trailers:

Type Vehicles	WD Numbers	Type Trailers	WD Numbers
¼ Ton Truck	20414430	¼ Ton 2 Wheel, Cargo	0627425
¼ Ton Truck	20153279-S		

4. Awards, Citations, Commendations: See over for details, if any.
5. Casualties: See over for details, if any.
6. Major Supply Problems: See over for details, if any.
7. Recommended Additions or Revisions to Training Program, Based on Field Experience: See over for details, if any.

(Signature of OIC of Team)
GERHARDT A. SCHUELER
1ST Lt AC
OIC IPW TEAM 120

CAPT BRUCE A. DE BOURBON CONDE 0350173 INF

Extract SO 220 12 September 1944

20. The following teams, consisting of named off, atchd unasgd Co "I", 3d MI Tng Bn and EM, asgd DEML Sec, are reld fr dy this sta and are trfd in gr held on date of departure to Shipment No RU-207-(d) and WP ASF Pers Replacement Dep, Camp Reynolds, Greenville, Pa, fr this sta 14 Sep 1944, for the purpose of awaiting Port Call of Port Comdr for eventual transshipment to overseas destination.

MI INTERPRETER TEAM (FRENCH)

Team No 315

Rank	Name	Serial No	Branch	MOS		Duty
CAPT	BRUCE A. DEBOURBON CONDE	0350173	INF	9332	86.548	Officer in Chge
2D LT	ARMAND N. MESSIER	01823626	FA	9332	02.409	Interpreter
M Sgt	ROBERT M. PINEAU	31310412		631	010	Asst Interp
S Sgt	EDWIN WOLF, II	33619146		631	010	Translator
Tec 3	FRANK J. FARUOLO, JR.	12066408		631	336	Typist Linguist
Tec 3	JAMES S. LINTON	33105828		631	010	Typist Linguist

GERMAN IPW TEAMS

Team No 316

Rank	Name	Serial No	Branch	MOS		Duty
CAPT	ROBERT W. ANDRAE	0456014	CAC	9316	11.326	Officer in Chge
2D LT	GERHARDT A. SCHUELER	01638458	AC	9316	86.552	Interrogator
M Sgt	WOLF D. GOELTZER	34050272		631	321	Asst Interrogat
Tec 3	MAX HIRSCHBERG	32009692		631	369	Document Exam
Tec 3	OTTO K. GRUENBAUM	32527211		631	021	Typist Linguist
Tec 5	JOSEPH M. KRAMAR	32965429		631	010	Chauffeur

Team No 317

Rank	Name	Serial No	Branch	MOS		Duty
CAPT	FRANK L. WOODS	0659946	AC	9316	86.523	Officer in Chge
2D LT	ERNEST L. STANGER	0798904	AC	9316	01.150	Interrogator
M Sgt	HERMAN MENDELS	33003067		631	055	Asst Interrogat
Tec 3	HENRY UNGER	36530391		631	186	Document Exam
Tec 3	ALEXANDER ECKSTEIN	39040665		631	426	Typist Linguist
Tec 5	LAWRENCE L. RHEE	18120727		631	010	Chauffeur

Auth: Ltr, Hq ASF, WD TAGO, file SPXOC-T-SPGAR 210.31 (5 Aug 44), dated 9 Aug 1944, and Ltr, Hq ASF, WD TAGO, file SPXOP-ASPGAR 210.31 (5 Aug 44), dated 16 Aug 1944.

DESTINATION: ETOUSA

****

XX Class MITC
FINAL STANDINGS 5-A, B, C, D, E SECTIONS
Inclusive Dates 18 June - 16 August 1944

NAME	RANK	BRANCH	SEC	Fluency of Language (1)	Organization (2)	Identification (3)	Classroom (4)	Interrogation Field X (5)	Tactics (6)	Map Reading (7)	Documents (8)	Score (9)	O I C (10)	Interrogator (11)	Document Examining (12)	General Utility VS (13)	S (14)	Not Recommended (15)
Coleman, J. E.	Cpl		A	VS	91	80	75	75		96	79					X		
Condakes, J. P.	Pfc		C	S	93	A	75	70		92	95					X	X	
David, K. S.	Sgt		A	E	93	90	75	76		90	89				X			
Dierker, F. W.	Pvt		D	VS	95	80	80	79		86	87				X			
Eckstein, A.	Pfc		A	E	96	86	75	77		90	87					X		
English, Wm. S.	Cpl		D	S	86	80	70	65		70	82							X
Feldman, H. J.	Cpl		D	S	93	87	70	73		85	83					X		
Flanz, G. H.	Pvt		A	SP	83	71	75	74		88	87				X			
Flesch, P.	Pvt		B	VS	89	99	75	75		87	81					X		
Fogg, N. W.	Pfc		C	VS	86	74	75	70		88	79						X	
Goeltzer, W. D.	Sgt		D	SP	98	95	80	80		87	94		X					
Gruenbaum, O. K.	Tec 5		B	E	97	98	80	77		90	85					X		
Hargrove, J. W.	Pfc		D	VS	99	85	75	71		97	97				X			

DECLASSIFIED
Authority NND 750122

Gruenbaum, Otto K.   TEC 3 ~~Tec 5~~ 32527211   Cl 20 Sec 5B

16 JUN 1944	ATCHD UNASGD CO. Y PAR 1 MEMO
16 AUG 1944	GRADUATE OF 20th CLASS LING #1 - GERMAN
6 AUG 1944	ATCHD UNASGD CO. K PAR 2 SO 197
23 AUG 1944	ALERTED
4 SEP 1944	Tfd DEML - par 2, SO 213
4 SEP 1944	PROM TEC 3 - par 3, SO 213
2 SEP 1944	RELD BY THIS STA - PAR VO SO 220

DECLASSIFIED
Authority UND957387

GRUENBAUM, Otto K.	Tec 3	32527211
(Last name first)	(Rank and Branch)	(Serial Number)

MITC Class No.   : 20   Specialty : IPW German   7995
                                                               (Certificate No.)
Post Graduate   :
Emergency Addressee : Susanna Gruenbaum (Wife)
                       31 Park Terrace West
                       New York, N.Y.
Place of Birth   : Austria   Date : 18 August 1918
Languages   : German, French

Overseas   : Yes   Assignment Book No. : VII - 952
Remarks   :

Lt. Hauser's letter to Otto's mother

Schongau, Bayern
3 January 1946

Dear Mrs. Jellinek,

The team on which your son Otto worked is quite small in comparison to other army units, consequently we grow to know one another very well. Otto commanded the respect of every one of us from the first day of his assignment because of the great amount of tolerance he had for his fellow's whims and by reason of his standards of clean living.

During the beginning of the Bavarian winter, all our thoughts turned toward American ways and customs and we grew more and more homesick for our loved ones there; at that time Otto proved to us how much we had grown to depend on him. He felt as lonely as any of we boys, yet he outdid himself playing the piano and, with his playing, he tried to alleviate our mental ills. He played long hours for our ammusement and was always very willing to lend a sympathetic ear to hear our personal problems.

His thoughtfulness evidenced itself toward the prisoners with whom we work. Otto very unselfishly instigated an education program for them which helps to clear their thoughts thereby providing more fertile fields on which the seeds of democracy can take root. He sponsored discussion groups for them and worked hard editing a library of some contemporary authors in order to ellicit interest from their tired, confused minds.

Otto's love for the outdoors was a tremendous thing. On free days he was out of his bed early and eager to seek out new peaks and views in the surrounding countryside. In fact this is what happened on the week end of November 18. Otto had made a casual remark Saturday evening about wishing to find a new peak the next morning if the weather permitted. When the breakfast table was assembled, it was discovered that your son had set off alone about three hours earlier. Every effort is being and has been made to discover his whereabouts and, you may rest assured, that some answer will result from this search.

2.

We shall be very glad to answer any further questions you may have, Mrs. Jellinek, and we shall notify you immediately concerning any developements in this problem.

Lt. Ernest F. Hauser
Hq XX Corps, G-2 Section
CIC # 10, APO 340
c/o Pm, New York

REPORT OF INVESTIGATION
(Under provisions of: (par. 1c(4)(c), AR 345-415) (par. 21, AR 600-550))*

Station or command Hq, XX Corps TUTZING, Germany   Date January 1946 (1)

1. Person (deceased)* GRUENBAUM, OTTO 32527211
   (Name, Army serial number, grade, and organization)
   M/Sgt. CIC Detachment (1)

2. (cause of death)* Unknown – missing (1)
   (Medical diagnosis)
   XC6193297

3. How incurred GRUENBAUM left his quarters early the morning 18th November 45 to
   (Complete details as to how, when, and where (injury) (death)* was incurred, including hour and date)
   climb mountains, vicinity GARMISH, Germany. Still missing. (1)

4. Investigation of the circumstances surrounding this (death)* has been made. All available witnesses were interrogated. The following pertinent facts were found to be correct:
   (a) Present for duty (yes) (no)*.
   (b) Absent (with) (without) authority.
       (1) Hour and date of commencement of absence Early morning, 18th Nov. 45 (1)
       (2) Hour and date of termination of absence _____
   (c) (Was) (was not)* within the territorial limits indicated by the authorization to be absent.
   (d) (Was) (was not)* under the influence of intoxicants. The use of intoxicants (was) (was not)* the proximate cause.
   (e) (Was) (was not)* under the influence of drugs. The use of drugs (was) (was not)* the proximate cause.
   (f) (Was) (was not)* exercising reasonable care for his own safety.
   (g) (Was) (was not)* violating a civil, moral, or military law, nor military orders or instructions, written or verbal. The violation (was) (was not)* the proximate cause.
   (h) (Was) (was not)* due to gross carelessness or negligence.
   (i) (Was) (was not)* mentally sound.

5. REMARKS: (1) These items as near to similar items on original report as available record and memory permit. Original report was submitted by the undersigned while serving in the G-2 section Hq, XX Corps from 28 December 45 to 26 January 46.

(See reverse side)

FINDINGS
(In line of duty)*
(Not due to his own misconduct)*

Frank A. Penn
FRANK A. PENN
Capt. Cav.
Investigating Officer.

APPROVED:

ERNEST F. HAUSER Commanding officer.
1st Lt. CIC
CIC CI DET.

RECEIVED
OCT 15 1946
RECORD VERIFICATION SECTION
Per _____

* Strike out inapplicable words.
[Additional sheets may be used for extension of remarks under paragraphs 2, 3, and 5.]

W.D., A.G.O. Form No. 51
October 13, 1942

38276ABCD

OTTO GFUNBAUM, MASTER SERGEANT, working in a CIC Detachment general vicinity of Garmish went for a hike in the mountains (vicinity Garmish) by himself early one Sunday morning, November 1945. This is the last time he was seen by anybody. Information received from his collegues indicate that he was contented and happily married, was about to be redeployed to the States (the week following his disappearance), was an ardent hiker and was well able to take care of himself.

Upon being missed, continuous searches were conducted the following two weeks by air and ground forces. The German Forestry Police combed the mountainous area, US troops searched the surrounding areas and Liaison planes flew over all the areas he could possibly have travelled into. Large posters carrying his picture and description were distributed throughout the area.

The latter part of the month an assistant G-2, XX Corps, conducted an investigation. The early part of January another investigation was conducted by the undersigned officer — results of both as to determining the whereabouts of the Enlisted Man were negative.

The information as determined by the two investigations was compiled and reported to higher Headquarters at that time. Who finally decided that the subject, Enlisted Man is dead, is not known by this officer.

AG 704 AGX-AGF   1st Ind.   CM/ns
HQ. US FORCES, EUROPEAN THEATER(REAR), APO 887, US ARMY, 3 SEPTEMBER 1946.

TO: The Adjutant General, Washington 25, D. C.

1. Approved. Soldier is buried in Grave 109, Row 10, Plot "NN", St.-Avold, France, Military Cemetery.

2. Burial report indicates cause of death as fractured skull and multiple lacerations.

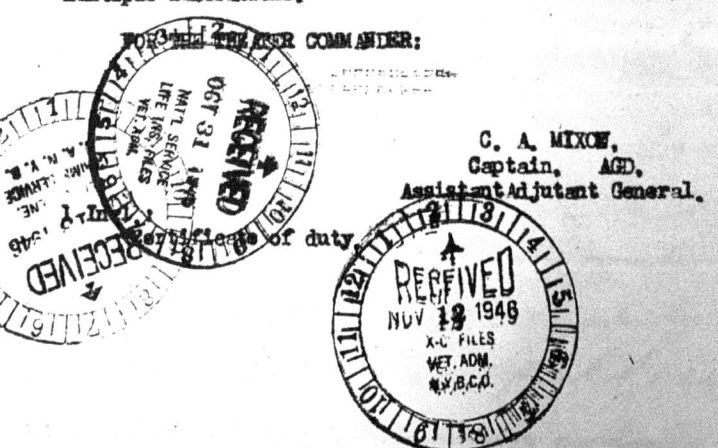

C. A. MIXON,
Captain, AGD.
Assistant Adjutant General.

HEADQUARTERS
UNITED STATES FORCES
EUROPEAN THEATER
AG CASUALTY BRANCH

16 May 1946

Mr. Otto Gruenbaum
110 rue Pasquier
Paris (8)

Dear Mr. Gruenbaum:

It is with the deepest regret that I am writing to you in reply to your letter of 6 March 1946 requesting more information about the disappearance of your son M/Sgt Otto Gruenbaum, 32527211, missing since 18 November 1945. Knowing how keenly his loss is felt by the members of his immediate family, I am taking the liberty of explaining the circumstances attending his death in the hope that despite its sadness, the news will be of some comfort to you.

M/Sgt Otto Gruenbaum departed Schongau, Germany on 18 November 1945. He planned to go mountain climbing and never came back. An intensive investigation has been conducted in view to obtain all information about your son's fate. I regret to inform you that the results of the searches concluded to his accidental death. His body was found in Mittenwald, Germany with fractured skull and multiple lacerations.

You may be certain that a Chaplain of his own faith officiated at his burial. He was buried on 22 April 1946 at a United States Military Cemetery. The exact location of his grave is U.S. Military Cemetery St. Avold, France, Plot NN, Row 10, Grave 109.

I know this tragedy has brought you an almost insurmountable burden of grief and can well imagine your sorrow and bitter disappointment in the disheartening news you received.

I extend my heartfelt sympathy and express the hope that the Almighty who saw fit to take your loved one will also give you the courage to bear your loss bravely.

Sincerely yours,

Robert A. Bowen

ROBERT A. BOWEN
2nd Lt., AGD
Asst. Adjutant General

SPECIAL

WAR DEPARTMENT
THE ADJUTANT GENERAL'S OFFICE
WASHINGTON 25, D. C.

NON-BATTLE CASUALTY REPORT

AG 201	NAME GRUENBAUM, OTTO K ASN 32 527 211	M SGT GRADE HUS		DATE CAS. REPORT RECEIVED 1946 MAY 28
NAME AND ADDRESS OF E.A.	MRS SUSANNE GRUENBAUM 30 PARK TERRACE WEST NEW YORK CITY NEW YORK		29 MAY 1946	DATE TELEGRAM SENT 10 15

THE INDIVIDUAL NAMED BELOW DESIGNATED THE ABOVE PERSON AS THE ONE TO BE NOTIFIED IN CASE OF EMERGENCY, AND THE OFFICIAL TELEGRAPHIC AND LETTER NOTIFICATIONS WILL BE SENT TO THIS PERSON. THE RELATIONSHIP, IF ANY, IS SHOWN BELOW. IT SHOULD BE NOTED THAT THIS PERSON IS NOT NECESSARILY THE NEXT-OF-KIN OR RELATIVE DESIGNATED TO BE PAID SIX MONTHS' PAY GRATUITY IN CASE OF DEATH.

THE SECRETARY OF WAR HAS ASKED ME TO EXPRESS HIS DEEP REGRET THAT YOUR **HUSBAND**

GRADE	NAME	SERIAL NUMBER	ARM OR SERVICE	REPORTING THEATRE	P OR J STATUS	SHIPMENT NUMBER
M/SGT	GRUENBAUM, OTTO K.	32527211	MIS	ETO		147086 U-1X
TYPE OF CASUALTY	PLACE OF CASUALTY	DATE OF CASUALTY DAY MONTH YEAR		CASUALTY CODE		
DIED	IN EUROPEAN AREA	18 NOV 45				

HE WAS PREVIOUSLY REPORTED MISSING PERIOD I REGRET THAT UNAVOIDABLE CIRCUMSTANCES MADE NECESSARY THE UNUSUAL LAPSE OF TIME IN REPORTING YOUR HUSBANDS DEATH TO YOU CONFIRMING LETTER FOLLOWS

EDWARD F WITSELL
XXXXXXXXXXXXXX

REMARKS AG 201 /27 MAY 46/   CORRECTED COPY   WT

MSG FM HQ USFET /REAR/ STATUS IS CHANGED TO DIE ACCORDING TO CIR 11, PARA 5A AND 6 BASED UPON RPT OF BURIAL. AMERICAN GRAVES REGISTRATION SERVICE, EUROPEAN THEATER AREA, STATES SOL BURIED IN GRAVE 109, ROW 10, PLOT NMNN ST. AVOLD, FRANCE, US MILITARY CEMETERY.
PL - ETO

ACTION BY COMPOSITE SECTION: REPORT VERIFIED ✓   FORM 45   AG 201 REQ
CASUALTY BRANCH FILE ATTACHED ✓   OR CHARGED TO   DATE
PREVIOUSLY REPORTED   NO   YES ✓   (AS INDICATED BELOW):
FILE NO. 120   MESSAGE NO.   TYPE DNB 18 Nov 45   DATE AND AREA   E.A. NOTIFIED No Action

FORWARDED TO →   SPEC. IDEN.   C. & P.   TELEGRAM ✓   LETTER   CERTIF.   F. REL.   CORRES.   REPAT.   S. N. & D.   NON-DEL.
REPORT NOT VERIFIED   NO FORM 45   NO CAS. BR. FILE   CHECKED BY   REVIEWED BY

DISTRIBUTION "A" ☐ 28 COPIES   DISTRIBUTION "B" ☐ COPIES
WD AGO FORM 0365
1 MAY 1945   EDITION OF 1 JAN. 1945 MAY BE USED.

Letter from Lt. LeRo. to Otto's father about finding Otto's body, Page 1

July x 6

Dear Mr. Gruenbaum,

I wish first to explain long'th lapse of time between your letter of 23 May 46 and my answer. I received your letter, after some delay, on the eve of of my departure for the U.S. I was never settled long enough during the long trip home to give a proper reply.

While I never knew your son personally, I am possibly possessed with more information surrounding his death than anyone else. I first recall the broadcasts requesting information concerning him as being received from A.F.N. Munich. These were in the latter part of November and first part of December, the year of 1945.

Now follows the circumstances by which I became connected with the recovery of his body, and the places in route to point of death, and description of locality.

On a night early in April I received a call from a detachment of men who had a station in Mittenwald, Bavaria, stating that a Germ-

forester had reported to them that he had located the body of an American soldier in the mountains near Mittenwald. I ascertained that the soldier had died some months previous and that the body had been preserved only by the snow.

Early the next morning, I, with several men, met the forester and proceeded, under his guidance, to again locate and recover the body. The route we took led from Mittenwald to the Lauter See and to a point midway between Lauter See and Ferchen See. This point may be recognized (see sketch) by boulders that lie on each side of road as it leaves a small meadow. At this point we left the jeep and proceeded into the woods where we hit a foot trail which led along the edge of the woods and then turned south into the mountains. After 30 minutes of hard walking and climbing we came upon the body of your son, Otto.

His body was located about two feet off the trail. It was at the base of a rock slide which extended steeply upwards for perhaps 150 feet and there ended at the base of a perpendicular cliff. Snow was about fifty feet above the body. The position of the body was with head nearest the trail, legs extended directly toward the cliff, left leg bent over ght leg and sug. "ring 2°Compound fracture, and body lying on back.

It is not my belief that he suffered from his fall. There was nothing to indicate he had ever moved. The position in which the body was lying was such that a man in even semiconsciousness would have changed, the head being much lower than the legs. The arms being in a very awkward position over head indicates he did not move them. The medical examiner, basing his opinion on certain broken bones in the head, expressed to me, unofficially, that death was instantaneous.

I found in the snow at the peak of the slide his glove, one glove only, and hat. There was nothing to indicate that he was the victim of a crime. I do not know whether he fell from the cliff to the slide and then rolled to bottom or merely fell from the top of the slide. My belief seemed up are that his death was instantaneous and resulted from an accidental fall.

If it is possible that you can visit the place, I suggest that you go first to the local police of Williams or to the S-2 office of 2D Bn, 47th Inf, who from their information files should be able to give you the name of the forester who first discovered the body. He could be your guide.

Please permit me to express my sorrow

deepest sympathies to you, his mother, and to his wife. From conversations with C.I.C. Agents who knew him, I know he was loved and respected by them all. Please feel free to call on me at any time for any information or service I may be able to give in your further locating the place of his death. I'm sorry that I am not now able to return and photograph the spot.

Yours respectfully,

Milton R. LeRoy
1ST LT. Inf.

Lt. MILTON R. LeRoy, Jr
RTE 3, NINETY SIX, S.C.

Route 3
Ninety Six, South Carolina,
U.S.A

269th MILITARY INTELLIGENCE DETACHMENT
HEADQUARTERS NINTH INFANTRY DIVISION
APO 9 US ARMY

22 July 1946

SUBJECT: Certificate

TO : Headquarters 9th Inf.Div. APO 9, US.Army
G-2 Section
Attn: Capt. Duke

I hereby certify that OTTO GRÜNBAUM, 32527211, M/Sgt., at the time of his death, on or about the 18 November 1945, was on a duty status.

ERNEST F. HAUSER
1st Lt. CWS
OIC MID 269

AG 201 Gruenbaum, Otto K.
32 527 211

War Department, A. G. O.   8 October 1946.

    Held by the War Department that this report will be accepted as the final report of investigation, without exhibits and testimonies, due to the lack of witnesses. Master Sergeant Otto K. Gruenbaum, 32,527,211, death occurred on 18 November 1945, result of a fractured skull and multiple lacerations, in line of duty and not the result of his own misconduct.

                    BY ORDER OF THE SECRETARY OF WAR:

                                            Adjutant General.

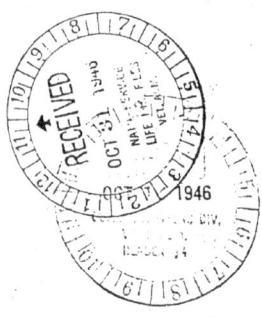

Part of the Individual Deceased Personnel File (IDPF) sent to me from NARA in St. Louis that first mentions that Otto hitch-hiked from Schongau to Garmisch

WAR DEPARTMENT
THE ADJUTANT GENERAL'S OFFICE
WASHINGTON 25, D.C.

NON—BATTLE CASUALTY REPORT

AG 201 — NAME: GRUENBAUM OTTO K — GRADE: M SGT
ASN 32 527 211 — HUS

NAME AND ADDRESS OF E.A.: MRS SUSANNE GRUENBAUM, 31 PARK TERRACE WEST, NEW YORK CITY NEW YORK

DATE TELEGRAM SENT: 13 DEC 1945

THE INDIVIDUAL NAMED BELOW DESIGNATED THE ABOVE PERSON AS THE ONE TO BE NOTIFIED IN CASE OF EMERGENCY, AND THE OFFICIAL TELEGRAPHIC AND LETTER NOTIFICATIONS WILL BE SENT TO THIS PERSON. THE RELATIONSHIP, IF ANY, IS SHOWN BELOW. IT SHOULD BE NOTED THAT THIS PERSON IS NOT NECESSARILY THE NEXT-OF-KIN OR RELATIVE DESIGNATED TO BE PAID SIX MONTHS' PAY GRATUITY IN CASE OF DEATH.

THE SECRETARY OF WAR HAS ASKED ME TO EXPRESS HIS DEEP REGRET THAT YOUR HUSBAND

GRADE	NAME	SERIAL NUMBER	ARM OR SERVICE	REPORTING THEATRE	F OR J STATUS	SHIPMENT NUMBER
M/SGT	GRUENBAUM, OTTO HAS BEEN	32527211	MIS	ETO		344007-BX-CC-1

TYPE OF CASUALTY	PLACE OF CASUALTY	DATE OF CASUALTY DAY / MONTH / YEAR	CASUALTY CODE
MISSING	IN GERMANY SINCE	18 NOV. 45	

IF FURTHER DETAILS OR OTHER INFORMATION ARE RECEIVED YOU WILL BE PROMPTLY NOTIFIED CONFIRMING LETTER FOLLOWS

EDWARD F WITSELL
ACTING
XXXXXXXX

REMARKS: AG 704 /7 DEC. 45/ — CORRECTED COPY — WT

PARIS, E 95333. CAS. MSG. 682. SOL. HITCH-HIKED FROM SCHONGAU GERMANY WHERE HE WAS STATIONED TO GARMISCH AND HAS NOT RETURNED.

APPENDIX C

OTTO'S LIFE IN MUSIC

In this newsletter of the Vienna Conservatory of March 1935, Otto's playing received special mention :"A certain personal note already today reveals the fundamental musicality of Otto Grünbaum's playing and one can, without hesitation, predict a promising future."

Prof. Engel-Weschler was the head teacher responsible for preparing students for their state's exam. Later, as a refugee in New York she taught at the New York College of Music, where Otto received a degree, and where I, as a child, also took piano lessons. Traute Meyer, also mentioned, was a close friend of Otto's whom I met years later, not knowing that the war probably caused her to lose a bright future in music too.

MITTEILUNGEN
des
Neuen Wiener Konservatoriums
Direktion: Prof. Josef Reitler

I., Bösendorferstraße 12 (Musikvereinsgebäude)   I., Himmelpfortgasse 11
Tel. U 46-4-37   Tel. R 28-1-75

25. Schuljahr   März 1935   Folge 1

Es gab ferner am 7. 8. und 9. Februar Aufführungen der von Regisseur Perfall geleiteten Tonfilm- und Kabarettklassen im „Simplizissimus", am 22. ein Abend der Operettenklasse im Thaliasaale und am 25. Februar ein Konzert der Klavier-Staatsprüfungsklasse Angela E n g e l - W e s c h l e r. Über die beiden letzten Veranstaltungen schrieb Dr. Hans Ewald Heller in der „Wiener Zeitung": „Eine wahre Freude bereitete der Klavierabend der Leiterin der Staatsprüfungskurse am N e u e n W i e n e r K o n s e r v a t o r i u m Engel-Weschler, ein Abend, der das gewohnte Niveau von Schülerkonzerten weit überstieg. Man hörte die talentierte Traute M e y e r, Hansi A l t und Anna K l e i n, die sich mit einer Polonaise von Chopin Separatbeifall holte. Eine gewisse persöhnliche Note verrät schon heute das grundmusikalische Spiel Otto G r ü n b a u m s, den man ohne Bedenken eine Zukunft prophezeien darf. Herta F i s c h e r ist keine

Otto's mother kept track of Otto's enthusiastic reviews.

"M O R G E N" 26.April 1937.

In erster Linie verdient hier Otto Grünbaum eine besondere Beachtung. Er ist heute schon ein Musiker(nicht nur Pianist)mit eigenem Profil, der jede Phase erlebt, ein Werk gross aufbauend zu gestalten versteht und auch in technischer Hinsicht erstaunliches Können zeigt.

"W I E N E R J O U R N A L" April 1937.

An der Spitze Otto Grünbaum, der mit seinem wohldurchdachten farbigen Chopin-Spiel aufhorchen machte.

"W I E N E R-A B E N D-B L A T T   4.Mai 1937.

Als die überragende Begabung des Abends fiel Otto Grünbaum auf. Er ist ein empfindsamer und empfindungsfähiger grundmusikalischer Pianist, der seiner Lehrrerin ungemein viel an Kultur und Noblesse verdankt.

"F R E I E P R E S S E", 4.Mai 1937.

Otto Grünbaum, den schon die Ruhe des gewiegten Pianisten auszeichnet, dazu ein farbiger Anschlag und technische Fähigkeiten, die seinem Chopin-Spiel starke Beschwigtheit verleihen und selbst die As-Dur Polonaise vortrefflich gelingen liessen.

"W I E N E R Z E I T U N G", 4.Mai 1937.

Wir greifen noch besonders Otto Grünbaum heraus, einem dem Knabenalter kaum entwachsenen Könner und Techniker.

Redaktion und Administration: Richard-Wagner-Straße, Haus „Am Lido", Parterre
Fernruf 2237

Klavierkonzert Otto Grünbaum.

Ein musikalisches Ereignis. — Ein Chopinspieler, wie es wenige auf der Welt gibt.

h. Achtzehn Jahre alt ist der Wiener Klaviervirtuose Otto Grünbaum, der sich dem internationalen Publikum des hochsommerlichen Karlsbads am Freitag abends mit einem eigenen Klavierkonzerte vorstellte. Das mag manchem als Wagnis erschienen sein. Aber das Wagnis wurde ein voller, ein strahlender Erfolg. Man ging, trotz der guten Pressestimmen Wiens über den jungen Virtuosen, etwas mißtrauisch in dieses Klavierkonzert. Und man ward Zeuge eines Erlebnisses, das weit über das Niveau des alltäglichen Konzertbetriebes der Welt hinausragte. Und dies trotz der Jugend des Pianisten, die vielleicht noch seelische und geistige Klärungsstufen vor sich liegen hat, die aber dem jungen Virtuosen kaum eine weitere technische Vervollkommnung offen läßt, weil diese technische Reife Grünbaums fast an restloser Vollkommenheit grenzt. Der Besuch des Konzertes war gut. Wir wollen vorneweg sagen, was wir an Grünbaum bewundern und was wir für ihn an Gefahren befürchten: Wir bewundern seine absolute Musikalität, sein wundervolles Ausdrucksvermögen, seine unendliche Sensibilität, doch wir befürchten auch, daß er durch eben diese Sensibilität einer leidenschaftlichen Seele verführt werden könnte, sich im Versinkenlassen in dem Stimmungs- und Gefühlswerte eines Teiles manches Werkes die große geistige Linie des Ganzen bei der Reproduktion eines Werkes zu übersehen und zu vernachlässigen. Mit Präludium und Fuge in D-dur von Johann Sebastian Bach, bearbeitet von D'Albert, hub das Konzert an. So virtuos Otto Grünbaum dieses Präludium spielte, muß doch gesagt werden, daß dem Bachschen Werke allzu große Blutwärme und Ueberschwenglichkeit des Gefühls nicht restlos jene Wirkung Bachscher Musik zu geben vermögen, die von einer geistig verklärten Seelenwärme und Tiefe der Auffassung auszuströmen pflegt. Das wunderbare Rondo in D-dur von Mozart folgte. Welch wundersame Weichheit des Anschlages, welche Leichtigkeit und Anmut des Spieles, welche Zartheit offenbarten sich hier! Die süßtönende Kantilene des Spieles Grünbaums entzückt und beglückt. Seine Gestaltung hat inneren Reichtum, hat Schönheit und jene erdentbundene Beschwingtheit des Besessenen, des Sichanjeneshingebenden. Und dann folgte die schwierige große Sonate in H-moll von Liszt, ein Werk, an das sich im Konzertsaal selbst reife und anerkannte Virtuosen nur zögernd heranwagen würden. Otto Grünbaum aber bewältigte dieses Werkes Brillanz in unerhört temperamentvollem Stile. Die schwierigsten Passagen funkeln und leuchten wie eine Schnur Diamanten reinsten Wassers. Verve, Schwung und Beseeltheit formen die Wiedergabe zum großen Erlebnis. Otto Grünbaums Wiedergabe ist von einer ungeheuer eindringlichen Plastik, die sich aber niemals in groben Licht- und Schatteneffekten verliert, die so reich nuanciert, wie nur ein großer Künstler vermag. Und vollends entzückend gestaltet er die gewählten Chopinschen Köstlichkeiten, die er im zweiten Teil des Konzertes spielte. Grandios spielte er vor allem die zwei Etüden und die Polonäse in As-dur. Rhythmisch filigran und bezaubernd ward auch die Mazurka wiedergegeben. Dabei stand dem Virtuosen nicht ein großer Konzertflügel, sondern nur ein normaler Försterflügel zur Verfügung. Aber wie polyphon klang dieser Flügel unter den Meisterhänden dieses großen Talentes! Wie füllig, wie orchestral ist sein Fortissimo, wie hauchfein, wie schwebend, wie zart das Pianissimo! Otto Grünbaums Erfolg ist durchschlagend. Der Achtzehnjährige hat heute schon die volle Konzertreife. Daß der junge Künstler eine bedeutende Karriere vor sich hat, daran läßt sich kaum zweifeln. Der Beifall nahm zeitweise den Charakter von Ovationen für den Virtuosen an. Als Chopinspieler wird Grünbaum sich Weltruhm erzwingen können. Aber auch der epische Glanz Lisztscher Konzertwerke findet in Grünbaum einen berufenen Künder. Angesichts der Fülle der künstlerischen Vorzüge Grünbaums hatte es die Opernsängerin Hilde Müller, Mitglied des Opernensembles des Wiener Volkstheaters schwer, sich durchzusetzen. Sie sang zwei Arien aus „Figaros Hochzeit". Frau Hilde Müller ist eine Schülerin der bekannten heimischen Gesangspädagogin Marth Manzer. Die Stimmittel Frau Hilde Müllers sind durchaus sympathisch, ihre Schulung nicht unbedeutend, aber Frau Müller schien an argem Trema zu leiden, intonierte nicht mit der nötigen Sicherheit und kam auch nicht zur effektvollen Gestaltung der beiden Arien, während sie die Zugabe bereits mit voller Sicherheit und daher auch recht gewinnend gestaltete. Am Flügel wurde Frau Müller ganz vortrefflich von der Karlsbader Klaviervirtuosin Margarete Löstl-Aller begleitet. Blumen gab es für Grünbaum und für Hilde Müller in Hülle und Fülle. Das Konzert, das mit einiger Verspätung begann, währte bis um die elfte Stunde.

KONZERTDIREKTION DR. ARTUR HOHENBERG
III, Lothringerstraße 20 (Konzerthaus) — Telephon U-16-1-79, U-16-1-80
Verkaufskasse: I, Operngebäude, Tel. R-27-2-11, von 10—1 und 3—6 Uhr

BRAHMS-SAAL im Musikverein

Montag, den 25. Oktober 1937, um ½8 Uhr abends

KLAVIERABEND
Otto GRÜNBAUM

PROGRAMM:

Bach-D'Albert	Praeludio und Fuge D-dur
Mozart	Rondo D-dur
Liszt	Sonate H-moll (in einem Satz)
	Allegro energico — Andante sostenuto — Fugato (Allegro energico presto)

===== PAUSE =====

Chopin	Ballade F-dur
	2 Etuden: op. 10, Nr. 3; op. 10, Nr. 12
	Nocturne B-moll, op. 9, Nr. 1
	2 Mazurkas: op. 33, Nr. 2; op. 63, Nr. 3
	Polonaise As-dur

Klavier: Bösendorfer

Preis des Programmes 30 Groschen

KURHAUS IN KARLSBAD

Freitag, den 23. Juli 1937:
EINMALIGES KLAVIERKONZERT
des jungen Wiener Künstlers
Otto GRÜNBAUM

PROGRAMM:

BACH – D'ALBERT: Praeludio und Fuge in D=Dur
MOZART: . . . . . Rondo in D=Dur
LISZT: . . . . Sonate in H=Moll
PAUSE
CHOPIN: . . . . . . Ballade in F=Dur
      Zwei Etüden
      Nocturne
      Mazurkas
      Polonaise in As=Dur

Förster=Flügel beigestellt von der Fa. B. Lang

Kartenvorverkauf: Buchhandlung Walter Heinisch, Alte Wiese
Friseurgeschäft Urban, Kurhaus

Bruno Walter's Recommendation Letter for Otto, 1937

STAATSOPER

Herr Otto Jokubaum hat mir beim Vortrag von Klavierstücken verschiedensten Charakters den Eindruck eines ausgezeichneten Musikers und eines sehr hoffnungsvollen Pianisten gemacht. Zweifellos ist er eine grund-musikalische Natur, versenkt sich mit Ernst und Verständnis in seine Aufgaben und hat seine vortrefflichen technischen Anlagen mit Fleiss bereits zu respektablen Leistungen entwickelt.

Bruno Walter

Wien 6. Oktober 1937

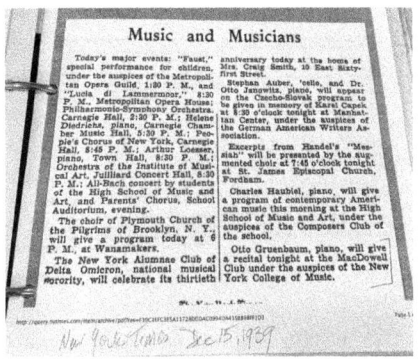

Music and Musicians

Today's major events: "Faust," special performance for children, under the auspices of the Metropolitan Opera Guild, 1:30 P. M., and "Lucia di Lammermoor," 8:30 P. M., Metropolitan Opera House; Philharmonic-Symphony Orchestra, Carnegie Hall, 2:30 P. M.; Helene Diedrichs, piano, Carnegie Chamber Music Hall, 5:30 P. M.; People's Chorus of New York, Carnegie Hall, 5:45 P. M.; Arthur Loesser, piano, Town Hall, 8:30 P. M.; Orchestra of the Institute of Musical Art, Juilliard Concert Hall, 8:30 P. M.; All-Bach concert by students of the High School of Music and Art, and Parents' Chorus, School Auditorium, evening.

The choir of Plymouth Church of the Pilgrims of Brooklyn, N. Y., will give a program today at 6 P. M. at Wanamakers.

The New York Alumnae Club of Delta Omicron, national musical sorority, will celebrate its thirtieth anniversary today at the home of Mrs. Craig Smith, 10 East Sixty-first Street.

Stephan Auber, 'cello, and Dr. Otto Janowitz, piano, will appear on the Czecho-Slovak program to be given in memory of Karel Capek, at 8:30 o'clock tonight at Manhattan Center, under the auspices of the German American Writers Association.

Excerpts from Handel's "Messiah" will be presented by the augmented choir at 7:45 o'clock tonight at St. James Episcopal Church, Fordham.

Charles Haubiel, piano, will give a program of contemporary American music this morning at the High School of Music and Art, under the auspices of the Composers Club of the school.

Otto Gruenbaum, piano, will give a recital tonight at the MacDowell Club under the auspices of the New York College of Music.

New York Times, Dec. 15, 1939

...opened the program with numbers by Bloch, Joseph Achron and Paul Kirman, admirably performed from the technical angle and projected with fiery intensity. Lazar Weiner provided competent support at the piano for both of the vocalists, and Otto Gruenbaum was Mr. Zadri's accompanist. Many encores were demanded by the large and responsive audience.

The New York Times
Published: December 28, 1941

...ington High School on Tuesday afternoon. The mural, entitled "Music," illustrates the evolution of music and musical instruments and will be placed in the music room of the school.

A musicale will be given this evening at 8:30 o'clock at the Vendome Gallery, 59 West Fifty-sixth Street, in connection with an exhibition of paintings by René Lopez. Enrico D'Amicis, tenor, will sing, assisted by Mildred Pelton, soprano, and Otto Gruenbaum at the piano.

Lithographs and original caricatures by Al Hirschfield are being shown in the art gallery of the Samuel J. Tilden High School, Brooklyn, until June 14.

The New York Times
Published: May 23, 1940

*Otto played Beethoven's Appassionata, and
Chopin's Ballade in G Minor, Etude in E Major and Polonaise in A Flat*

Morning Choral

presents

OTTO GRUENBAUM

Pianist

MORNING CHORAL

TWENTY-FIRST SEASON

Spring Concert

APRIL TWENTY-THIRD

1940

Academy of Music

HERBERT STAVELY SAMMOND

Conductor

ADA ZELLER

Accompanist

E. HAROLD DU VALL

at the Organ

AMUSEMENTS

Morning Choral Club Presents New Pianist

Otto Gruenbaum Appears as Soloist In Spring Concert at the Academy

By MILES KASTENDIECK

Into the world of song created by the Morning Choral in its Spring Concert at the Academy of Music last night came Otto Gruenbaum, a young pianist with a Viennese background. Unknown and unheralded, he won enthusiastic response from his audience last night for playing which marked him as a pianist of exceptional promise. While he is chiefly interesting at the moment for his pianistic accomplishment, he has the technique, the training, and the talent to become a fine musician.

At 21, Mr. Gruenbaum looks back to a successful career at the Vienna Conservatory of Music and praiseworthy appearances with orchestras in Austria and Czechoslovakia. He faces the future with so much in his favor that he should be heard from anon. In playing such works as Beethoven's Sonata Opus 57, the "Appassionata," Chopin's Ballade in G Minor, Etude in E Major, and Polonaise in A Flat, he adhered strictly to the standard repertoire, thereby challenging stiff appraisal.

That he could play these works with facility, clarity, and poise there was no question. How musical was his conception of them left the listener uncertain as to his sense of style and his interpretative ability. Two youthful handicaps militated against a well-fashioned realization of this music: a tendency to vary tempo out of all proportion to the nature of the composition and a tendency to sentimentalize. His chief interest appeared to be pianistic; that is, fastidious attention to tone and phrase with accompanying mannerisms quite unnecessary, and absorption in technical achievement. The niceties of piano playing were often in evidence as the result of this interest.

When it came to Beethoven, the pianist was most at home in the final movement; the appassionata of the first, and reflection of the Andante escaped him; even the finale was taken too fast. In his earnest and sincere performances, he played too carefully. Once in the Scriabin Etude, played as a second encore, there was the flash of temperament which would have enhanced his playing of the other works. Therein lies his future, for technically he is already doing big things.

In accordance with his regular policy, Herbert Stavely Sammond, the conductor, had arranged the choral program with an eye to some good music. The opening group of Handel, Bach and Franck set the keynote. But the most interesting works done and in many ways the best sung were Gustave Holst's Two Hymns from the Rig Veda: "To the Travellers" and "To the Waters," and the Rumanian Folk Song "The Village Gossip." The group listing Pauline Winslow's "My Saucy Sailor Boy," Boris Levenson's choral version of the folk song, and Mr. Sammond's "Spring is Here Again" was represented by all three composers present. In Joseph W. Clokey's "How Summer Came," Margaret P. Norman was the soloist; in Liszt's "The Loreley" Minna Gilsow. The program closed with Nicolai's "Woodland Sprites."

'Dr. Cyclops' Starts At the Fox Today

"Dr. Cyclops," Paramount's Technicolor drama of a power-mad scientist who turns helpless victims into capsule creatures one-fifth their normal size, is the screen attraction at the Fox Brooklyn Theater beginning today. The associate feature is "Adventure in Diamonds" with George Brent and Isa Miranda.

Albert Dekker, Janice Logan and Victor Kilian are cast in "Dr. Cyclops." Fired by the lust for power, a scientist tries his experiment upon five people who invade his hideaway and adventures follow.

The MacDowell Clubs were founded to honor composer Edward MacDowell and "to discuss and demonstrate the principles of the arts of music, literature, the drama, painting, sculpture and architecture, and to aid in the extension of knowledge of works especially fitted to exemplify the finer purposes of these arts. The New York club was the largest but was disbanded in 1942.

At the March 27th concert, Otto accompanied singer Elisabeth Schumann.

Gruenbaum Gives Piano Recital

Otto Gruenbaum, 23-year-old Viennese pianist, who made his New York debut last year at the MacDowell Club, last night gave a recital at Carnegie Chamber Music Hall. His program included Schumann's Fantasia in C major, Ravel's Scarbo, Albaniz's Triana and a Chopin group that consisted of the Barcarolle, two Mazurkas, the A flat major Ballade and the B flat minor Scherzo.

The New York Times
Published: March 24, 1942

Kulturabende der Austrian Action

In der Absicht, echte Kultur lebendig zu erhalten und zugleich jenem Teil eines künstlerischen Publikums, das sich den Luxus der grossen Musikabende in New York nicht oder nur sehr selten leisten kann, den Genuss erstklassiger Darbietungen zu ermöglichen, wird die "Kultursektion der Austrian Action" von nun an regelmässig und zu niedrigstem Eintrittspreis Abende unter der Devise: "Kunst und Wissenschaft, Anregung und Belehrung" veranstalten.

Der erste dieser Kulturabende findet Freitag, 27. März, 8:30 Uhr abends, in der MacDowell Club Hall, 166 E. 73rd St., statt. Kammersängerin *Elisabeth Schumann* wird, von Professor Leo Rosenek begleitet, eine Auswahl schönster Gesänge aus ihrem reichen Liederrepertoire zum Vortrag bringen. Mitwirken wird der bekannte Wiener Pianist *Otto Gruenbaum*.

CONCERT

UNDER THE AUSPICES OF

THE JEWISH NATIONAL FUND COUNCIL

OF GREATER BOSTON

Sun. Eve., April 5, 1942
Jeremiah Burke High School
Dorchester, Mass.

OTTO GRUENBAUM
Pianist

CARNEGIE CHAMBER MUSIC HALL
7th Avenue and 57th Street

Monday Evening, March 23rd
AT EIGHT-THIRTY O'CLOCK

PROGRAM

"THE STAR SPANGLED BANNER"	Key
ADAGIO	Bach-Busoni
FANTASY Op. 17	Schuman
SCARBO	Ravel
COMPOSITIONS ON HUNGARIAN FOLK-TUNES	Bartok
Lento	
Allegretto	
Poco andante	
Rondo	
TRIANA	Albeniz

BALLADE A FLAT MAJOR
BARCAROLLE Op. 60
TWO MAZURKAS C MINOR .... Chopin
               C MAJOR
SCHERZO B FLAT MINOR

STEINWAY PIANO

Tickets $1.65 to 55c (tax included) — On Sale at Box Office

SARAH GORBY
TOWN HALL
Wednesday evening, OCTOBER 30th, at 8:30 o'clock
Assisted by OTTO GRUENBAUM, *pianist*

Program

I

ROUMANIAN FOLK SONGS
- Love song and dance .... BREDICEANU
- Longing for Home .... D. KIRIAK
- Unfortunate Love .... BREDICEANU
- Of dor, dor (Humorous) .... BRAILOIOU

II

PIANO SOLOS
- Six Preludes
- Ballade f major .... CHOPIN

III

FRENCH FOLK SONGS
- Les trois Princesses (XV century) .... E. VUILLERMOZ
- En passant par la Lorraine (round for dancing) .... XVI CENTURY
- Ma poupée chérie (Berceuse pour la poupée) .... D. de SEVERAC
- Laissez moi planter le mai .... XVII CENTURY
- La coeur de ma vie .... J. DALCROZE
- Ca fait peur aux oiseaux .... F. BERNARD

INTERMISSION

IV

PALESTINIAN SONGS
- Ma yafim Haleilot K'naan (Invocation to the nights of Canaan) ... G. CHAJES
- Schir Haemek (Pioneer Song) .... G. GOROCHOV

OLD SPANISH SONGS — XVI CENTURY
- Atma y vida y corzzon (Romance of the Turkish ghetto) .... W. SIMONI
- Abram Avinu (Old Testament Song) .... W. SIMONI

V

PIANO SOLOS
- Sarabande et Toccata .... DEBUSSY
- Oiseaux tristes .... RAVEL
- Danse russe .... STRAVINSKY

VI

NEGRO SPIRITUALS
- Don't you weep when I'm gone .... H. BURLEIGH
- Oh, what a beautiful city .... E. BOATNER

TZIGANE SONGS
- Sad love song
- Gay love song

(Steinway Piano)

Tickets: $2.20, $1.65, $1.10, 83c, 55c, Loges, seating six, $16.50
Now at box office

Management NBC ARTISTS SERVICE
RCA Bldg., New York   GEORGE ENGLES, Managing Director

(OVER)

England Hospital Pianist To Play at Sunday Concert

Cpl. Otto Gruenbaum will be soloist and Pvt. Lawrence Anderson will be guest conductor at the Army Air Forces Redistribution Station No. 1 band concert tomorrow afternoon, scheduled for 3 o'clock in the Convention Hall Ballroom.

Warrant Officer Paul Hollinger, who will direct the band for the balance of the program, will hand over his baton to Pvt. Anderson, member of the band, for a special number, "The Legend of Sleepy Hollow" by David Bennett. A graduate of Crane Music College at Potsdam, New York, Anderson taught and directed a 50-piece orchestra regularly, at the Central High School in Cobleskill, N. Y. He studied conducting with Dr. Charles O'Neill, former president of the American Bandmasters Association. In the band he plays french horn.

Cpl. Gruenbaum, a pupil of Artur Schnabel and of the Vienna and Paris Conservatories of Music, has given New York recitals in Carnegie and Town Halls, and appeared as accompanist to leading artists in Buffalo, Detroit, Boston and Philadelphia. He is now stationed at England General Hospital.

The following program has been announced by the Station Special Services office for Sunday's concert:

1. Anchors Aweigh .... Zimmerman
2. Espana Rhapsodie .... Chabrier
   AAFRS No. 1 Band
   Mr. Hollinger, directing
3. Fantasie—Impromptu in C Sharp Minor .. Chopin
4. Polonaise in A flat major ..... Chopin
   Cpl. Otto Gruenbaum
5. Legend of Sleepy Hollow, David Bennett
   AAFRS No. 1 Band
   Mr. Hollinger, directing
6. Pavanne, from American Symphonette No. 2 . Morton Gould
7. Variations on "Pop Goes The Weasel" .. arr. Caillet
   AAFRS No. 1 Band
   Pvt. Lawrence Anderson—directing
8. March, from "Love Of Three Oranges" ... Prokofieff
9. Clair De Lune .... Debussy
10. Ritual Fire Dance .... De Falla
    Cpl. Gruenbaum
11. Waltz Potpourri ..... Johann Strauss
12. Introduction to Act Three of "Lohengrin" .. Wagner
    National Anthem.
    AAFRS No. 1 Band
    Mr. Hollinger, directing

Two Officers Are Decorated At Hospital

A Silver Star and an Air Medal with two Oak Leaf Clusters were presented to two officer-patients at England General Hospital last Tuesday for their battle achievements in the North African campaign.

With several hundred fellow patients, most of them veterans of Africa and Sicily drawn up at attention on North Carolina ave., the two officers stood before Col. Lloyd A. Kefauver, commanding officer of the hospital, and received the decorations.

The Silver Star was pinned on the uniform of Lt. Alfred Ramaglia, 23, of Syracuse, N. Y., for his gallantry in braving heavy German shelling in a reconnoitering mission near Mateur. The Air Medal went to Lt. Raymond R. Manley, also 23, of Colorado Springs, Colo., in honor of his serving as pilot or co-pilot of a Mitchell B-25 twin-engined bomber in 18 raids over Tunisia, Sicily, Sardinia and Pantelleria.

Described by his commanding officer as "the best soldier I have ever seen," Lt. Ramaglia was commissioned an officer on the same day of his reconnoitering mission, although at that time he didn't know it. He had gone through the African campaign as a sergeant, having enlisted in the Army three years ago because "I knew the war was coming and I wanted to be in it." He lost the hearing of his right ear in the invasion of Africa.

Witnessing the ceremony was Lt.

**U.S.O. COUNCIL
ATLANTIC COUNTY**

OFFICERS
AND
BOARD OF GOVERNORS

John C. Woulfe
  President
Harry Cassman
  Vice-President
Fred Chapman
  Vice-President
Frank Breder
  Vice-President
John Machise
  Vice-President
Paul M. Cope
  Treasurer
Frank M. McBroom
  Secretary

Wm. Carrington
Wm. Duffy
Mrs. James J. Farrell
Alfred T. Glenn, Jr.
Mrs. Henry Halpern
Rueben Jacoby
Rev. Geo. Lawrence
Andrew Littlefield
Wendell Norris
Miss Lucy Quinn
Miss Katherine Raedy
J. Potter Reilley
Harry Segel
Paul T. Wolcott

Committee
of Management
Mrs. Harry Cassman
Arthur S. Chenoweth
Paul M. Cope
Frank Daly
Saul Gorson
Miss Katherine Raedy

STAFF
Director
Philip W. Russ
Jewish Welfare Board
Assistant
Mrs. Tillie R. Segel
Jewish Welfare Board
Associate Directors
H. Darnell Brittin
Army and Navy Y. M. C. A.
Suzanne D. Cope
National Board, Y. W. C. A.
Frank J. Gilligan
National Catholic Community Service

USO CLUB
101 STATES AVENUE
ATLANTIC CITY, N. J.

PHONES 5-4033
       5-0032

ADDRESS REPLY TO:

February 17, 1943

Private Otto Gruenbaum
Medical Detachment
Atlantic City, N. J.

Dear Otto:

    Those who heard your very fine Concert of Monday are still talking about the fine quality of your playing. The fact that you had such a poor piano and could do so well on it is more than real accomplishment. I do want you to know that the members of the Staff and the men who were present had a real treat in your playing, and already I am planning if possible to have you give a repeat performance Monday March 15th. Won't you put that down somewheres as a date with the USO? Drop in to see us as often as you can. The offer to use my home piano still holds good, and I do hope you will avail yourself of the chance to play on it whenever you so desire.

    With kindest regards and good luck, to you.

Sincerely,

Tillie R. Segel
Assistant Director

TRS:FM

THE YOUNG MEN'S CHRISTIAN ASSOCIATIONS • THE NATIONAL CATHOLIC COMMUNITY SERVICE • THE SALVATION ARMY
THE YOUNG WOMEN'S CHRISTIAN ASSOCIATIONS • THE JEWISH WELFARE BOARD • THE NATIONAL TRAVELERS AID ASSOCIATION

PIANO RECITAL	STATION WBAB THURSDAY, APRIL 27, 1944 8:30 to 8:45 PM

MUSIC: (THEME --- UP AND FADE FOR)

ANNOUNCER: This is the Army Air Forces Redistribution Station No. 1. Tonight we again invite you to listen to a quarter hour of the world's great piano music. Waiting at the keyboard on the stage of the Ballroom of Convention Hall is Cpl. Otto Gruenbaum of England General Hospital. Gruenbaum is usually the accompanist on this program for Private First Class Ira Baker, Station Violinist, who is now away on furlough. Pvt. Baker and his violin will return to this program next Thursday. To open tonights program Cpl. Gruenbaum has chosen a selection from the work of the Polish pianist and composer, Frederick Chopin. It's titled Fantasy--Impromptu. The middle part contains a familiar melody which has been used for the popular song "I'm Always Chasing Rainbows." Chopin's Fantasy--Impromptu.

MUSIC: FANTASY---IMPROMPTU

ANNOUNCER: Several of Franz Schubert's most charming waltzes were later arranged into a paraphase by Franz Liszt, who decorated them with de[licate] variations. One of these, A Viennese Ev[ening] pictures the atmosphere of gaiety and

- 2 -

sentimentality of 19th century Vienna. We hear it now, a Viennese Evening, written by Franz Schubert, and arranged by Franz Liszt.

MUSIC: VIENNESE EVENING

ANNOUNCER: Manuel DeFalla is considered by many as one of the most original of contemporary Spanish composers. And one of his most original compositions is the "Ritual Fire Dance." It is taken from his ballet, "Il Amor Bruho." and is supposed to drive away any bad spirits that might dare be around. Cpl. Gruenbaum and DeFalla's "Ritual Fire Dance."

MUSIC: RITUAL FIRE DANCE

MUSIC: THEME (UP AND FADE FOR)

ANNOUNCER: You have been listening to fifteen minutes of the world's great piano music, presented by the Army Air Forces Redistribution Station No. 1, under the command of Col. A. W. Snyder. At the keyboard has been Cpl. Otto Gruenbaum. Listen again next week at this same time when Cpl. Gruenbaum joins Private First Class Ira Baker, violinist, in a quarter of music for the piano and violin. Your announcer has been S/Sgt. Robert A. Fuller.

END

NEW YORK HERALD TRIBUNE,

MUSIC
By VIRGIL THOMSON

NEW FRIENDS of MUSIC, Carnegie Hall, 8:45. Piano recital by Artur Schnabel. All-Beethoven program. Sonatas in A flat major, Op. 110; in F major, Op. 10, No. 2; in D minor, Op. 31, No. 2; in C, Op. 111.

Equalized Expressivity

ARTUR Schnabel, who played Monday night in Carnegie Hall the second of three recitals, presented by the New Friends of Music, devoted to the piano music of Beethoven, has for some thirty or forty years made this composer the object of his especial attention. He passes, indeed, and with reason, for an expert on the subject, by which is usually meant that his knowledge of it is extensive and that his judgments about it are respected. Any issue taken with him on details of tempo, of phraseology, of accent is risky and, at best, of minor import. Minor, too, are criticisms of his piano technique, which, though not first class is quite adequate for the expression of his ideas. His ideas about Beethoven's piano music in general, whether or not one finds his readings convincing, are not to be dismissed lightly.

* * *

Neither need they, I think, be taken as the voice of authority. For all the consistency and logic of his musicianship, there is too large a modicum of late-nineteenth-century Romanticism in Mr. Schnabel's own personality to make his Beethoven—who was, after all, a child of the late eighteenth—wholly convincing to musicians of the mid-twentieth. No one wishes to deny the Romantic element in Beethoven. But I do think that they are another kind of Romanticism from Schnabel's, which seems to be based on the Wagnerian theories of expressivity.

* * *

Mr. Schnabel does not admit, or plays as if he did not admit, any difference between the expressive functions of melody and of passage work. The neutral material of music—scales, arpeggiated basses, accompanying figures, ostinato chordal backgrounds, formal cadences—he plays as if they were an intense communication, as if they were saying something as important as the main thematic material. They are important to Beethoven's composition, of course; but they are not directly expressive musical elements. They serve as amplification, as underpinning, frequently as mere acoustical brilliance. To execute them all with climactic emphasis is to rob the

Artur Schnabel

Whom the New Friends of Music presented in a piano recital at Carnegie Hall Monday night

melodic material, the expressive phrases, of their singing power.

This equalized expressivity ends by making Beethoven sound sometimes a little meretricious as a composer. His large-scale forms include, of necessity, a large amount of material that has a structural rather than a directly expressive function. Emphasizing all this as if it were phrase by phrase of the deepest emotional portent not only reduces the emotional portent of the original material; it blows up the commonplaces of musical rhetoric and communication into a form of bombast that makes Beethoven's early sonatas, which have many formal observances in them, sound empty of meaning and the later ones, which sometimes skip formal transitions, sound like the improvisations of a talented youth.

The work that suffered least Monday night from the disportionate emphasizing of secondary material was the Sonata, Opus III. Here Mr. Schnabel achieved a more convincing relation in the first movement than one currently hears between the declamatory and the lyrical subjects. And in the finale he produced for us that beatific tranquillity that was a characteristic part of Beethoven's mature expression and that had been noticeably wanting, though there were plenty of occasions for it, in the earlier part of the evening.

T. D.

Hollywood News

Otto's Letter in response to Virgil Thomas' column on Arthur Schnabel's concert.
Otto studied with Arthur Schnabel when he first came to New York.

Otto K. Gruenbaum
T/5 Med. Det., 1272 S. C. U. T.
Atlantic City, New Jersey

29 March 1944

Dear Mr. Thomson:

Reading your article about Artur Schnabel I noticed the fact that your way of criticizing him is entirely controversial to the way this artist has often been criticised in this country. As a rule he was called "overexacting", too deliberate— the word pedantry appeared frequently, on the other hand you consider him tooromantic for Beethoven and expressiv in passage work and minor parts of the composition.

As little as I agree with any of those opinions, I recognize the superiority of your criticism expressing adefinite point of view and I remember similar objections made to Mr. Schnabels way of playning in Europe.

But to call him a Wagnerian Romanticist is indeed quite far off. Even without knowing his personal feelings towards Wagnerism, it is quite obvious that his rather chasteand simple way of playing is not at all Wagnerian. The great emphasis on broad melodies, brass-like effects a la Liszt, the following of the "great line", the big tone, the massive sensousness— these are not at all attributes of Schnabels playing, nor is his whole approach to music wagnerien.

Schnabel is the type of musician coming from the stringquartett (as a symbol), from the inside of music - not from outside considerations. There is a difference between the conductor who interpretes th 3rd Sinfonie of Beethoven in a certain way because it is called "Eroica", and the one who states after studying the score: This work is indeed heroic. The first one is inspired by the thoughts his imaginations associates with the word heroic, the other one gets his inpiration only by the music itself. Wagner is the first type and he is right for himself (there is no right or wrong for the ceative artist, only good or bad), but of course for the performer of Pre wagnerian music this attitude would be dangerous.(this is mentioned in connection with your previous articles on Wagner).

Wagner did not have two different talents, poetry and music, - it was the same talent in all his different artistic activities, the same way of expressing his message, even if the results are not equally good. He uses the logic of th mind to devellop his musical ideas, and the the specific musical way of thinking in writing poetry.

I feel that this is the main difference to Beethoven, who despite of the deep phylosophical content of his work - always devellops his material in a purely musical way, using something undiscribable: "the musical logic".

To come back to Schnabel: I consider his way of thinking entirely on the Beethoven side -little influenced by extra-musical thoughts. If you insist of calling him a romantic, so only in the Schubertian way.

To speak of your "equalized expressivity": the word equal does not seem to be qite correct, because the grade and character of expression varies greatly in any interpretation. To play continouly espressivo would indeed be very tiring to listen to. But Schnabel plays continously with a certain musical meaning- could that be called distorting the music?

Mr. Schnabel is very sensitive to harmony progressions and feels intensely for instance a chord of the 7th or a ninth triad. So he interprets all passagework according to its harmonic developement. Certain neglected details become more significant due to their harmonic back ground. There is always something happening musically, in every run, in every arpeggio- for some people these happenings might seem to be unimportant- there is no reason of continously underestimating the value of those supposingly minor details and if we look closer into the works of Mozart and Beethoven we recognize the big difference between their passagework and what you call "common place". This way of playing tends nearer to improvisation, (this statement is correct), but it comes nearer to the creative mood of the composer too, a mood in which he's felt stronger and more intense than any performer ever can be able to feel.

Schnabel's method shows more enjoyement in music than the ordinary performer experiences, more pleasure in the natural sources of music A man who sees beauty in every little detail, is he to be criticised for that? If the others don't see all this, is it his fault? He plays one whole and not "melodies and runs". I never heard Schnabel emphazice mere accompaniments or embellishments of any sort.

As much as I understand that one's liking or not liking of an artist is highly individual and cannot be discussed, I still feel that the sincere, serious and strongly idealistic approach of Artur Schnabel could be considered with more justice and with more friendly understanding.

Very truly yours

April 12, 1944

Pvt. Otto K. Gruenbaum
T/5 Med. Det., 1272 S. C. S. U.
Atlantic City, New Jersey

Dear Mr. Gruenbaum:

    I thank you for the charming and extremely interesting letter. I suspect that many of our seeming differences of opinion about musical matters are due to the different meanings that we attach to words like Romanticism, Wagnerian and "the commonplaces of musical communication."

    Very sincerely yours,

Virgil Thomson

APPENDIX D

**Notes on the Ritchie Boys,
IPW Teams, and Interrogations**

A book of snapshots take of American soldiers, Spring 1945

RESTRICTED

HEADQUARTERS
ARMY GROUND FORCES
Army War College
Washington 25, D.C.

354.2/12(Maneuvers-1943)(R)(15 Mar 43)GNGBI   12 August 1943.

SUBJECT: Interrogator of Prisoners of War Teams.

TO: Commanding Generals,
    Second Army,
    Third Army,
    IV Corps,
    XIII Corps,
    Desert Training Center.

1. The Military Intelligence Training Center, Camp Ritchie, Maryland, has been requested to make available Interrogator of Prisoner of War Teams to Army Ground Forces units undergoing combined training. A team consists of approximately two officers and four enlisted men, complete with T/BA equipment, less transportation. The initial request for these teams will be made direct to the Commandant, Military Intelligence Training Center.

2. The commanding general of the maneuver area will furnish, on a loan status, two $\frac{1}{4}$-ton trucks and one $\frac{1}{4}$-ton trailer to each team upon its arrival in the maneuver area. In the event that $\frac{1}{4}$-ton trucks and trailers are not available, suitable vehicles may be substituted. If additional vehicles are required to meet this need, they may be requisitioned in accordance with War Department memorandum 850-32-43, 4 July 1943, "Distribution of Ordnance Vehicles."

3. The War Department has been requested to make Interrogator of Prisoner of War Teams available for maneuvers and to work with divisions engaged in combined training on the basis of one team per division as a minimum, or three per division as a maximum. It is the desire of this headquarters that full use be made of these teams during maneuvers. Their use during the combined training period in the D series is authorized.

4. The Commandant, Military Intelligence Training Center, has been informed that direct communication with the Commanding Generals of the maneuver areas with respect to detailed arrangements is authorized.

5. This letter supersedes Par. 10 of Weekly Directive No. 11, Headquarters Army Ground Forces, 16 March 1943.

By command of LT. GEN. McNAIR:

J. R. DRYDEN,
Lt. Col., A.G.D.,
Ass't Ground Adjutant General.

A TRUE COPY:

Two items specific to Otto's team IPW 20
The first reports the terrible losses to his team on 20 December 1944
The second shows what equipment was needed

```
a.  ROBERT W. ANDRAE        Capt.  CAV  O456014
    Wolf D. Goeltzer        M/Sgt        34050272
    Joesoh M. Kramer        Tec 5        32965429
b.  30 December 1944
c.  Capt Robert W. Andrae and M/Sgt Wolf D. Goeltzer: DOW
    Tec 5 Joesph M. Kramer: SWA
d.  Geographical site:  Surburg, Alsace, France
e.  Hqs. 14th Arm'd Div.
f.  Evacuated through 84 Med Bn., 14th A.D.
g.  Date of evacuation to hospital 30 December 1944
Note:  The above named personnel were relieved from IPW Team 12
       as casualties and replacements were assigned per Par. 19
       SO F17 Hq. MIS ETOUSA 17 Jan 45
```

```
c.  Capt Robert W. Andrae and M/Sgt Wolf D. Goeltzer: DOW
    Tec 5 Joesph M. Kramer: SWA
d.  Geographical site:  Surburg, Alsace, France
e.  Hqs. 14th Arm'd Div.
f.  Evacuated through 84 Med Bn., 14th A.D.
g.  Date of evacuation to hospital 30 December 1944
Note:  The above named personnel were relieved from IPW Team 120
       as casualties and replacements were assigned per Par. 19 and 20
       SO F17 Hq. MIS ETOUSA 17 Jan 45

Par. 6.  Major Supply Problems:
    a.  IPW Team 120 has on hand the following team equipment:
            2-Ton Trucks (Nos. 2041430 and 20153279-S)
            1-Trailer, ¼Ton, 2 wheel, cargo (No 0697425)
            1-Camouflage net
            2-Portable typewriters
            1-Knife Trench M3, and scabbard
            1-Bag of tools (minus jack and tire lugs wrench)
            1-Knife TL-29 and Pouch Type CS-34
            1-American Gas Lamp
            1-Burner, Stove
            1-Bucket, Canvas, Water
            2-Field Telephones
            1-Trouble Lamp with wire extension
            3-Clip Boards
    b.  The following team equipment lost or destroyed due to enemy action
        at Surburg, Alsace, France on 30 Dec 44, has not been replaced:
            2-Alidade, Boxwood
            1-Case, Canvas, Dispatch
            1-Chair, Folding, Wood
            1-Desk, Field Hq Type
            2-Goggles, M-1943
            3-Knife, Trench M3
            1-Machine, paper fastener
            2-Protractor, Semi-circ
            1-Table, camp, folding
            2-Tube, flexible, nozzle
            1-Wire, W-130 on reel
            1-Binoculars, M1 3 w/case
    c.  Other items of team equipment authorized according to TBA, SPX 400
        4 April 1944 OB-S-Spmoo-M, were never issued to IPW Team 120.
    d.  ¼ Ton Truck No. 20153279-S is in poor and unserviceable condition
        through fair wear and tear and is a handicap to the team because
        of repeated break-downs. Request replacement of this vehicle.
```

DECLASSIFIED
Authority NND 745001

All the following pages as well as the three preceding ones were found and copies at the National Archives in College Park, MD

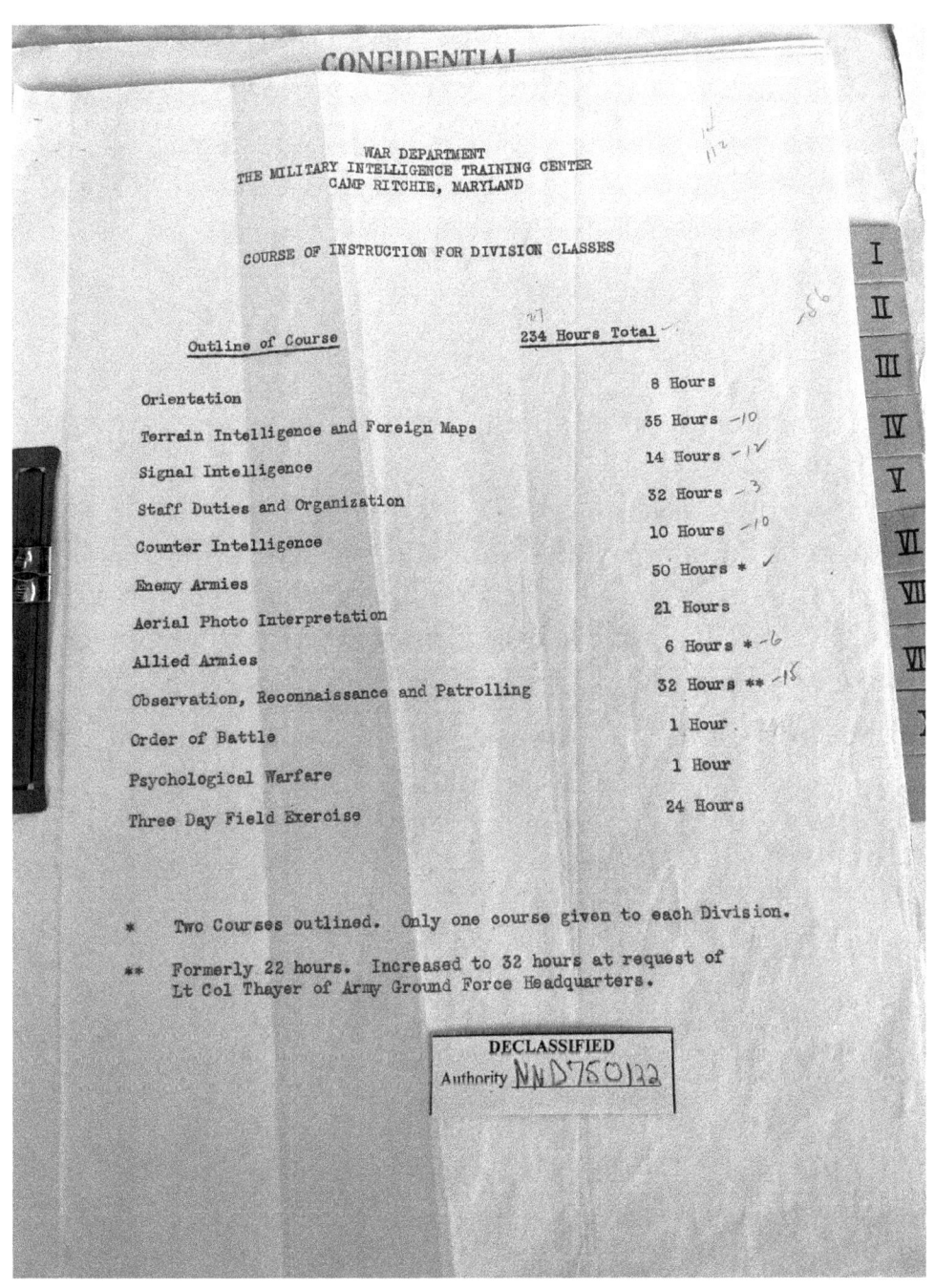

CONFIDENTIAL

WAR DEPARTMENT
THE MILITARY INTELLIGENCE TRAINING CENTER
CAMP RITCHIE, MARYLAND

COURSE OF INSTRUCTION FOR DIVISION CLASSES

Outline of Course — 234 Hours Total

Orientation	8 Hours
Terrain Intelligence and Foreign Maps	35 Hours
Signal Intelligence	14 Hours
Staff Duties and Organization	32 Hours
Counter Intelligence	10 Hours
Enemy Armies	50 Hours *
Aerial Photo Interpretation	21 Hours
Allied Armies	6 Hours *
Observation, Reconnaissance and Patrolling	32 Hours **
Order of Battle	1 Hour
Psychological Warfare	1 Hour
Three Day Field Exercise	24 Hours

*   Two Courses outlined. Only one course given to each Division.

** Formerly 22 hours. Increased to 32 hours at request of Lt Col Thayer of Army Ground Force Headquarters.

DECLASSIFIED
Authority NND750122

The first document below is a training script of how an interrogation might be conducted.

To hear what such an interrogation might sound like, and to see how the interrogator assesses the tone he should take with each prisoner go to YouTube and look for *"World War 2 Interrogation Techniques/ Intelligence Gathering/ WW2 Military Training Film/1943 (Watch?v=c_SjWqF1Xc0)*

Reproduced from the Unclassified/Declassified holdings of the National Archives.

RESTRICTED

INTERROGATION
OF
PRISONERS
OF
WAR

9 Feb 1945   MITC – Ritchie
                   Section IX

RESTRICTED

DEMONSTRATION

INTERROGATION OF PRISONERS OF WAR

(The house is darkened. After a moment, a spotlight comes up center stage and Capt Norton steps through the center opening of the curtains.)

Capt Norton: Good afternoon. No matter who our enemy is we're always interested in finding out the strength, location, and composition of his forces. And reports we receive today from all fronts indicate that most of our information will be obtained from captured enemy personnel and documents. You will see this afternoon how to get that information and how to exploit it properly.

Let's say an outfit has taken some prisoners. First you want to segregate them, that is, to separate the officers from the non-coms, and non-coms from the privates. You see, a German private is accustomed to having someone tell him what, when and where to do everything. Separate him from the men who have been giving him his orders and . . . well, you can start giving the orders yourself and in all likelihood he'll obey them. In all likelihood, too, he'll be inclined to tell you what he knows if he hasn't anyone around to encourage him and bolster his morale.

Capt Graham: (Who has been sitting in the audience.) Excuse me for interrupting, Captain, but I'd like to ask a question, if you don't mind.

Capt Norton: Why, certainly, sir, go right ahead.

Capt Graham: I'd like to know what you do when you get a large crowd of prisoners. How do you handle them?

Capt Norton: Get the commissioned officers out of sight immediately. Then, on the basis of recognition of rank, segregate the privates and non-coms. If the men have come into battle stripped of insignia, and this happens quite often, call out the senior non-commissioned officer and order him to do the segregating. Just in case you're wondering, he'll do it all right, because he's used to taking orders and giving them, and remember, he hasn't been asked to give any military information or to do anything else he hasn't been trained to do.

Capt Graham: All right, what happens if your prisoners aren't segregated right away?

Capt Norton: I could talk about that for hours, Captain, but instead, suppose I tell you what happened shortly after American troops landed at Gela. They moved up the Sicilian coast past Licata in the direction of Agrigento. Germans based at Canicatti started toward Marina in an effort to cut off the American advance. A group of prisoners were being taken back to the collecting station immediately after they had been disarmed.

(Captain Norton exits between the curtains as they part. An American Lt leads 5 German PW's on stage. A slightly wounded American doughboy acts as guard. Lt gives the private his instructions.)

Lt: No look, soldier, your job right now is to watch those PW's and nothing else. Don't let 'em get away. Understand?

Pvt: Yes, sir.

Pvt: What do I do then?

Lt: Tell the Lt that these men have been captured by B Co of the 52d Infantry and a damn good job they did too. Only don't tell him that !

Pvt: Yes, sir.

Lt: By then you should be recovered from that knock on your head, so come on up forward and report to your company again. They're not much farther on than when you left them.

Pvt: Yes, Sir. (Salutes, officer exits.)

(The German prisoner, an officer, looks to the American private and walks toward him.)

Ger Off: (Offering a pack of cigarettes.) Cigarette?

Pvt: Oh...thanks ! I'll smoke it later. You speak English.

Ger Off: Yes. I studied a little in school. Did you study German in your American School?

Pvt: No, I only speak English.

Ger Off: I see. (He wanders back towards his men.)

Pvt: Well, you guys make yourselves comfortable. It'll be a long wait if I know those guys. Probably'll get lost on the way, anyhow.

Ger Off: We are tired . . . .

(The American private walks down R makes himself comfortable and begins to read a letter.)

Mannschaften ! Achtung !

Germans: Jawohl, herr Lt. Ja, mein Herr, etc.

Ger Off: Hierher, schnell! Jetzt passt mal gut auf! Obwohl wir Kriegsgefangenen sind dürfen wir unsere soldaten Pflichten nicht vergessen. Gut zuhören! Wir sollen keine militärischen Angelegenheiten besprechen.

PW 1: Dürfen wir gar nichts sagen?

Ger Off: Nach den Internazionalen Gesetzen, braucht Ihr nur Namen, Dienstgrad und Nummer anzugeben.

PW 2: Können wir unsere Geburtstage und Begurtsorte geben?

Ger Off: Ja, wenn Ihr wolt. Das is nicht sehr wichtig.

PW 3: Nichts anderes?

Ger Off: Nichts anderes! Nur Name, Dienstgrad, und Nummer! Keine Militarischen Angelegenheiten! Das ist alles. (The prisoners start to sit.) Noch etwas. Mir ist etwas anderes eingefallen. Um den Feind zu tauschen können wir unsere Schulterklappen abnehmen.

PW's: (The PW's remove shoulder straps amid ad lib.)

Ger Off: Jetzt nehmt alle Dokumente, Landkarten, Bilder und was Ihr sonst noch habt aus den Taschen und gebt es mir schnell.

PW 4: Auch unsere Soldbücher?

Ger Off: Nein, die könnt Ihr behalten. Zerreisst alle Papiere in kleine Stücke und vergrabt sie dort . . . .
Die Amerikaner! Setzt Euch!

(The PW's resume positions of rest.)

(Lt Darrow and S Sgt Williams enter.

Lt Darrow: Guard!

Pvt: (jumping to attention and coming over to the officer.) Yes, sir.

Lt Darrow: What the hell goes on here? Why haven't these men been separated?

Pvt: I don't know, sir. Lt Black just told me not to let any of 'em get away. And I didn't. Started out with five and I still got five.

Lt Darrow: What else did he tell you?

Pvt: Well, he said that these men were captured by B Company of the 52d Infantry. That's my outfit and then after I've turned 'em over to you I was to come forward.

Lt Darrow: Anything else?

Pvt: Well, sir, he said we did a damn good job...Oh....I wasn't supposed to tell you that.

Lt Darrow: Did he have these men separated according to rank when he gave them to you?

Pvt: No, sir. They were just like they are now.

Lt Darrow: Did you hear them say anything?

Pvt: Well that little guy in the middle speaks a little English. He kept hollering something like hagen bagen schlagen...or something...to his men... but nobody said nothin' about not lettin' 'em talk.

Lt Darrow: How about the documents? Were they searched?

Pvt: I don't know, sir.

Lt Darrow: (The Sgt hands him a few scraps of paper which he's found near the prisoners.) Did you tear up any papers in the last hour?

Pvt: No, sir.

Lt Darrow: Well, where did these come from?

Pvt: I don't know, sir.

Lt Darrow: OK. Stick around until I release you. (The Pvt salutes and exits. Then to the Sgt.) Some of these days I'm going to get one of those Infantry Lieutenants and ... well.. what do we have here?

Sgt: Well, there's one officer but I can't tell what the rest of them are.

Lt Darrow: The officer probably wised them up by now.

Sgt: Yes, sir. We'll have trouble with these men.

Lt Darrow: Take them out under the trees and we'll try them one at a time. Have Stevens search them, but don't set up the equipment. I don't think we'll need it.

Sgt: Yes, sir. Gefangene ! Achtung ! Stillgestanden. In einer Linie hier in der Mitte antreten....Marsch ! Links um ! Vorwärts marsch. (The PW's march out.) (Reentering with the first PW) Halt. Stillgestanden.

Lt Darrow: Soldbuch vorzeigen. Wie heissen Sie?

PW 1: Kurt Schliessen.

Lt Darrow: Dienstgrad?

PW 1: Grenadier.

Lt Darrow: Nummer?

PW 1: 3989

Lt Darrow: Feldpost nummer?

PW 1: Es tut mir leid, aber ich werde Ihre Fragen nicht beantworten.

Lt Darrow: Take him away. Bring in another one.

Sgt: Kehrt. Vorwärts marsch. (They exit.)

Lt Darrow: They've removed their shoulder straps and won't say a word.

Sgt: (Entering with another prisoner.) Halt!

Lt Darrow: Wie heissen Sie?

Ger Off: Ruprecht von Bargen.

Lt Darrow: Dienstgrad?

Ger Off: Leutnant.

Lt Darrow: Nummer?

Ger Off: 09937.

Lt Darrow: Zu welcher Truppenteil gehören Sie?

Ger Off: Ich habe nichts mehr zu sagen. Nach den international Gesetzen brauchen wir nur unser Namen, Dienstgrad, und Nummer anzugeben.

Sgt: Ich glaube dass er diese Gesetze seinen Mannschaften erklärt hat?

Ger Off: Naturlich.

Lt Darrow: Take this man away. They've had too much time to prepare their answers and every damn thing.

Sgt: Kehrt. Vorwärts marsch.

Lt Darrow: We'll not get anything out of these men. We should have stayed over at Regiment. Norton's got a lot of work to do over there alone.

Sgt: (entering with another prisoner.) Halt!

Lt Darrow: Wie heissen Sie?

PW 3: Muller.

Lt Darrow: Dienstgrad?

PW 3: Obergefreiter.

Lt Darrow: Nummer?

PW 3: 5674

Lt Darrow: Feldpostnummer?

PW 3: Mein deutsche Soldatenehre verbietet mir Ihnen etwas zu sagen.

Lt Darrow: Oh blow it out of your barracks bag. Get him out of here. Oh, wait a minute. Did Stevens find anything on them?

Sgt: No sir. No maps, no pictures, no documents, nothing. Not even a scrap of paper.

Lt Darrow: That's the answer! (looks at scrap of paper in his hand.) We could find the rest of it and put it together but it might take hours and we don't have the time. Put him back, and let's get out of here.

(The curtains close, and Capt Norton returns to the front of the stage.)

Capt Norton: There you are, Captain. Does that make it any clearer?

Capt Graham: Well, my college German is pretty rusty, but I think I got most of it. Those prisoners mixed things up so badly the officer couldn't get anything out of them. Is that it?

Capt Norton: Oh, he could have gotten something out of them eventually, but at this point there just wasn't enough to make the effort worth while. We're after quantity here. We want a lot of information and we want it quickly, and the dazed prisoner, still under the shock of battle, is our likeliest customer. During the march from the front lines to the Interrogation point, guards must maintain strict prisoner discipline at all times. They must not allow the prisoners to

Capt Norton: (cont'd) smoke, talk, eat or drink, for such bits of kindness may spoil prisoners for the interrogation team. Incidentally, all members of the team are trained interrogators and are qualified to examine documents and make accurate and concise reports on all information derived from prisoners. Naturally all members of the team are fluent in the enemy's language. Teams are attached to combat units by Theater Headquarters and go into the line with their own transportation, namely, 2 jeeps and a quarter-ton trailer, operating at the Divisional or Regimental collecting points. Frequently, however, they may go even farther forward if the prisoners are not evacuated immediately. But let's continue the story I started before, and you can get an idea about how to handle prisoners correctly, particularly the technique of the search, which is very important. Here's what happened a little later that same day.

(Capt Norton walks offstage as spot goes down. Curtain opens. Lt Darrow, the Assistant Interrogator, and S Sgt Williams are awaiting PW's at the enclosure.)

Lt Darrow: They've received a new batch of prisoners at the collecting point, and they're bringing them over right away. Only five, I think. Captured down there by F Company of the 151st. Hope to hell they know something.

Sgt: You're right, sir, we did run into trouble this morning. By the way, where do you want them put this time....same place?

Lt Darrow: That's ok...Here they come now, and it looks as though those dofoots have the enlisted men separated from their officers this time.

(Enter MP's with 4 PW's. Three enlisted men, one non-com, one officer. They are separated.)

MP: Halt. (Turns and salutes Lt.) Sir, these five prisoners were captured by F Company, 82d Infantry, in the vicinity of Palma. They have been separated and searched for weapons and ammunition, only.

Lt Darrow: Very good. That's all. I'll take over from here.

MP: Yes, sir. (Salutes, goes behind PW's left.)

Lt Darrow: Stillgestanden! Links um! (PW's come to attention.) Take this man to the non-com's pen.

Sgt: Yes, sir. Vorwärts marsch.

PW: Keine militärischen Angelegenheiten besprechen....

Lt Darrow: Schweigen! (To MP) Take him to the Officer's pen. Have him searched.

MP: Yes, sir. (Pushes G. O. out with his rifle. G. O. continues to shout excitedly).

PW: Vergessen Sie nicht. Nur Namen, Dienstgrad und Nummer.

Sgt: Halts Maul'!

Lt Darrow: Mannschaften, achtung!

Sgt: Fuhlüng nehmen. Einen schritt zwischen raum nehmen. Kehrt! Hände auf den rücken.

Lt Darrow: We'll start with this man in the center. Search him from top to bottom...you know, the whole routine.

Sgt: Yes, sir. (Points) Sie, einen Schritt rückwärts. Kehrt! Füsse auseinander. We'll start with his helmet. Nothing in here, sir. Beide haende anfassen.

(At this point the search is described as lie by Capt Norton various essential elements involved in the search.)

MP: (returns) Sir, I found this on the Officer prisoner.

Lt Darrow: Hmmm ! Looks very interesting. Regiment Angriff Berehl. (To Sgt.) It's an attack order and it's dated today. Write the Officer's name on it and take it to Capt Norton for translation; you can arrange for transportation to send the translated order to the S-2. Norton will phone in the gist of it, but I think we should be ready to get the map to the S-2 as soon as possible. How can you get it there?

Sgt: We can send a runner, sir.

Lt Darrow: Runner, hell ! This is important. Grab a motorcycle, and get this attack order to Capt Norton right away.

MP: Yes, sir. (Salutes and leaves.)

Lt Darrow: As soon as you finish, call the guard to watch these birds and don't let 'em talk to each other. We'll send out for them as we want them, one at a time.

(The curtains close and Capt Norton appears once more on the fore-stage.)

Capt Norton: Well, so much for the proper method of segregation and search.

Capt Graham: Captain, in that last scene I noticed there was quite a bit of emphasis on military courtesy and discipline. Is there any particular reason for that?

Capt Norton: A very good reason. Those soldiers handling or coming into contact with PW's are instructed to emphasize military courtesy to an even greater extent than usual, in order to impress prisoners with the efficiency and alertness of the American soldier.

Capt Graham: I see; well, what happens from here on?

Capt Norton: Let's get on with the interrogation itself. Our interrogator picks out his most likely victims for questioning and later sends the rest along to the clearing point for evacuation to the rear.

Capt Graham: Does he just pick a certain number, depending on how much time he has?

Capt Norton: That's one consideration, of course, but he also has to keep in mind the different branches of service ... the usual choice is several from each branch and at least one from each unit. Now, the examiner arranges to have the prisoners brought to him one at a time. The stenographer should be hidden from the prisoners, but in such a position that he can take down all that is said in German shorthand. One of the team members will act as the guard, and the remainder of the team will be set up hastily nearby to go over the documents.

Capt Graham: That reminds me, Captain, quite a few documents were taken from the prisoners just searched. Now I know German soldiers are instructed not to carry any papers at all into combat, so wasn't that an exaggeration?

Capt Norton: You're right. They are instructed not to. Fortunately for us, most German prisoners carry diaries and other papers of great value. These can be best exploited if the examiner looks at them before the interrogation. Then he can refer to them when he's questioning the prisoner. Incidentally, the interrogator has no other papers in front of him, and he takes

Capt Norton: (contd) no notes because the prisoner is likely to spill a lot more valuable information if he thinks he's just in conversation, and not talking for the record.

Capt Graham: When your examiner questions prisoners, does he try to stick to the same line of questioning?

Capt Norton: No, it all depends on the prisoner. However, he does have a general outline to follow and certain questions about important information wanted. This questionnaire is based on essential elements of information furnished him by G-2 or S-2 and sometimes pluss the strategic information desired by higher headquarters. However, the interrogator's primary job at first examination is to get tactical information and to pass it on immediately to the S-2 whom he serves. Obviously, information of this type that arrives late is worthless. Suppose we take a look at one of these tactical interrogations. Oh, by the way, we'll have a little trouble at first, because the prisoner is German and there's no German-speaking interrogator available...Just some officer who happened to be around. This will prove the advantage of having properly trained personnel do the interrogating.

(Capt Norton walks stage right and exits. The curtains part. Lt Tanner is discovered at a field desk.)

Lt Tanner: Well, here goes nothing.

Sgt: (entering with PW.) Sir, here's the man you wanted.

Lt Tanner: That'll be all. Wait outside and send Sgt Williams of the IPW team in to me.

Sgt: Yes, sir. (Salutes and exits.)

Sgt Williams: (entering) You sent for me, sir?

Lt Tanner: Yes, Williams, I know I'm not a member of your I.P.W. Team, but I want to ask this prisoner some questions and I want you to translate for me ...

Sgt Williams: But I'm an Interpreter, sir; my job is to .....

Lt Tanner: Yes, I know, but that'll be O.K. I know just how it's done. I've watched them do it loads and loads of times. I'll ask the questions and you put 'em in German.

Sgt Williams: Yes, sir.

Lt Tanner: Well! Get him to stand where he belongs!

Sgt W: Stellen Sie sich hierher.

Lt Tanner: Ask him his name.

Sgt W: Wie heissen Sie?

PW: Wolfgang von Eulenspiegel.

Lt Tanner: Thanks! Can you translate that?

Sgt W: You can't translate it, sir, it's just a name.

Lt Tanner: Can you spell it?

Sgt W: W-O-L-F as in Wolf. G-A-N-G as in gang.

Lt Tanner: Fine. Now ask him...

Sgt W: Just a minute, sir. That's only his first name. Then comes von, V-O-N-.

Lt Tanner: That's his middle name.

Sgt W: No, sir, that is just a title. You know, like in von Hindenburg.

Lt Tanner: Yeah, I got it. What's the rest of his name.

Sgt W: Eulenspiegel. E-U-L-E-N-S-P-I-E-G-E-L.

Lt Tanner: Quite a mouthful, isn't it? All right, now what's his rank?

Sgt W: He's an Obergefreiter.

Lt Tanner: What the hell's an Obergefreiter.

Sgt W: It's pretty hard to translate, sir. An Obergefreiter is about a corporal in our army, but in the German army he's not considered a non-com. In any event, his rank is between a pfc and a sgt.

Lt Tanner: My God! All we have so far is his name. It certainly seems to have taken a hell of a while to get it, too.

Sgt W: I'm doing the best I can, sir. I have to get the question from you in English; translate the question into German; ask him the question in German, get his answer in German, and then translate it back into English for you, sir.

Lt Tanner: Sgt, you're confusing me. You're doing all right but it takes too damn long. (To PW) What is your unit? (To Sgt.) Ask him what his unit is.

Sgt W: Zu welcher Einheit gehören Sie?

PW: Divisions Aufklärungsabteilung Nummer achtundzwanzig.

Sgt W: Reconnaissance Bn Number 28. Does that sound right?

Lt Tanner: (Looking in his Order of Battle.) Did he say which troop he belonged to?

Sgt W: No, sir, he didn't. I didn't ask him. Should I ask him now?

Lt Tanner: Certainly.

Sgt W: In welcher Schwadron waren Sie?

PW: In der ersten.

Sgt W: In the first.

Lt Tanner: Is that the horse troop?

Sgt W: I don't know, sir, should I ask him?

Lt Tanner: Of course.

- 15 -

Sgt W: Ist das die Reiter-Schwadron?

PW: Nein.

Sgt W: No.

Lt Tanner: No, what? Just "no" doesn't do me any good.

Sgt W: Sir, I asked him what you told me to. I am sure I translated the question properly. Should I ask him something else?

Lt Tanner: I wish Capt Morton was able to talk to this man. He can speak German the way a German soldier speaks it. Military terms and all that. Ask him what kind of an outfit it is, of course.

Sgt W: Was für eine Schwadron ist das?

PW: Eine Radfahr-Schwadron.

Sgt W: He says it's a bicycle troop. Can that be?

Lt Tanner: It says here it's a mounted troop; the men who got the information of this Order of Battle are no dopes. They didn't just dream this up. Ask him if it wasn't a horse troop at one time.

Sgt W: War Ihre Schwadron nicht früher eine Reiter-Schwadron?

PW: Ja, aber sie hat sehr viele Verluste erlitten. Die meisten Pferde wurden getötet. Unsere Abteilung war nicht mehr vollständig. Darum wurde die Reiter-Schwadron durch eine Radfahr-Schwadron ersetzt.

Sgt W: Yes.

Lt Tanner: Yes, what?

Sgt W: Yes, he says it was a horse troop at one time, but that the battalion suffered severe losses and most of the horses were killed. Because they were no longer at full strength, the

– 16 –

Sgt W: contd. horse troop was replaced by a second bicycle troop.

Lt Tanner: Why the hell couldn't he have said that in the first place. It's just like pulling teeth to get a simple little bit of information like that. We're supposed to do this damn thing in ten minutes. We'll never get finished at this rate. (Capt Norton enters.)

Lt Tanner: Oh, Captain, am I glad to see you. Have you finished the translation yet?

Capt Norton: Yes.

Lt Tanner: Yes, what? Oh, excuse me, Captain, I've been trying to interrogate this guy here through an interpreter and I'm not doing too damn well. Ya gotta speak the language.

Capt Norton: I'll talk to him. What have you gotten so far?

Lt Tanner: I got yes, and some horrible name. I can't remember.

Capt Norton: Is he willing to talk?

Lt Tanner: He's willing enough, but I can't understand it.

Capt Norton: I've just been interrogating 19 willing PW's but they didn't have any information of value. I'll have a go at this one.

Lt Tanner: You'd better start from the beginning. We might have screwed up some of it. (To Sgt) You come along with me.

Capt Norton: Stellen Sie sich hier her. Legen Sie Ihre Mütze am Tisch und geben Sie mir Ihr Soldbuch. (Prisoner does so). Nun, Obergefreiter Wolfgang von Eulenspiegel zu welcher Trup enteil gehören Sie?

PW: Division Aufklaerungsabteilung Nummer 28.

Capt Norton: In welcher Schwadron?

PW:	In der ersten.
Capt Norton:	Ist das die Reiter-Schwadron?
PW:	Nein, das ist eine Radfahr-Schwadron.
Capt Norton:	Wieso?
PW:	Unsere Reiter-Schwadron hat sehr viele Verluste erlitten. Die meisten Pferde wurden getötet. Unsere Abteilung verblieb nicht mehr vollständig. Darum wurde die Reiter-Schwadron durch eine Radfahr-Schwadron ersetzt.
Capt Norton:	Is this your map?
PW:	Yes.
Capt Norton:	When did you reach the front line?
PW:	Two days ago.
Capt Norton:	Where was your first position?
PW:	Near Serradifalco.
Capt Norton:	Where were you before you came into action?
PW:	Near Enna.
Capt Norton:	What was your assignment?
PW:	I was the leader of a small patrol that was on the road from Canicatti to Palma.
Capt Norton:	How were you taken prisoner?
PW:	My patrol was surprised and overpowered by your troops north of Palma.
Capt Norton:	Which unit held Ravanusa Ridge?
PW:	The 39th Infantry Regiment.
Capt Norton:	How are the companies of the 39th Regiment placed along the ridge?

PW: I don't know that, but yesterday evening I saw the 4th Company on the Palma Road. I also saw the 3d Battalion in the woods southeast of Naro.

Capt Norton: What other infantry regiments belong to your Division?

PW: The 77th and 78th Infantry Regiments.

Capt Norton: Do you know where those Regiments are?

PW: I know the 78th is in the front line with the 59th. I think the 77th is in reserve near Cannicatti.

Capt Norton: Why do you think that?

PW: When we came through Cannicatti I saw the commander of the 3d Battalion, who used to lead my troop.

Capt Norton: Which division is to the right of yours?

PW: I don't know.

Capt Norton: But surely there must be troops on both sides of your division?

PW: Yes there are, but I don't know which units.

Capt Norton: What was your patrol supposed to find out on the road from Cannicatti to Palma?

PW: We were supposed to see whether there were any road blocks or tank traps on the road leading to the sea.

Capt Norton: Do you often do that kind of road reconnaissance?

PW: Yes. Whenever preparations are being made for an attack.

Capt Norton: Do you think an attack is being planned now?

PW: I don't know, but I heard an officer say our division will attack soon in the direction of the coastal road to cut off your troops. We have received a great many replacements, possibly for this purpose.

Capt Norton:	And provisions also?
PW:	Yes, we've received all kinds of provisions.
Capt Norton:	What troops did your patrol run into?
PW:	There was some heavy artillery in position in the vicinity of Campobello di Licata.
Capt Norton:	What other troops did you see?
PW:	I saw engineers.
Capt Norton:	What equipment did these engineers have?
PW:	They had only barbed wire in their combat wagons.
Capt Norton:	Where did you see these engineers?
PW:	At the foot of Ravenusa Ridge.
Capt Norton:	(calling) Sgt Haggerty. (He enters.) Take him away, Sgt.
Sgt:	Rechts um ! Vorwärts marsch ! (They exit.)
Lt Tanner:	(entering) Sounded OK. You must have gotten a hell of a lot more out of him than I ever could.
Capt Norton:	It's pretty difficult to work through another man.
Lt Tanner:	You're telling me. Who's next?
Capt Norton:	I think I'll check on his story; I'm going to try Hans Richter. He's the non-com.
Lt Tanner:	Thought maybe you would. I brought along his shoulder-claps... ...... straps ... ah ... shoulder.... !
Capt Norton:	Schulter-clappen !
Lt Tanner:	Clappen...Clappen....
Capt Norton:	Your German.... !
Lt Tanner:	No, sir, I'm from Brooklyn.

Capt Norton:	He's an Oberfeldwebel. That's 1st Sgt to you. And in the 2d Infantry Regiment. I'll bet his officers have told him a 100 times that those are not to be taken into combat because they can be a real help to us.
Lt Tanner:	I thought they would...Here I got some of his papers found on him.
Capt Norton:	Well, how long have you had them....?
Lt Tanner:	Just got 'em...just got 'em....
Capt Norton:	(Going through the papers) Driving license, fishing license, three-day pass.
Lt Tanner:	I always wanted to see one of those.
Capt Norton:	(Calls) Sgt Haggerty.
Sgt Haggerty:	(enters, reports.) Yes, sir.
Capt Norton:	Bring in Richter. Oh, and Sgt, don't be surprised at any names I might call you in the next few minutes.
Sgt:	I understand, sir. (exits.)
Lt Tanner:	Wish to hell I did. Think I'll listen in on this one, too.
Capt Norton:	I don't know why. You can't understand German anyhow.
Lt Tanner:	I know, but there's something fascinating about knowing that a German is squirmin'. (exits.)
Sgt:	(enters with PW) Stillgestanden! Sir, here's Richter.
Capt Norton:	That'll be all, Sgt. (Sgt exits) Nun, was ist Ihnen geschehen?
Richter:	Ich bin überrascht worden.
Capt Norton:	Das ganze Regiment?
Richter:	Nein! Die Deutsche Soldaten sind nicht so dumm....
Capt Norton:	Zu welchen Regiment gehören Sie.

- 21 -

Richter:	(relaxes to a sloppy position.)
Capt Norton:	Stillgestanden! (The PW jumps to attention.) What is your Regiment?
Richter:	I'm not going to give any military information.
Capt Norton:	Quiet! That's not the way to talk to an officer. You're going to do as you're told.
Richter:	You can't give me orders.
Capt Norton:	Is that so? Well, you are a prisoner and I'm your superior officer. You'd better get that in your head or we have means of hammering it in.
Richter:	I am protected by International Law.
Capt Norton:	Oh, I see. A schlaumeier! Well, you're in for some surprises. How long have you been in the army?
Richter:	Three years. I am also three years in the SA.
Capt Norton:	Oh, the SA?
Richter:	Yah, I was Unterstümführer.
Capt Norton:	Well, then, you probably know how the SA takes care of prisoners who don't behave. You can expect the same treatment here, only a little worse. Now, what is your regiment.
Richter:	My Captain told me not to give any military information.
Capt Norton:	I don't give a damn what your Captain told you. Besides, he's dead anyway. Now, what is your Regiment?
Richter:	I am in the ....infantry.
Capt Norton:	I said Regiment! Regiment! (The PW stubbornly comes to attention.) All right, if that's the way you want it. My guards are all Polish and they know how to handle German prisoners who won't talk. (Call) Sgt Pulaski!

(Sgt enters and stands threateningly behind PW)

Richter: I belong to the 44th Infantry Regiment.

Capt Norton: (Flashes shoulder straps.) What about the 2d Infantry. Don't lie to me.

Richter: (Caught) All right, I'm in the 2d Infantry.

Capt Norton: Division?

Richter: 11th.

Capt Norton: Commander?

Richter: General-Major von Acheen.

Capt Norton: Give me your Soldbuch. (The PW hands him his paybook.) What is your company?

Richter: I am in the 13th Company.

Capt Norton: What arms did you use?

Richter: Infantry howitzers.

Capt Norton: Caliber?

Richter: 7.5 cm.

Capt Norton: Where were you captured?

Richter: Oh, right behind the village over there?

Capt Norton: What do you mean, right behind the village? What village?

Richter: Maybe it was Favara.

Capt Norton: What kind of an answer is that? Maybe? Listen, I'm getting fed up with your attitude. You'd better become a little more precise or else....(Indicates Sgt) Was it Favara or wasn't it?

Capt Norton: You said behind the village. What did you mean by that?

Richter: Well, you know where the village comes to an end and the little woods starts.....

- 23 -

Capt Norton:	Is there a road there?
Richter:	Yes.
Capt Norton:	Where does it lead to?
Richter:	It is the road to Canicatti.
Capt Norton:	To Canicatti?
Richter:	Yes.
Capt Norton:	Where's the rest of your company?
Richter:	Also at Canicatti.
Capt Norton:	When did you come into the line?
Richter:	We have been fighting constantly against your inferior American troops for a week.
Capt Norton:	You don't seem to be doing so well against those inferior American troops. Whom were you supporting?
Richter:	The 3d Battalion.
Capt Norton:	What were your sector boundaries?
Richter:	I do not know.
Capt Norton:	Who was on your left flank?
Richter:	The rest of the Regiment.
Capt Norton:	Right flank?
Richter:	The 64th Infantry Regiment.
Capt Norton:	How do you know?
Richter:	My cousin is in it. I saw him in Canicatti this morning.
Capt Norton:	Who is in reserve?
Richter:	I don't know...I think it was the 83d Infantry Regiment.
Capt Norton:	What was the mission of your company?

Richter: (Lying) I don't know.

Capt Norton: You don't know or you won't tell?

Richter: I said I don't know.

Capt Norton: An oberfeldwebel, the first Sgt of your company, and you don't even know your own mission. Well, I guess your captain doesn't have much confidence in you, I can see that.

Richter: Yes, sir, he does. I am told everything.

Capt Norton: Then what was your mission?

Richter: To support the 3d Battalion.

Capt Norton: It seems rather peculiar that the whole 13th Company would support one battalion. When are you going to attack?

Richter: I am not required to answer that question.

Capt Norton: You may not be by International Law, but you certainly are by me because you're my prisoner. And besides, that Polish sergeant may need a little exercise before long. When is the attack to take place?

Richter: As soon as we receive ammunition.

Capt Norton: At what time?

Richter: I am a German soldier and I will not betray my comrades.

Capt Norton: Speak!

Richter: I will not answer that question.

Capt Norton: What is the full strength of your company?

Richter: We are full strength. Last night we received 24 new men as replacements.

Capt Norton: What kind of replacements?

Richter: Men who were wounded on the Russian front, got well, and were sent here.

Capt Norton: What was your company doing when you were captured?

Richter: Ach, our guns got stuck in the mud. We worked like dogs for three hours to get the battery out of the mud, but no success. Just as we were about to take a rest, we were surprised by a gang of damned snipers. This isn't fair. It is also against International Law.

Capt Norton: Stop babbling about International Law. Incidentally, how did that gun get stuck in the mud?

Richter: We had no more horses, so we had to try to pull them out by ourselves.

Capt Norton: Don't you have any horses left?

Richter: Oh, yes, Captain. There are always 2 guns in our company which are still drawn by horses.

Capt Norton: What kind of guns are they?

Richter: The heavy guns, naturally.

Capt Norton: How about the other guns?

Richter: They are drawn by the soldiers.

Capt Norton: I don't believe that. You could never transport your ammunition that way.

Richter: This does not cause us any difficulties.

Capt Norton: How come?

Richter: We have no ammunition left.

Capt Norton: That's a lie.

Richter: It's the truth. However, we expect supplies tonight.

Capt Norton: Where from?

Richter: Condotti.

Capt Norton: How do you know that?

Richter:	My Captain promised me that definitely. We ex-ect even 120 high explosives for each gun tonight.
Capt Norton:	How do you know the ammunition would come from Canicatti?
Richter:	My Captain told me so.
Capt Norton:	Oh, he was just telling you some cock-and-bull story because your supply system has been broken down.
Richter:	That's not true. When we marched through Canicatti, I myself saw the ammunition piled up.
Capt Norton:	Where was that?
Richter:	Near the freight station where we left the train.
Capt Norton:	At what time?
Richter:	About eleven this morning.
Capt Norton:	Eleven? They couldn't have piled up much by then.
Richter:	Oh, yes, Captain. At least 1200 high explosives were piled up.
Capt Norton:	How do you know that?
Richter:	A Captain from a divisional supply detachment told me so.
Capt Norton:	How could he know? He had nothing to do with the matter.
Richter:	Quite to the contrary. He was in charge of all the unloading at the freight train.
Capt Norton:	Thank you. That's all. Sgt, take him away.
Sgt:	Stillgestanden ! Rechts um ! Vorwärts marsch !
	(Richter and Sgt march off.)
	(The curtains close and Capt Norton walks between them)
Capt Norton:	Of course, our stenographer makes a quick translation and we get it down to S-2 immediately.

- 27 -

Capt Graham: I've been wondering, Captain, whether the methods you've outlined for the handling of German prisoners apply as well with Japanese prisoners?

Capt Norton: Well, as you know, the total number of Japanese prisoners taken by our forces in this war is very small. This is for several reasons: first, the hatred of Allied troops toward the Japanese; second, the Shinto religion which requires that a Jap soldier commit suicide rather than submit to capture; third, the fear of disgrace at home leads the Jap to commit suicide, since if he is captured he is officially declared dead anyway; fourth, Japanese officers are instructed to shoot their enlisted men when capture is imminent; and finally, the Japs' fear of Allied treatment, since we have been pictured to them as barbarians. Of course, this attitude towards capture is changing as the war is prolonged and the Japanese suffer defeats on a major scale. There are not any important differences in the processing and handling of prisoners, except in the search. Japanese prisoners are stripped completely because they have been known to conceal handgrenades in their loin cloths. The composition of the team is slightly different. It generally consists of an officer and two enlisted men, the enlisted men are mostly Nisei, that is, second generation Americans of Japanese descent. Since few Nisei speak both English and Japanese fluently, it is necessary for interrogators to work as teams in order to get the best results. In the actual interrogation, according to reports of interrogators in the Pacific, the best method of getting information from the Japanese is by showing kindness. Once a Jap has been convinced that he is not in the hands of barbarians and that he will be treated with kindness, he will in all likelihood talk freely. He is under no restraint as far as security is concerned, since he is dead, according to all that he has been taught. In fact, Japanese instruction to soldiers doesn't even take into consideration the remotest possibility of capture. As for documents, the Jap is very similar to the German: they carry excellent map-sketches and diaries which can be extremely valuable to intelligence personnel. But let's get back to the European theatre.

Capt Graham: Very well. What's your next step with a tough prisoner such as the one you just questioned.

Capt Norton: He's evacuated with the rest of the prisoners to the rear, but segregation is still maintained. After they have been processed they are removed to prisoner-of-war camps in England and in the United States.

Capt Graham: And that's the end of them?

Capt Norton: Not necessarily. Certain selected prisoners may be further examined to develop certain technical, strategical, political, and economic information and order of battle. Since this special examination is conducted in detail, it may last several days, and of course it's tougher to break down a stubborn prisoner at this time than previously because he's had time to recover from the shock of battle.

Capt Graham: How do you select these prisoners, Captain?

Capt Norton:	Well, those who show some signs of having technical knowledge in some particular field may be questioned on some specific topic. For example, a prisoner from a Panzer Division may be questioned at length about the latest German tanks, armor, weapons, construction, weakness and all other characteristics.
Capt Graham:	Would it be possible for us to see one of these special examinations, Captain?
Capt Norton:	I think it can be arranged. As a matter of fact, I know very well it can. It's in the script. Remember the tough guy we captured in Sicily? Hans Richter? It seems that before he was transferred to the Infantry, he was with a coast artillery outfit on the Channel. Well, one of our special interrogators had the job of finding out the locations of certain gun emplacements along the French coast, so he called in Richter ....
	(The curtain opens.)
Lt Darrow:	(Seated at desk.) I see by your records that you were with the occupation troops in France.
Richter:	That's right.
Lt Darrow:	Sit down.
Richter:	Thank you.
Lt Darrow:	I want to ask you some questions.
Richter:	Ask anything you want.
Lt Darrow:	I'm glad you're being sensible about this thing.
Richter:	Ask anything you want. I won't answer.
Lt Darrow:	Oh, so it's like that.

Richter: It's like that.

Lt Darrow: Just who do you think you are?

Richter: I'm a soldier of the German Reich and I shall always be one!

Lt Darrow: Well, I must say you're a fine looking specimen of the master race at this moment.

Richter: Bad luck, that's all.

Lt Darrow: Your press called it the consolidation of a new defense line.

Richter: Call it what you like. It was bad luck.

Lt Darrow: Suppose I tell you I don't believe you're a German soldier at all, or even a soldier.

Richter: Believe what you like.

Lt Darrow: Can you prove you're a soldier?

Richter: Yes, I can prove it.

Lt Darrow: Then prove it.

Richter: (Tosses Soldbuch on the table.) Here are my papers.

Lt Darrow: What's that?

Richter: You know what that is.

Lt Darrow: I said what's that?

Richter: It's my Soldbuch.

Lt Darrow: What's a Soldbuch?

Richter: My pay-book...my service record.

Lt Darrow: How do I know it's yours.

Richter: It has my name on it.

Lt Darrow: What's your name?

Richter: Richter. Hans Richter.

Lt Darrow:	(Looks at book casually, then throws it on the desk.) You call that proof? If you had a Soldbuch with Fritz Mueller's name on it, that would make you Fritz Mueller, I suppose.
Richter:	I don't know what you're talking about. My name is Richter, not Mueller.
Lt Darrow:	I'vt got a dozen books here.....French, Italian, German... (Tosses some books on the table.) Here, take one. I said take one ! (Richter picks one up gingerly.) Now you're Francois Perrier. (PW looks puzzled.) Take another one. (PW picks up another.) Now you're Domenico Scarpa.
Richter:	I don't know what you're talking about.
Lt Darrow:	Just this, as far as I'm concerned that book doesn't mean a damn thing.
Richter:	I tell you I'm Hans Richter.
Lt Darrow:	And I tell you I don't believe you.
Richter:	Then don't believe me. (Lt Darrow rises and walks in back of PW.)
Lt Darrow:	You know what happens to guerrillas....?
Richter:	I'm no guerrilla !
Lt Darrow:	I didn't say you were.
Richter:	Then don't talk like that.
Lt Darrow:	Why, does it make you nervous?
Richter:	No...No...it doesn't make me nervous...
Lt Darrow:	Then why did you jump? What do you Germans do with guerrillas?
Richter:	We kill them quick.
Lt Darrow:	Why?

Richter: They are dangerous...and they are not protected by International Law.

Lt Darrow: Oh, we're up to International Law now, are we? What do you know about International Law?

Richter: Enough.

Lt Darrow: Answer my question.

Richter: I know enough to know I don't have to answer your questions.

Lt Darrow: You have to tell me your name.

Richter: I've told you my name.

Lt Darrow: I don't believe you're Richter. I don't believe you're a German soldier. I don't know what you might be. Where were you born? Where were you born?

Richter: I don't have to answer that.

Lt Darrow: Are you afraid?

Richter: I'm not afraid.

Lt Darrow: Then why don't you answer?

Richter: Under International Law I don't have to.

Lt Darrow: You do know a lot about International Law, don't you?

Richter: I said I know enough.

Lt Darrow: Then what's it for?

Richter: What?

Lt Darrow: International Law.

Richter: It's to protect people from injustice.

Lt Darrow: Like civilians, for example?

Richter: Yes, like civilians.

Lt Darrow: Like Dutch civilians, for example?

Richter: Yes, like Dutch civilians.

Lt Darrow:	And Belgian civilians?
Richter:	And Belgian civilians.
Lt Darrow:	And French civilians?
Richter:	And French civilians....
Lt Darrow:	What army are you in?
Richter:	The army of the German Reich.
Lt Darrow:	What branch of service?
Richter:	Infantry...before that the Artillery.
Lt Darrow:	And the Germans...they have an Air Force, haven't they?
Richter:	The best in the world.
Lt Darrow:	So you're proud of your brothers in the air force?
Richter:	They are great fliers.
Lt Darrow:	Did you see Rotterdam?
Richter:	Yes...
Lt Darrow:	A magnificent job, wasn't it?
Richter:	Magnificent.
Lt Darrow:	Thirty thousand at one time, right?
Richter:	I don't know....maybe....
Lt Darrow:	Thirty thousand....at one time...CIVILIANS!
Richter:	Maybe....
Lt Darrow:	Where was your International Law then?
Richter:	I don't know what you're talking about.
Lt Darrow:	Where was your International Law then? Answer my question!
Richter:	It had to be done, that's all.
Lt Darrow:	Then you make your own International Law as it suits you, is that it?
Richter:	It was a matter of military necessity.

Lt Darrow: The cold-blooded murder of thirty thousand civilians... You call that a matter of military necessity?

Richter: They interfered with the rightful expansion of the German Reich.

Lt Darrow: And the Belgian hostages...they, too, interfered with the expansion of the German Reich?

Richter: Yes.

Lt Darrow: So they had to be killed, is that it?

Richter: If they were killed it was out of necessity.

Lt Darrow: Without trial?

Richter: I don't know.

Lt Darrow: Where was your International Law then? What happened to it? Did it get lost? Do you lose it conveniently whenever you don't need it?

Richter: Leave me alone.

Lt Darrow: Wait a minute...You went down the main roads of France. I mean, if you are Richter, and a German soldier. Did you see anything?

Richter: I saw hills and valley and ruined cities.

Lt Darrow: On the roads though, did you see any civilians, any dead civilians, women and children, machine-gunned by your gallant airmen?

Richter: They were....in our way. They clogged the roads.

Lt Darrow: So your brave fliers ... dived down and machine-gunned them, didn't they?

Richter: Necessity.

Lt Darrow: But there was your International Law, what happened to it then?

Richter: I don't know. I'm only a German soldier. I don't know about International Law and I don't make plans for the General Staff.

Lt Darrow: All right, then, listen to me for a minute and I'll tell you something about International Law. You may think you're a German soldier and entitled to all kinds of protection but I can tell you that so far as we're concerned you're nothing more than a common criminal and that's the way you're going to be handled. You're a member of a band of outlaws who have never had any regard for International Law or anything else, and you're not going to start running to the law now, for protection. Did you hear what President Roosevelt said about the trials for criminals after the war?

Richter: No, I didn't hear it.

Lt Darrow: Well, he said that an account is being kept of the criminal record of every Nazi in Europe both before and during this war, and when it is over, everyone of them will be tried and punished. Now you were with the occupation troops in France and you might as well know that when this war is over a thorough report of your activities will be in our hands and you'll be tried accordingly.

Richter: I'm not afraid.

Lt Darrow: Well, maybe you haven't any reason to be. I doubt, but maybe you haven't. Only you might as well know that isn't the point. I want some information from you and I'm going to get it. If I don't, I'll see to it that your trial is the very last one on the docket.

Richter: What do I care?

Lt Darrow: Just stop and think a moment. Conservatively...100,000 prisoners; 100,000 trials. Conservatively...four days for each trial...400,000 days before they get to you. 400,000 divided by 365....1096 years. 96 years more than your Fuehrer gave the Third Reich even when he was drunkest with power. Somehow, I don't think you'll be around when your case comes up for trial. Are you married? Be nice to go home, wouldn't it?

Richter: But this is inhuman!

Lt Darrow: We're not talking about humanity now...we're talking about International Law, a subject you kноww too much about. And I'll tell you something else. Not all the prisoner of war camps will be in the United States. They're building a nice new one near Murmansk...that's in Northern Russia, in case you don't know....And I can arrange to have you lodged there until we're ready for your trial. Now, are we straight on International Law? Of course, if you could prove that you're a German ....a soldier....a German soldier and not a brigand or a guerrilla. If you can prove you are not guilty of these crimes we've been talking about, you wouldn't have to stand trial. Maybe you could go back home after the war is over. But you'd have to give conclusive proof.....

Richter: (Very quietly and completely broken.) How can I prove it?

Lt Darrow: Let's start at the beginning. Where were you born?

Richter: Stuttgart.

Lt Darrow: When?

Richter: 14th October 1918

Lt Darrow: School?

Richter: Realschule.

Lt Darrow: What then?

Richter: Labor service.

Lt Darrow: Army?

Richter: Three years.

Lt Darrow: Occupation?

Richter: Lathe operator.

Lt Darrow: Where?

Richter: Weinsberg.

Lt Darrow: Inducted?

Richter: January 1940.

Lt Darrow: Where?

Richter: Munich.

Lt Darrow: Company.

Richter: 13th Company 470th, Infantry Regiment.

Lt Darrow: Artillery training?

Richter: Bremen, Coast Artillery Training Regiment 1st Bn, 128.

Lt Darrow: When

Richter: May 1942

Lt Darrow: Then?

Richter: My regular unit, coastal battery 801.

Lt Darrow: Tell me exactly where this battery is located.

Richter: I don't know exactly. We were east of Dunkerque and south of the highway.

Lt Darrow: Can you show it to me on a map?

Richter: Yes, I can do that....it was right here.

Lt Darrow: What caliber was your gun?

Richter: 150 mm.

Lt Darrow: And the other guns in your battery?

Richter: Two more 150s and one 210.

Lt Darrow: Anything else?

Richter: Two light machine guns.

Lt Darrow: How far were you from the beach?

Richter: Mile....maybe..

Lt Darrow: What was on your right?

Richter: A road leading to the beach.

Lt Darrow: And on your left?

Richter: The canal.

Lt Darrow: Is the canal mined?

Richter: Yes, heavily mined.

Lt Darrow: Controlled mines?

Richter: Some controlled, some uncontrolled.

Lt Darrow: Is there barbed wire on the beach?

Richter: Of course, much barbed wire.

Lt Darrow: Mine fields?

Richter: Directly in front of our battery there is a minefield.

Lt Darrow: Then....?

Richter: Barbed wire...then the highway...then tank traps...then our battery.

Lt Darrow:	Are there any special obstacles an invading force might encounter?
Richter:	Well, to the right of the mines in front of the canal there is barbed wire hidden in the water.
Lt Darrow:	To the right as you face the ocean?
Richter:	Yes...to the right of our gun position.
Lt Darrow:	Anything else?
Richter:	In the shallow water where the beach is not steep we have steel stakes and wooden logs.
Lt Darrow:	What are they for?
Richter:	They are to catch your landing barges.
Lt Darrow:	Then you expect us to try an invasion at this point?
Richter:	How do I know where you plan to invade!
Lt Darrow:	Would an invasion attempt there be successful?
Richter:	I don't know...I don't know...
	(The curtain closes. Capt Norton steps in front.)
Capt Norton:	Now some prisoners crack more easily and others are tougher than this baby. But once the prisoners are ready to talk, continual concentration on the subject is required and here, too, a set of general prearranged questions relating to the subject is required.
Capt Graham:	Just one more question, Captain. Did that scene really happen---- or was it just put together by one of your writers?

Capt Norton: This interrogation happens to be based on an actual interrogation in England some months prior to the invasion last June. It's been rearranged the least bit, but for all practical purposes this is the real thing. Any further questions?

Capt Graham: No, Captain, I think I have the hang of it now.

Capt Norton: Well, I know I don't have any more questions from you. Thank you very much for your close attention, gentlemen.

(Exit.)

THE END

WAR DEPARTMENT
THE MILITARY INTELLIGENCE TRAINING CENTER
CAMP RITCHIE, MARYLAND

26 October 1944

GENERAL COURSE OF INSTRUCTION
(Scope of Course)

IX. VISUAL DEMONSTRATION (3 hours total)

Hitler's Secret Weapon   1 hr

An instructional demonstration to show the student how seemingly unimportant scraps of information can, when collected and fitted together by Nazi agents, build a complete picture for the enemy. The demonstration is in dramatic form. In the prologue a German Intelligence Officer tells his staff that one of their greatest weapons is the American soldier's inability to keep his mouth shut. The four scenes of the play proper show an agent picking up seemingly unrelated bits of information from American soldiers which, when pieced together, spell the doom of an American convoy. The epilogue shows the same German Intelligence Officer reviewing for his staff the way careless talk from American soldiers eventually gave them a complete picture of our activities.

Interrogation of Prisoners of War   1 hr

An instructional demonstration illustrating the proper method of handling, evacuation and interrogation of prisoners of war. It also shows the inefficacy of attempted interrogation by those not specially trained as interrogators. As a security lesson it shows the student some of the methods that might be used on him if he is ever captured and impresses him with the necessity of giving only name, rank and serial number in such an event. The demonstration is in dramatic form with further instructional explanations of the operation of Interrogation Teams being given between the scenes. The first and second scenes concern the handling of prisoners by capturing troops and the proper method of search. The third scene deals with tactical interrogation at Division level. The fourth and final scene deals with a strategic interrogation in the zone of Communication or zone of Interrior.

CHAPTER III

INTERROGATION AT VARIOUS LEVELS
INTERROGATION BELOW REGIMENTAL LEVEL

Interrogation below regimental level was not generally practiced except in emergency cases. Battalion interrogation proved utterly impractical, since not enough prisoners were taken at this level to warrant the use of an entire interrogation team. Also, many dangers, general confusion, and lack of adequate working facilities prevailed at battalion and lower levels.

Some teams, however, reported sending members even down to squad level to question prisoners on the spot immediately after their capture, but this practice was more fool-hardy than advisable for obvious reasons. IPW personnel could not afford to take unnecessary chances because their number was too limited. Furthermore, the atmosphere at these lower levels was not conducive to satisfactory

It must be pointed out that in some instances, however, officers-in-charge of IPW teams reported that during the early stages of their work their services were looked upon by the G-2 and allied agencies with a cold and suspicious reservation of uncertainty. This attitude was easily understood since IPW work was a new venture in serving as an auxiliary agency attached to G-2; and since G-2's and S-2's in many cases had not been properly indoctrinated as to the full exploitation of this particular type of intelligence gathering agency. Therefore, the chief task which confronted some teams was that of convincing their G-2's or S-2's as to the value and significance of IPW work. This fact had to be established through practical operational work in the field. Consequently, IPW had to justify its existence and continuation by the quality of work it performed while serving with combat units. Needless to say, this situation along with the many unanticipated and unrelated problems and emergencies which constantly arose, imposed a rather tedious strain upon some of the IPW teams during the early stages of interrogation work. However, fate was generally kind from the very beginning in furnishing sufficient fruitful and satisfactory results. When once the fact was established that IPW work had been greatly misjudged and underestimated, the former attitude of the G-2 and associated intelligence agencies was quickly dissolved and replaced by a feeling of respect and appreciation. This change of heart was usually augmented by a spirit of cooperation almost invariably resulting in inter-intelligence coordination. Many G-2's expressed their firm convictions in their letters of commendation to FID Headquarters on the field activities of IPW teams (and other MIS team units) by referring to such units as: "An intelligence agency we cannot do without"; and other similar complimentary statements.

It was always recognized that a team once attached to a combat unit was under the operational control of the G-2. During the early stages there was a good deal of discussion as to possible shifting of the teams from one division or army to another and also as to the position of G-2 Section, ETOUSA, in respect thereto.

trouble in handling as well as in interrogation. Firm and harsh handling was often necessary to make such prisoners realize that there was a limit to Hitler's power and jurisdiction. However, once these soldiers were broken, they were usually as meek as lambs. They also responded well to orders since they were accustomed to obeying without question.

Since most Germans resembled a machine more closely than a human being, they were generally controlled and handled with greater ease than would have been the case if individuality had been allowed them in the past. All that was needed was the proper formula, and it could be utilized again and again with equal assurance of similar results. We owe thanks to Hitler for making his people so much alike, thus making our burden lighter and helping to solve the problems which confronted us. This factor helped us gauge the reliability of prisoner statements by comparing them to the general picture given by the majority of prisoners. Any deviation from this trend conspicuously indicated its falsehood. Such offenders were properly dealt with.

All prisoners of war when in official hands were treated in conformity with the rules of the Geneva Convention. The use of violence in the handling of PW's was refrained from with the exception of a number of reprisals which were reported and which took place without official sanction. Infractions of this type were firmly dealt with when the perpetrators were apprehended.

Discipline was strictly enforced at all times. The formation system was used whenever possible in order to save time, avoid confusion, and execute an orderly procedure. Nothing was done to add to the discomfort of the prisoner as long as he did not present any disciplinary problems; also nothing was done to add to his comfort. No talking was permitted in ranks or during transfer from one place to another. No special privileges were extended to any prisoners. No promises were given in exchange for valuable information. Information at its best was obtained when the prisoners were in a rather hopeless, uncertain and uncomfortable state.

During the course of the interrogation of PW's it was entirely up to the individual interrogator as to what method of treatment to apply in obtaining information. The interrogator in turn adapted his treatment of the prisoner in accordance to the prisoner's attitude and the type of response to the questions asked. The important issue was to obtain information and if kind treatment and perhaps a cigarette with an "at ease" for smoking proved fruitful, it was used in preference to any other method. When this method failed to produce the proper results, other methods were improvised to suit the particular subject. Prisoners were perhaps threatened in many ways, but were never subjected to a third degree or corporal punishment.

In many instances the prisoners themselves have voiced surprise regarding the good treatment they received after they had reached the prisoner-of-war cages. Up to this point however, it was rough going

TREATMENT OF PRISONERS

Part of the secret in the handling of prisoners was the use of firm authority by those in charge. The proper command given sharply in German usually brought a somewhat magic automatic response. This is merely the application of the traditional disciplinary routine to which all German soldiers (and civilians) were subjected in upholding the Nazi Doctrine. This was especially representative of the younger generation, emanating from the various Hitler Youth and other Nazi organizations where this doctrine was deeply inculcated within their immature minds.

It was this fanatical type of German which caused the most

The value to the intelligence organization of the interrogation of prisoners of war and the interviewing of friendly and enemy civilians has long been recognized. It was chiefly due to the efforts of Lt. Colonel Hochschild and Major Ryser that such practices came to hold such an important place in operations, and due to the caliber of the personnel and to that of the training which they received that interrogation and interpreter teams had the success which they did.

About 47 per cent, or nearly half, of all combat intelligence gathered by the United States Army in the European Theater of Operations, World War II, was the product of Field Interrogation Detachment teams, Interrogator of Prisoner of War teams alone accounting for 36 per cent of all ETO combat intelligence.[1]

for the prisoners in most cages. Most reports of mistreatment of prisoners were traced to the lower echelons and took place soon after their capture. Front-line troops, company and battalions, and the military police all had their own version as to how prisoners of war should be treated. Rough treatment of PW's was therefore common and an evil which was difficult to control. Prisoners were sometimes treated very harshly but few cases of torture were reported. The common practice of front-line troops and other army personnel of company and battalion level was the pilfering of the PW's. Sometimes even the military police participated in this all-out souvenir hunt. These operations often relieved the prisoners of all their personal belongings, such as watches, cameras, rings, jewelery, money, etc. This practice not only constituted unethical treatment but it also placed the prisoners in a very unreceptive state of mind for interrogation later on. Much important enemy information was purposely withheld by prisoners as a means of silent protest in this injustice. Many prisoners demanded an explanation for such treatment, especially in those cases when they were armed only with the safe conduct leaflets dropped by our troops guaranteeing them fair and proper treatment in return for laying down their arms. Many of the prisoners were not of German origin and were victims of circumstances in being compelled to serve with the German Army. This practice was generally improved and discontinued by some units after

interrogation under any circumstances, since the lives of both the team members and the prisoners were in constant danger. Experience proved that the prisoner must be given time to stabilize his shaken mind to permit him to give a coherent story. This can only be fully accomplished by conducting him first to a place of safety.

INTERROGATION AT REGIMENTAL LEVEL

Enemy information obtained at this level was generally of such great importance, because of its highly tactical nature, that the regimental level was considered the most important echelon of prisoner of war interrogation. Because no IPW teams were directly attached to regiments, they had to be obtained from the respective divisions. Since two IPW teams were attached to each division and each division was made up of three regimental combat units, it was found most practical to split these teams into four three-man teams. One of these teams was sent to each regiment to serve in processing and interrogating prisoners, while the remaining team assumed charge of the prisoner of war enclosure (PWE) at division level.

The type of interrogation which took place at regimental level was exclusively devoted to the obtaining of tactical information. Documents other than the usual 'sold buch' carried by every German soldier were seldom of importance at this level.

Most of the interrogation work at this level was done under the direction of the Regimental S-2. As a rule the work of the S-2 and the IPW team was very closely coordinated, since the S-2 was quite dependent upon the work performed by the IPW team and the IPW team was dependent upon the S-2 for the furnishing of briefing and an accurate picture of the existing tactical situation.

After the prisoners were interrogated, a composite and detailed report was prepared by some designated member of the team and submitted to the S-2, whose duty it was to relay the information to adjacent, lower and higher echelons. A copy was immediately dispatched to the Division G-2 even though the prisoners were evacuated to the same echelon. Many teams found it most convenient and practical to forward immediately after interrogation a summary of their findings to S-2 and G-2 by phone. These reports by phone were received by the officer-in-charge of the G-2 Section. As the message came in, facts which were later to become a part of the chronological record of the day's events were taken down in short-hand by the journal clerk, who listened in on the headphones. As the pages of the journal were filled, they were mimeographed and distributed within the division staff. An original copy of all IPW information was given to the divisional Order of Battle Team, whose duty it was to have situation maps posted with all current information and to keep a chronological and category filing system concerning all enemy information received both through IPW reports and from captured enemy documents. Documents found on prisoners which indicated immediate value were forwarded to the local OB team for proper disposition.

After being processed and interrogated, the prisoners at regiment were evacuated to division where the process described above was repeated on a wider scope.

INTERROGATION AT DIVISION LEVEL

Interrogation procedure at division level was very similar to that at regimental level; in fact, it had the appearance of duplication of effort. However, the Division Commander was mostly interested in obtaining enemy information directly concerned with his sector. Interrogators were therefore usually well briefed by the G-2 as to the type of tactical information desired. IPW reports coming from regiment were rechecked and in some cases elaborated upon by further interrogation. The questioning of prisoners at both regimental and divisional cages necessarily entailed some duplication, but it enabled the interrogators to check on the reliability of the information supplied by the prisoners at the previous interrogation. Although tactical questioning was still predominant here, organizational details, unit movements, rear installations, morale and health of the enemy facing the division also entered the picture.

At this level a thorough search was conducted for documents and important papers. These findings were fully exploited and evaluated. Documents of tactical significance were immediately translated by IPW personnel and the information forwarded to the G-2. Documents of immediate strategic value were forwarded to the division OB Team.

Since most of the personnel of the two IPW teams attached to division usually worked at regimental level, the three-man unit remaining at division was mostly engaged in screening and processing prisoners at the divisional enclosure. This proved to be a full-time job in most cases, particularly since prisoners usually arrived by the thousands. When the time arrived for interrogation at division there usually existed a shortage of IPW personnel. At such times requests were made to corps which sent some of its teams to help relieve the situation.

Sometimes IPW personnel was supplemented by members of the Counter Intelligence Corps (CIC), whose primary function was to question civilian suspects. German Military Intelligence Interpreter Teams (MII), in many instances, were employed to assist in interrogation when large number of prisoners had to be processed and interrogated, and time was short.

INTERROGATOR TEAMS AT CORPS LEVEL

Since corps was not the normal channel for either evacuation or interrogation of prisoners, this level was usually by-passed. The three IPW teams attached to corps had specific duties to perform. Their chief mission was to coordinate and disseminate the work of IPW teams attached to lower levels. Another function was that of examining enemy documents for strategic information and reporting the findings to higher echelons. (Tactical information was also reported when found.)

Aside from the regular duties of IPW teams attached to corps, these teams also constituted a reserve pool from which IPW personnel was supplied to lower echelons. This system was put into practice quite often because the influx of prisoners was usually too great for the regular IPW teams to handle properly.

INTERROGATION AT ARMY LEVEL

Many of the prisoners who had been previously interrogated at lower levels were again questioned at Army level to check further some of their previous statements. Although interrogation at this level was chiefly conducted to obtain strategic information, immediate tactical and long-range tactical information of an important nature were not overlooked.

Due to the wide scope of interrogation at this level, it was soon discovered that four IPW teams attached here could produce better results if less attention were paid to the functioning of individual teams and if more attention were given to the idea of a working organization, the foremost thought being that of serving as a production unit for G-2. Experience demonstrated that the best results were forthcoming when the members of the various teams assumed an indifferent attitude with regard to their team and rank, and were assigned specific tasks for which they were best qualified. IPW work, therefore, became departmentalized. Each interrogator concentrated his efforts upon a few special subjects in which he had a wide range of knowledge and experience. This system of specialization was instituted in every department and was generally found to increase both speed and efficiency to a very high degree. Certain IPW members were therefore in permanent and exclusive charge of interrogation, screening, documents, reports, editing, general office work, etc.

An IPW team attached to the United States Third Army Headquarters made the following report as to the distribution of the IPW personnel attached there:

Interrogation Section, usually taken care of by fourteen permanent members with the assignment of additional members when needed. Most of the interrogators specialized in certain types of work or units. Sometimes one group of interrogators worked for a certain period of time exclusively on one or two German units and at another time on one of the German branches of service, such as the artillery, engineers, etc. Some interrogators specialized in accumulating information pertaining to industrial targets, bridges, railroads, etc. All interrogation became specialized.

SCREENING SECTION, usually supervised by three IPW members assisted by four or five military police. One member usually selected subjects for interrogation, another member searched for documents and papers and made spot evaluations, while the third member busied himself in translating the documents and passing the information to the proper channels.

The military police assisted wherever possible in carrying out the work in an orderly fashion. A locally improvised Essential Elements of Information helped to speed up the screening process.

Editing and Briefing Section, usually taken care of by three IPW members whose duty was to compile, collate, evaluate (to a certain extent), and edit this material in final form to be included in the consolidated daily report. There were usually three such reports issued daily:

1. <u>Tactical IPW Report</u>. This was a consolidated report which incorporated material on Order of Battle. The criterion which determined the inclusion of material in this report was its immediate value to G-2.

2. <u>Detailed IPW Report</u>. This report embodied the results of long-range interrogation data on such subjects as strategic air-targets, effects of tactical and strategic bombing, railroad information, war crimes, and the replacement system in all parts of Germany. These reports appeared irregularly but were usually attempted on a bi-weekly schedule.

3. <u>Counter Intelligence IPW Report</u>. This report included information concerning the political machinery of Germany and the forces working for the overthrow of the Nazi Regime. All information determined necessary for an estimate of the Anti-Nazi potential in Germany was included. Such reports usually appeared weekly.

It was further reported by this Third Army IPW Team that about fifteen agencies submitted detailed lists of Essential Elements of Information to the local G-2. Ways and means were also found in formulating an EEI to facilitate local IPW work, especially in screening and interrogation. A system was developed whereby a great number of prisoners could be processed and interrogated with a high degree of accuracy and speed and thoroughness within a

~~AIDS IN FIELD INTERROGATION~~
BRIEFING AND COORDINATION BY G-2

In addition to knowing the tactical and the strategic situation of the enemy, it was necessary that our teams have an up-to-the-minute estimate of our own tactical situation. In order to make this possible the G-2 usually delegated one of his representatives to serve in an advisory capacity as coordinator of the activities of both the G-2 and the IPW teams. The respective teams were instructed as to what type of information was to be obtained through prisoner interrogation at the various levels. This requirement naturally varied inasmuch as each team represented a different combat unit at the regimental level and each regiment had its own individual tactical problems. This fact called for a frequent and detailed perspective of the rapidly changing tactical situation on the part of the coordinator.

The response to questions on briefing from IPW teams in the field denotes a general picture of satisfaction. In a number of instances expressions of appreciation for the cooperation of the G-2 in furnishing desired information and permitting access to maps and other research materials were volunteered. However, IPW teams in general did not seem to be conscious of the full responsibility of G-2 for leadership and guidance in their work. Most teams reported that the briefings received from the G-2 or S-2 were adequate while only a few teams reported the briefings as having been inadequate. Nevertheless, certain facts seemed to indicate that many teams were not fully aware of the advantages of thorough and systematic briefing.

Reports from IPW teams in the field indicated that the teams on the whole were given freedom for work with opportunity for initiative. This, at times, resulted in inadequate guidance and direction from the G-2. The following complaints were registered by a number of OIC's: briefings were too infrequent and irregular, not detailed enough, oral (instead of oral and written), given only to the OIC instead of the entire interrogational personnel, and in some cases not given at all.

These situations were relieved, in some instances, however, by the various teams themselves who inaugurated the necessary steps to secure that information which proved helpful in gauging their interrogation activities. Furthermore, after IPW teams made special efforts to acquire needed information pertaining to briefing etc., the S-2's and the G-2's often became conscious of their laxness and improved conditions on their own initiative. However, there were times when IPW teams were too much enveloped in their own work to be able to maintain the proper perspective and balance in the rapidly changing tactical situations. Some teams suggested a better overall view of the general war situation within their respective areas and also of the G-3 operations. It was further suggested that a clear-cut and well-organized briefing system should always be in operation to expedite both economy and efficiency. Both written and oral briefings should be given to all members of the interrogation staff. A regular time and place of meeting should be the established policy, if possible. For purposes of economy and efficiency, the intelligence agency should furnish regularly in both written and oral form specific items deemed most valuable at the moment. The written briefings are valuable for references purposes; the verbal briefings permit the exchange of ideas and clarification of doubtful points. A well-prescribed system of briefing is not only necessary for the establishment of coordination and efficiency, but enables the IPW personnel to gauge their activities and achievements in terms of the Army's needs.

G-2 coordination was accomplished with varied enthusiasm. During the early stages of interrogation, the general concensus of opinion held by some G-2's and S-2's was that IPW work appeared to be an unnecessary extravagance. In a number of instances, where the full significance of IPW work was not realized from the start, those agencies were commonly quite cool and reserved with their treatment of IPW teams. This fact often made it difficult for the teams to enlist the necessary assistance of the various G-2's and S-2's adding to the many problems to which the teams were already subjected. However, as the various teams proved their worth and the continuation of IPW work was substantially justified, the close coordination between the G-2's and the IPW personnel developed. Fortunately, in the early stages of interrogation work, both the G-2 and the IPW personnel became conscious of the interdependence which existed between them. It was necessary for the teams to have the full support of their respective G-2's or S-2's. Likewise, G-2 was highly dependent upon the findings of the IPW teams.

Originally, the work of all IPW teams, as well as all Military Intelligence Service Teams, was officially integrated into a closely woven pattern according to the prescribed policy handed down by the Assistant Chief of Staff of G-2. In this respect the G-2 regarded the work performed by the numerous specialist teams as a unified agency set up for the collection of all available combat intelligence.

Although these various specialist teams had their own individual function to perform, they learned, through practical application, the value of coordinating their work with allied G-2 agencies. This cooperation brought about the vivid demonstration that much time and duplication of effort could be spared if these agencies reinforced

one another. IPW work was closely coordinated by the unit G-2's with that of intelligence agencies of all the Allied Armies, wherein many mutual benefits were derived through the exchange of important enemy information.

The cooperation given by G-2 in many instances allowed the IPW teams to make the most of their assignments and to fulfill their respective missions more efficiently. Many times when the problem of insufficient personnel arose, the G-2 helped alleviate the situation by assigning some of his personnel to the task. In like manner, the G-2 often sent veteran specialists to newly committed divisions for the purpose of orienting inexperienced intelligence teams.

The successful fulfillment of all missions by the G-2's and their respective IPW teams depended upon their common understanding and mutual cooperation. It is clearly indicated by the information received from team officers-in-charge that satisfactory relationships and adequate coordination existed between the teams and the G-2's. It was generally true that where a lack of coordination existed between these two agencies, this situation was almost always brought about due to the lack of a common understanding of mutual problems and situations.

ORDER OF BATTLE

The enemy Order of Battle was a publication compiled

by the Order of Battle Center consisting of about five hundred pages comprising a complete classified list of all enemy information at our disposal. This information was compiled by specialists who had been trained and designated for this particular type of work. Necessary revisions and the adding of supplementary material was also done by these specialists. The chief source of such information was supplied by enemy documents. Upon their discovery, all enemy documents were immediately forwarded to the various OB teams, for translation, study, evaluation, and the listing of new information. Documents disclosing tactical information were held by IPW personnel and the information recorded before being forwarded to OB. Much of the Order of Battle information was originally supplied through IPW interrogation reports, which were studied by the local OB teams as they were turned in to the respective S-2's and G-2's.

This OB publication included such information as identifications of units of the German Army and their deployment and estimated strength; a complete catalogue of all enemy weapons including their nomenclature and potential destructive qualities; and enemy military signs and symbols.

By a thorough knowledge of the enemy Order of Battle the individual interrogator was not only well oriented on the enemy's military situation and history, but was also

enemy objectives of a tactical nature, etc. Through the use of maps and overlays, this operation could be performed with a great deal of accuracy and within a short span of time. To facilitate the prisoner's speed and accuracy these maps were printed in German. The usual scale of maps at regimental and division levels was 1 : 25.000. A supply for the use of IPW teams was usually arranged by the respective S-2's and G-2's.

G-2 SITUATION MAP

It was necessary for interrogators to frequently consult the enemy situation map which was kept up to date at the S-2 or G-2 section by either the G-2 personnel or the members of the local OB team. Both the friendly and the enemy tactical situations were noted on this map. Interrogators were able to grasp the situation at a glance.

~~MOSAICS~~ Aerial Photographs

In many cases, interrogators used photo-maps which were commonly known as mosaics. In making these mosaics, a group of photos taken from the air and covering specific areas were taken and the terrain features were blended until they coincided. When this operation was completed the overlapping portions were cut away. Mosaics were used whenever they were obtainable. Oftentimes, however, they were unobtainable because of the inability to obtain photo-

45.

covering for many specific areas. These photo-maps proved more helpful and practicable than the regular maps because the actual features of the terrain were represented, which not only facilitated orientation of the terrain features, but in many instances actual enemy positions could be located, identified, or confirmed with the help of prisoners. Often prisoners were able to pin-point highly camouflaged positions or newly created positions which photo-intelligence had been unable to pick up. It was quite common for prisoners to become hopelessly confused due to their inability to read maps regardless of their simplicity of construction. On the other hand, practically any type of prisoner was able, with little outside help, to orient himself properly on a photo-map. Another point in favor of mosaics was that they were larger scale than regular maps, the scale usually being 1 : 15,000. Such maps were generally obtained from the local Photo Intelligence Center, either from the distribution department or from photo-interpreters teams. Some interrogators used Photo-Intelligence Reports in order to check and verify prisoner statements. This fact brings forward a conscious realization of the prime necessity of having the proper tools in order to accomplish a given task quickly and accurately.

The importance of the Soldbuch

THE SOLDBUCH

The soldbuch was the most valuable single document found on the person of German prisoners. This document constituted a combination pay-book and army service record which was carried by the soldiers at all times, even in combat and after their capture. Other personal information concerning the soldiers listed in the soldbuch were promotions, present rank, supply record, record of hospitalization, etc. Prisoners were instructed, however, to tear out certain pages of this document upon being captured in order to withhold important information concerning the identity of the unit to which the prisoner was last assigned and other items of information which the enemy considered confidential.

This document served as a means of prisoner identification (Another means of identification was the German equivalent of our dog tags known as the Erkennungsmarke which the soldier wore about his neck and which bore only the identity of the unit to which the prisoner was assigned upon being inducted into the army) and was looked upon by the soldiers with a great deal of personal pride, since it carried a complete record of the soldier's military history and achievements. It also served as an inventory record of all supplies issued to the soldier since his induction. Therefore, as a rule, the prisoners were not relieved of their soldbuch as long as the possibility of interrogation existed and even then, in most cases, it was allowed to remain on the prisoner's person.

The soldbuch proved very valuable during interrogations. Usually the first question directed to the prisoner by the interrogator was a demand for his soldbuch. After directing a number of routine questions concerning this document, the interrogator usually handed it back to the prisoner. This document sometimes proved helpful in checking the reliability of prisoner's stories, provided the prisoner had not torn out the important pages for security reasons. Much information from the soldbuch, when compiled on a large scale, was helpful in ascertaining the history as well as the strength of certain units. Sometimes, when the soldbuch was in the possession of the interrogator, stubborn prisoners were prodded into revealing important information upon the application of psychological pressure. Furthermore, this document, itself also indicated important issues which would otherwise have been overlooked by the interrogator. Hence, the soldbuch served as a chief reference document while the prisoner was being interrogated and as a means of identification at other times.

PROPER SETTING

It was very important that the interrogation be held

PART ONE

Interrogator of Prisoners of War Team

INTERROGATION IN ACTION

INTRODUCTION

Interrogator of Prisoner of War Teams (IPW) proved to be one of the most valuable sources from which first-hand and last-minute vital information pertaining to enemy strength, organization, reinforcements, operations, plans, capabilities, morals, etc. was obtained. Furthermore, through this same medium, the authenticity of information received through other sources was checked and confirmed.

The correct handling of prisoners and the speed of disseminating enemy information were two items of utmost importance. The prisoner of war interrogation teams were designated to exploit the full knowledge of prisoners in their quest for needed information. These teams were especially well organized and prepared to handle enemy identification, tactical questioning, evaluation and translation of enemy documents, and a limited degree of strategic interrogation. The obtaining of tactical information played the major role since all combat echelons were primarily interested in information of immediate value which could be utilized in adjusting the offensive or defensive disposition of troops within their own sectors. Detailed interrogation pertaining to longrange tactical, technical, and strategic information was conducted in the higher echelons to the rear. This chapter is a treatment of methods used by the men who performed interrogation functions in the zones of combat.

CHARACTERISTICS OF THE SUCCESSFUL INTERROGATOR

It has been pointed out in chapter I that efficient interrogation required a full knowledge of German Army organization and identification on the part of the interrogator. But more important yet, was that the man who asked the questions had to show profound enthusiasm for his work and be a good psychologist. It was important that he fashion his interrogation technique to cope with the personality of the particular prisoner confronting him. In addition, he had to be able to evaluate any type of information that came his way and ascertain its approximate degree of reliability on the spot. Furthermore, the good interrogator had to be able to sense the particular point when the prisoner's limit of knowledge had been reached in order not to waste any further time in collecting fragments of little or no value. Finally, the interrogator had to have in his possession sufficient fortitude to withstand prolonged periods of interrogation without noticeably impairing his efficiency as an interrogator.

TECHNIQUES FOR SUCCESSFUL INTERROGATION

Although the general procedure of interrogating prisoners of war was fundamentally the same, the techniques varied with both the personalities of the respective interrogators and their individual subjects. Old techniques were constantly revised and new techniques improvised to cope with the demands of the numerous situations confronted.

Some prisoners were arrogant, others were expert liars, some preferred not to talk at all, while many talked too freely. Still others were ideal subjects for interrogation from both the standpoint of cooperation and reliability. Consequently, there could be no standard operating procedure (SOP) by which to extract enemy information. Hence, flexibility in technique employed by the various interrogators was the best prerequisite for proper and efficient interrogation. The interrogator had to bear in mind at all times that the prisoner was confined in hostile hands and enemy territory, which fact in many cases contributed to his nervousness and general uneasiness and was often responsible in preventing prisoners from thinking and expressing themselves as clearly as they could under normal conditions. This applied to the reticent as well as to the talkative kind. Therefore, the interrogator had to exercise caution at all times to avoid obtaining misleading information.

The attitude of the well-trained interrogator toward his subject was usually friendly, if only for the reason of obtaining the desired results. However, familiarity had its bounds and was seldom used in excess. Prisoners considered kindness with suspicion and disrespect, since they were not accustomed to such type of treatment. All German people had been subjugated to firm and strict discipline in the past, and consequently, they respected rather than resented firm treatment. This was especially true of the younger Hitler Youth Generation.

Experience indicated that prisoners revealed more information when they were tired, hungry, or uncomfortable. In such cases the doors of security were often left wide open in preference to receiving immediate and proper personal attention and in getting the required routine of interrogation over with in a hurry. The interrogator, therefore, had to be alert in recognizing any such weaknesses and in exploiting them to the fullest degree. This necessitated on his part a firm mental grip of the complete situation at all times, accompanied by sufficient self-confidence to assert these attributes in a forceful, complete, quiet and dignified manner.

The successful interrogator had to have a good command of the enemy's language and a well-rounded knowledge of the organization and materials of the German Army, the armed party formations (such as the Sturm Soldaten), German uniforms and insignia, enemy tactics, military map symbols, abbreviations and military slang (which the German soldier used in abundance). If the interrogator had to interrupt the prisoner to ask the meaning of such abbreviations as "LIG" for "light infantry howitzer", or "KOMMIS" for "army", etc., he was soon at the mercy of an intelligent or stubborn prisoner. When the interrogator demonstrated a profound knowledge of such matters, the prisoners were usually very much impressed and were very liberal in supplying desired information. In many such instances the prisoners felt free to talk because they were undoubtedly of the impression that the interrogator was already in possession of such information, and that perhaps a little added information might possibly lead to the granting of some concession on the part of the interrogator.

The interrogator also had to be familiar with German Geography, History, Culture, and Economics. The knowledge of German regional likes, dislikes, rivalries, party personalities and scandals concerning them was most helpful in softening up unwilling customers and in appealing to the officer class in the quest for needed information. Interrogations were never opened by asking the prisoner the location of his command-post. But if a prisoner from Sudenland whose <u>soldbuch</u> showed that he was a musician in civilian life were asked whether Professor Furtwaengler was still conducting the Berlin Philarmonie, or how the tourist trade was in Karlsbad (during peace-time), or whether Konrad Henlein was still Gauleiter, the interrogator was usually well on his way toward obtaining any information within the range of his subject. Sometimes these finer points were not always recognized or approved by outsiders, but they brought results, according to a survey of field reports. This merely brings forth the element of human emotion to which the Germans are known to be more susceptible than any other national group, and when once the road to opposition was opened, the rest followed as a matter of course and time.

The interrogator's night-mare was the spoiling of a prisoner by the front-line troops and lower echelon personnel (company and battalion), who often took it upon themselves to conduct their own personnel interrogations. These self-styled experts almost invariably did much more harm than good and oftentimes spoiled the prisoner for all future interrogation. Quite a few cases were reported as having taken place, whereby such individuals upon looking at a soldbuch, discovered that the prisoner belonged to a unit not previously identified within their particular sector. Shortly thereafter, everyone was on the lookout for this particular unit, which of course was not to be located, because these experts not knowing how to read a soldbuch had confused the prisoner's field unit with his replacement unit.

The taking of notes under the direct observation of the prisoner was not practiced as such action prevented the prisoner from talking freely. Notes were taken as scantily as possible at a point out of the prisoner's sight. This led him to believe that what he was saying was not too important and was not being put into writing.

An atmosphere which encouraged prisoners to talk freely was created by the skilled interrogator. It was, however, necessary to be skeptical of loose tongues. An unconscious remark was often the prelude to a storehouse of important enemy information. The interrogator had to be able to sift the wheat from the chaff during the operation of unveiling information.

It must be remembered that most prisoners taken constituted a low-ranking category and consequently were not in possession of a great deal of valuable information. This was conforming with the German way of keeping those not sharing responsibility in the dark as to what was happening. It was a matter of practice that the German private was concerned only with his platoon and company and seldom knew any facts concerning his battalion. On the other hand, high-ranking non-coms knew a good deal, but they were also more security minded. However, the good interrogator usually had enough tricks in his bag to break down the most stubborn resistance and get the information desired.

The interrogator also had to realize that he was only one of many agencies collecting enemy information. He had to be able to recognize any type of important information when he heard it, regardless of its nature and quantity. Sometimes important fragments served as leads to an entire situation of great importance. In such cases careful and detailed probing of the prisoners was considered a necessity.

It was wrong to generalize that all prisoners talked. The majority did talk with various degrees of willingness after the proper application of the appropriate techniques on the part of the interrogator in charge. It was generally true that many prisoners were willing to supply information of their own accord. There were also those prisoners who were willing to supply helpful information out of the gratitude of being relieved of the burden of war. Those prisoners who were forcibly pressed into service, such as Bohemians, Poles, and other foreigners, were highly cooperative in furnishing all information possible. Deserters were generally but not always helpful subjects. In some cases, information supplied through such sources was pre-arranged and sugar-coated. Needless to say, much of such information was unreliable. The chief handicap which usually accompanied the capture of foreign prisoners was the language problem. This was, however sufficiently taken care of in many cases by some member of the respective IPW teams who was able to speak the particular language represented. But usually the amount of time spent in obtaining such information was none too productive, since most of these subjects, not knowing the German language, possessed very limited useable information. As the war progressed and the number of desertions increased, the Germans got wise and withdrew all non-Germans from the front-line zones and used them in rear echelons where their chances for escape were greatly lessened.

Ideal prisoners were those Germans who realized that a few master criminals were systematically and most assuredly exterminating the German race. There were surprisingly many anti-Nazis who were mostly intellectuals and belonged to the upper classes. They were able to see through Hitler's selfish desires for world domination and they, like the battle-scarred and shell-shocked NCO's were very favorable subjects for interrogation.

The interrogator had to be ever on the alert to intercept and exploit intentional or accidental leads given by the prisoner. Not only the recognition but also the proper pursuit of such leads constituted some of the characteristics of a successful or outstanding interrogator. The interrogator had to be careful not to become confused with his own eagerness to obtain incidental or unrelated information and neglect the main program. After such information had been apprehended and properly tracked down, the interrogator had to remember where he left off and resume his work from this point. Since the finished report would indicate whether or not orderly sequence of questions existed throughout the course of interrogation, it was generally practiced that a tentative plan of some sort was drawn up in advance, to be used as a guide in limiting the bounds of an ordinary interrogation. Interrogation was often a strenuous task in taxing the patience and endurance of the interrogator, but the satisfaction of having obtained favorable results was ample compensation in most cases.

Frequently, after short periods of unsuccessful interrogation, impatient interrogators often considered the prisoner incapable of answering intelligibly or as not in possession of important information, while in reality the blame often rested upon the interrogator, who was short-sighted and short handed in applying the proper technique in tapping the prisoner's resources.

The efficient interrogator timed his questions in smooth coordination and in such a manner that the existence of gaps between questions were minimized as greatly as possible, since wide gaps not only wasted time, but also added to the tension and suspense of both interrogator and the prisoner. Poor timing of questions often led the prisoner to think the interrogator inferior and encouraged the clever prisoner to take advantage of the situation by becoming a hard customer to handle and from whom to extract information. The well-trained interrogator was at all times in complete control of the situation and at the same time maintained the full confidence of his subjects.

Questions were always brief and to the point. Questions which could be answered by yes or no were avoided as much as possible because answers could be too easily fashioned to suit the whims of the prisoner. They also encouraged prisoners to make wild guesses when ignorant or in doubt of the correct answer. The trained interrogator did not ask more than one question in the same sentence, thus avoiding confused and misleading answers. Furthermore, a question once given was not altered by the interrogator until an answer was given. Suggestive questions were naturally avoided because they merely encouraged prisoners to lie or to give the wrong answer through ignorance. Questions, except those designed to gain the prisoner's confidence, were confined to matters of military importance and a reflection upon personalities or personal problems were usually avoided.

Every prisoner had human weaknesses pertaining to his character and personality. It was therefore the task of the interrogator to be able to recognize these weaknesses at a glance and base his reactions in accordance with their full exploitation. The most important thing for the interrogator to remember was that the prisoner was the star witness and that a style of interrogation had to be administered which blended with the character and personality of the prisoner. However, each individual prisoner could indirectly choose his own style of interrogation. It was very important that the interrogator have in his possession a technique to fit every type of prisoner reaction.

One point on which interrogators were somewhat "touchy" was the presence of unessential onlookers during important and difficult interrogations, especially when they chose to disrupt the pre-organized interrogational program by volunteering help from the side-lines. Many teams complained of having too many visitors dropping in on them while they were engaged in interrogation. This action was not only most distressing to the interrogator in charge but also helped to make the situation more confusing to the prisoner. Such persons failed to realize that these interrogations were not mere chats or informal discussions, but rather rotated on a well pre-arranged program in which concessions were allotted only to certain categories in accordance with their immediate or ultimate importance, which all in all made the matter of interrogation a difficult, delicate, and specialized proposition.

Experience in the field demonstrated that the most desired results were obtained when the interrogator and the prisoner were alone. Prisoners talked most freely when they were certain that other prisoners were not within hearing distance and when there was no side-line audience. The psychological effect that witnesses had upon prisoners placed an unconscious and automatic inhibition in keeping him from revealing information detrimental to his own troops. This was, however, mostly due to the prisoner's fear of retribution to their kin in Germany, since even fellow prisoners could not be trusted not to report such traitorous actions via the Gestapo grapevine. Members of the Gestapo organization had infiltrated into every branch of German military service and no prisoner could be certain that his best friend was not spying on him. This fear of surveillance sometimes followed the prisoners far into captivity. This did not necessarily mean that successful interrogation could not be done with a third or more persons present. Prisoners whose statements were of particular interest to one specific arm of service such as the artillery, engineers, ordnance, etc., were often questioned in the presence of representatives of such arms. In fact, it was at times almost a necessity for such officers to be present in order to be able to point out to the interrogator questions of a specialized or technical nature, which in all probability would have been either overlooked or not thought of by the interrogator because of his limited knowledge. This was, however, not the general practice and occurred only in exceptional cases. As a general rule, the interrogator was left to his own initiative in handling the prisoners and in administering the duties involved in interrogation with whatever facilities available, since time did not always permit the setting-up of elaborate preliminary aids.

As has been pointed out previously, it was very necessary that the interrogator be properly briefed at all times by the G-2 or S-2 coordinator. It was reported in a number of instances that the coordinator sat in on interrogations to check whether or not his briefings were carried out properly. However, this was not necessary. Although the interrogator was much in need of the support of G-2 and S-2, he was usually trusted by these agencies to carry out his work as directed and to be the sole judge in applying techniques and in evaluating the information which he collected.

Another important item which the interrogator had to remember was that the chief purpose of interrogation was not that of obtaining colorful and headline stories but to get the true story and let the facts alone indicate the degree of significance. Many thousands of prisoners were interrogated without bringing to light any startling new information. In many cases nothing was gained except their unit identification.

Just as the regimental echelon was the most important interrogation point, _time_ was the main element involved in carrying out successful interrogations. A delay in transporting prisoners to the various collecting points often spelled the difference between success and failure in interrogation work. It was very important that the first formal and comprehensive interrogation be conducted as soon as possible after the capture of prisoners in order to capitalize upon their emotional state and to enable the obtaining of important tactical enemy information before it became obsolete and valueless. These timely last-minute "news flashes" of the enemy received through prisoner interrogations were in many instances responsible for saving the lives of many friendly troops. Since time was the greatest neutralizer of tactical information, it was necessary that the transportation facilities be adjusted to bring about speedy evacuation of the prisoners to the various echelons where they were needed for processing and interrogation.

During the early stages of interrogation when IPW was still in its embryonic stage, IPW teams naturally lacked the full sense of foresight which developed later as the result of practical experience. However, as the various IPW teams continued to face problems which demanded alterations and improvements, the entire system of interrogation was subsequently strengthened as well as popularized. As is to be expected, techniques which evolved through field operational work differed from those included in the training program in many respects. It also frequently happened that techniques which applied in particular situations were not always applicable in situations presenting similar problems. This led to the development of local SOP's, which themselves were subject to revision as the local tactical situation was altered. The important feature, therefore, concerning IPW operational work was that techniques were almost as fluid as the tactical situation and that trail and error played the leading role in many new and unanticipated situations.

The best results were gained in interrogation when the prisoners were properly screened and when the prisoners to be interrogated were separated from those already interrogated. This prevented the possibility of prisoners collaborating on a "cooked-up" story in order to side-track the interrogators.

Interrogation revealed in many instances that when prisoners were willing to talk of their own accord, they generally told the truth, while on the other hand, when some form of force was applied, a very noticeable drift toward falsehood prevailed. Generally, appeal proved better in obtaining information than the use of force or threats.

Sometimes prisoners were induced to go back to the enemy lines to try to persuade other members of their unit to lay down their arms and surrender. This was done by the prisoners informing these troops that further resistance would only add to their own misery and bloodshed. This procedure often resulted in the capture of many additional prisoners. The practice of going right up to the enemy lines often involved danger on the part of both IPW members and the prisoners, but in most cases the results were well worth the chances they took.

Prisoners often volunteered to accompany troops to the front in order to direct artillery fire upon their own positions. The interrogation of prisoners captured later brought out the accuracy of such operations.

Many times IPW members served as emissaries in establishing contact with the enemy, in acting as interpreters during negociations for surrender, in the exchange of prisoners of war, in returning enemy nurses and medics back to the enemy lines, etc.

chiefly included pill-boxes, bunkers, underground fortifications, and gun emplacements, it was necessary that interrogators draw from the prisoners specific and detailed information. This proved quite difficult until prisoners who had been living in these fortifications for years were captured and interrogated. After several fruitful interrogations, a comprehensive chart was developed designing the number and type of defenses, including the calibre of guns, amount of ammunition, fields of fire, range of fire, number of troops manning the various defenses, etc. Much of this information later proved invaluable to commanders in charge of assault troops.

The task of obtaining enemy information was not always an easy matter. This was especially true during the period immediately following D-Day, as well as during all other periods during which the enemy was able to present strong opposition, or even take the initiative as was the case in the Ardennes breakthrough. During such times, there was usually a scarcity of prisoners, and those prisoners we captured had a high morale which tended to make them more security minded. This was especially true in the Bulge operations, where the best and most fanatical of the remaining German soldiers were used. Most of the prisoners captured here held the opinion that the time had come to push the Allies back into the sea; also they were convinced that Germany would win the war. Furthermore, it was at such times that the well-known German character traits of arrogance and stubborness came to the foreground. During such periods flare-ups between the interrogators and the prisoners were common, often reaching a very advanced stage. Sometimes prisoners had to be threatened and disciplined to serve as a reminder that they were in enemy hands. It was also during such periods that many deliberate attempts were made to deceive the interrogators. It was not until the Germans had received their major set-backs, augmented by the fury of the Allied guns and bombings, that the enemy began to show signs of softening up. However, when this attitude changed, it usually reverted to that of the opposite extreme. Prisoners were then not only willing to advance information when questioned, but often volunteered to do so. Sometimes, it was necessary to shut off these human talking-machines. This was usually the best indication that the German morale was in a definite state of deterioration and that the enemy was finally beginning to rot at the core.

As the war was drawing to the closing stages, the general attitude represented and expressed by prisoners and civilians alike was as follows: "Well, we have lost the war, now let us be friends". Nevertheless, the Germans were still vague in realizing or in admitting that they were responsible for causing the war. They revealed no apparent change of heart or sense of shame for the many atrocities committed by their troops. No one would admit having taken an active part in any of the many atrocities reported and war guilt seemed to have no significant meaning for them. Most prisoners and civilians especially, seemed to be puzzled that they were treated so coldly. Country people said that they had been interested in one thing only, that of being able to make proper disposal of their farm products. This was only possible after becoming a member of the Nazi Party. In the larger cities, as they were captured, the men put on their "Sunday-best" treatment because they were frightened, and the women were glad because the bombings and the artillery barrages were all over with. Many prisoners openly denounced Hitler and his associates for having been responsible for the destruction of Germany, but none of them would admit having stood behind the "Fuhrer" one-hundred percent until the tide began to swing against them. Many of them said they only joined the Nazi Party because they were compelled to, because every one else joined, because their continued operation in business demanded it, and a variety of other flimsy reasons. Practically all admitted that their membership took place primarily as a matter of expediency, which was very obviously a gross misrepresentation of the truth. Many German civilians could not be convinced that their soldiers had committed any atrocities against the Greeks, Poles, Russians, etc. To them this was merely enemy propaganda. At the same time these very people were constantly able to observe all around them the struggling of the many thousands of imported slave laborers, going about in rags and their faces white and pinched from malnutrition. To the Germans, the misfortune of others had no significance, until it started knocking at their own doors.

REPORTING IPW FINDINGS TO S-2 AND G-2

As each prisoner departed, after being interrogated, the information gained was hurriedly assimilated and placed in readiness for consolidation into the final report, which was compiled by the interrogators and type-written by the team typist. This formal report was known as the Interrogation of Prisoner of War Summary which later became a part of the appendix to the G-2 Periodic Report.

Immediately upon the termination of interrogation of prisoners, it was the responsibility of the officer-in-charge to relay this information to the local S-2 or G-2. In the lower echelons, many OIC's constantly reported their findings to both the regimental S-2 and the division G-2.

IPW teams realized the importance of reporting their findings as soon as possible in order that they could be disseminated by the G-2 in like manner. There was constant emphasis on speed in transmitting this information to the G-2 and S-2, and wherever time could be gained, new methods were improvised. For this purpose the teams with the armored units made use of the radio, while other teams relied heavily on the telephone. Where these rapid means of communication were not available, messenger service via the motor transport was of paramount importance. At such times, when the team members themselves had to deliver these reports by jeep, speed was sometimes impaired due to the inability on the part of some team members to drive properly. This happened frequently, especially where three-man teams operated.

Oral messages by phone were invariably followed by, or later incorporated into, the regular and formal typewritten reports. These reports were usually issued daily and contained such information as identifications, locations, organization, strength, mission, equipment, supplies, losses, replacements, morale, reserves, rear installations, and supporting units of the enemy. Such items were usually SOP.

The form of reports varied. In general, three sections were noted:

and effort but also avoi[DECLASSIFIED Authority NND 745001]formation.

It must not be overlooked that much enemy information was supplied through civilian sources. Throughout the various campaigns in France and Belgium, close contact was kept with the various underground resistance movements through which much valuable information was gained. Often, these civilians had first-hand information because they had served forced labor battalions which helped construct enemy installations and fortifications. Cases were reported where alert civilians counted the number of guns, noted the calibre of these guns, knew the fields of fire, the amount of ammunition, and the number of men engaged at the various points. The Counter Intelligence Corps (CIC), was very cooperative in apprehending civilians with possible tactical information and in forwarding them to IPW teams for interrogation. Frequently, CIC passed valuable information which they had uncovered, on to IPW teams for disposition. In Holland and Germany civilians were interrogated for tactical information. The fact that most IPW teams had French speaking personnel proved quite an asset throughout the various campaigns in France. The information gained from civilians, necessarily, had to be evaluated and confirmed. Civilians were often advised on how to gain additional information and what type of information was needed. More than once, the communication system of various forts was discovered by civilians who informed our troops of such findings. The cutting of the wires by our troops often proved to be directly responsible for the early capitulation of these forts.

Due to the intensive defense system of the Siegfried Line which

(1) statistical data in which new information was emphasized in relation to facts already known; (2) details of individual interrogations; (3) summary of the essential information presented in a concise manner. This form lent itself to wide usage, since the summary could be quickly grasped and easily distributed while the statistical and detailed interrogation sections could be referred to by those agencies desiring more information.

It was only in a few instances that periodic daily reports were not made. Sometimes no report was submitted until after a shipment of prisoners had been completely processed and interrogated. Invariably, however, any valuable information was reported immediately.

According to the information received from teams in the field, the reporting of information, although far from uniform, was handled to the satisfaction of both the teams and the G-2. All realized that proper and timely reporting was the main instrument by which the whole work of IPW teams became effective. It was in this regard that the inability of IPW team members to drive, type, or write English properly showed up conspicuously as the most common weakness of IPW teams in the field.

The Army's Military Intelligence Community on the Eve of the Cold War

World War II greatly expanded and thoroughly professionalized Army intelligence. Opening in June 1942, the Military Intelligence Training Center at Ft. Ritchie, Maryland, trained thousands of G.I.s as prisoner-of-war interrogators, military interpreters, photo interpreters, and order-of-battle specialists. Following an eight-week course, the Army grouped the recruits into military intelligence specialist teams and deployed them overseas, principally to Europe.

A good number of "Ritchie Boys" were German émigrés who had left their country for political reasons under the Nazis, and many were Jewish.[5] The émigrés' generally superior level of education and intimate knowledge of Germany proved valuable assets as they pursued their Army intelligence duties during the war, and some continued to work for the Army during the occupation period.

As an organization, Army intelligence during that period is best described as a fluid community, composed of several agencies of varying size and different, if often overlapping, responsibilities. Unlike many other intelligence agencies, it was not a single entity with a clear structure and hierarchy, its administrative history being neither static nor monolithic. Between 1944 and 1947, the War Department and the Army managed over half a dozen agencies which dealt with the collection, evaluation, dissemination, and safeguarding of militarily and politically relevant information in Germany.

At the apex of Army intelligence stood the War Department's Military Intelligence Division (MID), whose director doubled as assistant chief of staff of the G-2 (second section of the General Staff). The MID held overall responsibility for the development of strategic intelligence, establishing the Army's intelligence priorities and requirements, collecting the appropriate information from subordinate agencies and other sources, processing the acquired data into finished intelligence, and passing the results to other agencies inside and outside the War Department. For its operating functions—collecting, analyzing, and disseminating intelligence—the MID relied on its executive arm, the Military Intelligence Service (MIS).[6]

The two most important intelligence organizations under the MID were the Army Security Agency (ASA) and the Counter Intelligence Corps (CIC). The ASA was responsible for the interception and decryption of foreign communications.[7] The CIC had the task of countering enemy espionage and sabotage. Toward the end of the war, the CIC acquired a number of additional duties, including intelligence collection through espionage.[8]

During World War II, the Army relied mainly on the OSS for intelligence gathering, but when OSS was dissolved in September 1945, its espionage and counterespionage sections were briefly attached to the War Department as the Strategic Services Unit (SSU). The SSU reported directly to the office of the assistant secretary of war, not to the MID, and thus remained on the periphery of the Army's intelligence community.[9]

The Military Attaché Branch also produced a steady stream of information for the G-2. The War Department appointed military attaches to US diplomatic missions, and one of the tasks of the attachés was the collection of militarily relevant information in their host countries. Typically, they used open sources, such as newspapers or information gleaned from conversations with local officials. The attachés reported their insights directly to the MID in Washington.[10]

APPENDIX E

LETTERS, DOCUMENTS, INTERVIEWS and INFORMATION ON FAMILY AND FRIENDS

U.S. Holocaust Museum's Interview with Trude Grünbaum Ludwig (Otto's sister)
Interviewer was Anthony Di Iorio

December 10, 1991 - Trude was 74

Could you please start by telling us your name when you were first born?

My name when I was first born was Gertrud Grunbaum and I was born in Vienna on March 26, 1917.

And your parents?

My parents was - my father's name was Otto Grünbaum and my mothers name was Melanie gebore Wöhrer

Also born in Vienna?

My mother was born in Yugoslavia and my father was born in Vienna. Not true? Now Romania, then it was Yugoslavia.

Well it was still the Austro-Hungarian Empire. Right.

Yes.

What did your father do when you lived in Vienna?

My father had a fur store. He was a furrier and dresses.

And your mother?

My mother was just at home.

Housewife.

Housewife, yes.

Did you have any brothers and sisters?

I had a younger brother who was born on August 18, 1918.

Also Vienna?

Also Vienna.

And his name?

Was Otto, Otto Karl Grünbaum.

Which religion did your family?

My father was Jewish, my mother was Catholic and we were protestants.

You were Protestants. Do you mean you were raised as Protestants?

As protestants, ja, we were raised as Protestants.

Any particular church? The Evangelical or Lutheran or..

Lutheran

Any particular reason for this combination?

I don't really know. I think my father didn't want to become a Catholic and my mother did not become Jewish so the middle was Protestant - I expect you had a lot of people like this in Vienna.

In Vienna

Ja

And they liked each other enough to marry one another even though they were Catholic and Jewish?

Yes

Okay so you both were born baptized as Protestants then?

Yes

Was it a religious family?

No Everybody another religion. We were not very religious.

What languages were spoken in the home?

German

Just German?

Yes

How about schooling? What kind of schools did you attend?

Elementary school and Gymnasium

Public?

Public schools, yes.

Public schools in Vienna?

In Vienna.

How about your parents' politics? For example, you were born towards the end of World War I. Your brother was born in the last year of the Austro-Hungarian Empire. Must have been period of tremendous turmoil and change. Was your father a Republican or was he still Kaisertreu as they used to say.

I really don't know. We didn't talk very much about politics at home.

Did he serve in the army?

Yes. He served in the army in World War I.

So one way or another he had to serve the empire?

Oh ja

You can't tell whether or not he was glad or sad that the old empire had come to an end?

I think they were more or less sad.

How about the politics in the 1920s and 1930s during the republic. Do you recall any political parties that your father..?

No my father was in no political party.

Apolitical

Ja, and we didn't talk much about politics at home because at this time you didn't talk politics to your children - at least in our home we didn't.

Could you recall when the Nazis were first mentioned if at all?

Oh yes I remember that very well because it was when they killed Dollfuss. This was I think 1934.

Dollfuss being the Chancellor of Austria?

Chancellor of Austria at the time and the Nazis killed him.

That made a big impression on you?

Yes it made a very big impression and then when I started working in the theater we had some people from Germany. Of course Jewish people because the others wouldn't come and they were told a lot of terrible stories and we were very much impressed at least I was very much impressed. Most of our friends did not believe it could happen in Austria.

So you knew of Jews who had left Germany to come to Austria

Yes.

They told you stories of...?
Some of them were in camps but at this time it was not extermination camps yet I think but they told us stories and I was very impressed and I know a lot of people - it could never happen in Austria.

Do you remember any stories in particular when you were listening to these refugees in Austria?
Yes we had a young actor whose father was a very famous actor as a matter of fact in Germany and he told us that he was in a camp andnthat they treated him very badly but I mean they did not talk too much about it.

And they settled in Austria?
They settled in Austria or tried to settle in Austria.

Did your family feel safe in Austria even after 1934?
Yes actually yes.

Was there any experience with antisemitism in Vienna itself?
Oh yes.

By Austrians?
Oh yes, a lot, a lot of antisemitism.

Do you recall any incidents either in the theater or in public or in school?
I went to school with a daughter of Seyss-Inquart. She was sitting next to me and she was .....

Do you recall her first name?
Oh yes Inge, Inge Seyss-Inquart and she would brush her sleeves when she touched us. There were a lot of Jewish girls in the class. Half of the class was Jewish.

So she had to wipe her blouse of what - Jewish breath or Jewish germs?
Jewish germs yes I guess so.

So they knew you were Jewish or part Jewish in this class?
Oh yes with the name of Grünbaum there was no doubt.

There was no doubt. How about your father did he have any experiences with antisemitism? You mentioned that he was an army war veteran?
Well when he was in the army he never told anything about it to us, no.

How about as a furrier?

Well he never talked about it. He certainly had some experience because there was a lot of antisemitism in Austria at the time.

Do you recall what neighborhood you lived in Vienna? Was it a mixed neighborhood or...?

Mixed - but in the neighborhood I really cannot say that I had antisemitism, we felt it in school.

You had friends who were Protestant, Catholic and Jewish?

Yes but mainly Jewish.

Mainly Jewish friends - of your own age - both genders or just girls?

At this time just girls.

How about your brother did he have any - do you recall any experiences?

Not before Hitler came not that he talked about.

You mentioned that you were in the theater. Did you have dreams as you grew up of becoming an actress?

Oh sure - we went to the Vienna Conservatory when we were children already, my brother and I, both of us and we took up - this was called Kinderkonservatorium - conservatory for children. I was seven and my brother was six when we entered and you know we had all kinds of music lessons - piano, singing, gymnastic

So you were musicians?

No I was not a musician. I go for dancing. My brother was studying piano and violin.

So at age seven already you were dancing and acting?

Oh ja

And your brother was beginning studies in music?

Ja, he studied piano and he gave his first concert when he was fourteen.

Do you recall what he played?

Yes I recall he played with - there was a very famous opera singer - her name was Elizabeth Schumann and when she gave a concert she always had in between a young musician so she could rest. My brother played with her the first time when he was fourteen and then every concert she gave he played.

In Vienna?

In Vienna, ja.

And what was your brother's great dream as he grew up? This is your younger brother..

He wanted to be a pianist and a conductor.

in Austria - In Vienna? Salzburg?

Well at this time, yeah, in Vienna, Sure.

That was the preference?

Oh sure Vienna was always for music.

There was no talk of leaving Austria - of going..

No not when we were children.

Now do things become better or worse after the Dolfuss incident?

It became worse. First of all there was a lot of unemployment. It was very hard to find a job and the antisemitism was pretty bad.

Even before Hitler came.

Yeah

Did you follow the career of Inge Seyss-Inquart?

No

Did you know who her father was at that time?

Well ja, we know something that he was a Nazi but you know how old was I, fifteen or so. We were not so interested in this.

You were more interested in art?

Yes much more.

Do you recall any classmates who were Nazis?

Oh yes we had quite a few. I couldn't tell you the name now because this is too long ago but we had quite a few.

They cause any problems in the class - did they try to...?

Well they separated.

They just tried to stay away. Did they attack any students?

No.

How about the teachers. Did you find them to be sympathetic or loyal to the republic?

Well we had a lot of Jewish teachers in this school and a few who were not Jewish and were more or less antisemitic. We had a few of them too but it was not too bad.

You could live with that?

We could live with it, ja.

Do you remember where you were when the Nazis finally took over Austria?

I was in Italy.

You were in Italy. How did you get to Italy? How could a nice little Austrian girl go to Italy?

Go to Italy? It started out that I was looking for an engagement in the theater and I had a contract to teach in Bodenbach which is in the Sudentenland and ...

Czechoslovakia then?

Sudentenland, ja, but they were already thinking - German.

And you had to submit all your papers, of course.

And I had a stage name. My stage name was Hermann, Trude Hermann. Of course I had to submit my real name and with Grünbaum right away they wouldn't give me the contract.

This is in Sudentenland?

Yes and the same happened to me in Linz. I had a contract there too and they wouldn't take me when they found out that I was not an aryan..

This was before Hitler's time?

This was in 1937.

That's interesting because your Jewish name - even though you were a protestant ...

Yes this didn't cut any ice with them.

Linz and then the Sudentenland. Do you remember any of the towns in the Sudentenland?

Tetschen-Bodenbach [Podmokly] it was called. Tetschen-Bodenbach. And then my agent , you know you had to have an agent, he suggested that I go to Italy because he said I will not get any contract in a German speaking country.

What did your parents think of your career in the theater and then going to Italy of all places?

Well, I was twenty then and could do whatever..

So you had relatively liberal parents?

Yes, and I went to Italy and I was in Milano when the Anschluss came and my mother wrote me immediately please don't come back because our contract in Italy was not expired but had one more month I think to go and she said try to stay in Italy

And you recall when you went to Italy?

Yes in September 1937.

And you had what a one year, six months..?

No we had a three months contract and then we were another three months so we were in Italy in March when the Anschluss happened - in Milano.

And you obviously did not experience employment discrimination?

Not in Italy, no.

Your mother said, "Don't come back."

"Don't come back, be glad you are in Italy."

Were you glad?

Yes, very much.

So you remained in Milan?

I remained in Milano. We had to go to vote. The German embassy came to the theater, took all our passports away because we were thirty girls from Vienna.

You had Austrian passports?

Austrian passports, ja, and they told us we had to go to the consulate and when we were there they said we had to go to vote on the torpedo boat "Wolf" which was in Genoa. We would be brought there from the German Embassy.

So the German consulate in Genoa..

No it was a German boat and on this you voted because a boat is territory, right?

Okay so a German boat in Genoa was going to be your voting booth?

Yes.

And they gave you of course free transportation?

Free transportation. And I didn't want to go but there was a very intelligent, I don't know what he was, attache or something, who called me in his office and said go and vote because you won't stop Hitler but he could stop you.

This is a German attache at the consulate in Milan?

In Milan, yeah.

So he advised you to vote in the plebiscite approving...

He said vote what you want but go to vote.

And you voted?

I voted, yes.

Do you want to tell us how you voted?

Oh you had to say yes because you had to give the thing, the slip you voted on, you had to give in an envelope and were not allowed to close the envelope. You had to leave it open and then you handed it to some of the soldiers who were standing there and he took your passport, looked at your passport - so - what chance did you have to say no?

Right and besides they would have known who you were and it would have defeated the purpose.

Immediately ,ja.

And were they surprised in any way that you were voting?

Yes.

They could tell you had a Jewish name.

Yes. One soldier said to me I think you are on the wrong boat. We don't go to Palestine.

Sense of humor. This is a Nazi, possibly?

Possibly not. Because otherwise he would probably not let me vote.

And the real reason why you voted?

Because this gentleman told me it would be better for me if I do it. I alone could not stop Hitler but he could stop me and he would have.

And of course your real sentiment was..

Not very friendly, no.

What were the rest of your family doing? They were still in Vienna?

My father was in Switzerland on business and he stayed there and did not come back. My mother and my brother were in Vienna. My brother tried to get out of the country which wasn't easy because you needed an exit visa in order to get out but he had applied for an international music - piano - competition in Brussels and with this he got the exit visa and he went to Brussels. They didn't let him play because for them he was a German. And he tried to go to France and he couldn't get a visa to France either so I wrote him a letter from Italy telling him that I was very sick and he should immediately come and visit me and he went to the Italian consulate and they gave him a visa to enter Italy and so he got a transit visa from France and got off the train.

Did he discover that you were sick or did he discover that you made up the story?

Oh he knew I made up the story. He knew I wasn't sick. But he had the transit visa in France and he got off the train and went to Paris and my father was in Paris at this time and so he got always I think a three weeks or six weeks visa, I don't remember, and always to apply again and again.

So basically you faked an illness in order to justify this transit visa through France ..

And the Italians gave him the visa.

Which then allowed him to go France? To get the transit visa from France. And your mother meanwhile..?

My mother was in Prague in the meantime.

She left Vienna?

She left Vienna for good, yes.

What had happened to your brother's musical career if you back up just a little bit?

Well he started in Paris with Claude Arrau

If we could go further back. He had begun at age fourteen in Vienna and then in 1938 the Nazis come. At that point where was his career?

He was still a student in the Conservatory conducting classes and he gave concerts in Czechoslovakia and gave a concert in Karlsbatd [Karlovy Vary]. He gave several concerts in Vienna and then he went to France and he studied. There he never worked. He studied there with Claude Arrau. He tried to go to the United States but he didn't have a sponsor so my mother wrote a letter to a very famous violinist who my brother knew, Fritz Kreisler and Fritz Kreisler went with him to the consulate and got him a student visa for America and he came here as a student.

Do you recall when?

Yes in '39.

In '39. Before the war?

I think in August '39.

And you were still in Italy?

I was in Italy. I didn't have a sponsor.

Still in Milan?

No. In Rome, Milan, - we traveled. In Italy you traveled.

So you had work?

I had work. I always had work.

How about your passport? After the Germans took over Austria, you voted. Were you still with an Austrian passport or did you...?

No, the Austrian passport was good till the end of '38. I had an Austrian passport as long as possible.

When you had to renew your passport?

I renewed my passport. I wrote to one of my aunts in Vienna. Please send me an aryanmacher. Do you know what that is?

Proof of aryan.

This is very hard when you have a Jewish father. So she sent me all the documents of my mother and my maternal grandparents and my mother's certificate of matrimony. This was the funniest thing that I got a German passport without a J. I'll never know because in this said that my father was the son of Ivor Grunbaum and Zara geborene Cohen.

This is really not real.

So it was falsified?

No, no I got it

Through anybody's help? Was it a mistake or was it just that you had a nice guy?

A nice guy.

A nice guy, but he certainly wasn't Jewish. This was the German consulate?

It was the German consulate.

In Milan.

In Milan, no, in Rome. He gave it to me and once you had a German passport, you were okay. The Italians didn't ask any questions.

So you had a non-Jewish passport even though your name is still Jewish?

Ja

Were there any changes when the war breaks out?. Your brother is in the United States?

My mother was in France and my father, too. My father was in Paris and my mother was in Lyon with her second husband.

Oh, so your parents had divorced. Were they divorced before the Anschluss?

Before, much before that.

Before you even went to Italy?

Yes, I was seventeen when my parents divorced so that must have been '34.

The year Dollfus..

The Dollfus year, yes.

But it had nothing to do with Dolffus?

No it had nothing to do with Dolffus?

Nothing to do with being Jewish or Protestant or Catholic?

No, in fact her second husband was Jewish too.

So your mother was pro- Jewish.

Was pro-Jewish ,ja.

Did your father remarry?

No but my mother came with her second husband. They went from Prague ... He was Czechoslovakian nationality, lived always in Vienna.

Jellinek is the

Jellinek, ja. He and his brother were born in Russia, by coincidence because their father worked there for several years and when they applied for a visa to the United States - they came on the Russian quota which was wide open - and got immediately a visa because they thought they were coming on the Czechoslovakian quota which was waiting list for years. But they didn't know that in American law your nationality where you were born and not what passport you have so these two were born in Odessa and my mother was married to a Russian. They got immediately the visa and they came via Casablanca because they could not go through France anymore and could not go to Spain. Spain wouldn't let them in so they had to go Casablanca and from Casablanca to Portugal and from Portugal they went to Cuba and from Cuba they went to the United States.

Do you recall when this was?

This must have been '40, no '41, no '40.

Had the Germans gone into Paris yet? ..in the Vichy?

No, I think before that.

But after the beginning of the war?

No they were in Paris already, the Germans, when my mother left. My brother was ...

In the United States

In '39, he came in '39

So it would have been after June of 1940

I think so, yes. I don't quite recall.

Was it winter?

I don't recall that.

Well, maybe we'll remember later. But anyway by 1941 they were here.

They were here, yeah. I think they came 1940, the end of 1940. It was certainly not '41 because I think they came in the fall of 1940.

That would make sense. After the Germans had occupied France but still the freedom of Vichy because in Vichy you could go to Casablanca.

Yes. It certainly was 1940 because '41 was already Pearl Harbor and they were here already in Pearl Harbor.

Meanwhile you're still in Italy.

I was still in Italy.

And Italy is in the war in 1940.

It was in the war. That's why I don't recall. We could not correspond too well then. The mail took very long. I mean it was still possible because America was not in the war. But a letter took months.

As a German passport holder you were an ally of Fascist Italy in 1940.

Yes, but the Fascists didn't bother you.

Did you get even better treatment?

No. We always got good treatment.

How about the anti-Jewish laws that Mussolini introduced. Did they have any affect on you?

No

Were there any examples of anti-semitism?

No I'd never seen anti-semitism in Italy. No, never.

Were you working - in Rome mainly?

I was working - no, we traveled around because in Italy you don't work in a theater. You work in a company and the company travels around

And who were you working with? Were they mixed, Italians, foreigners?

All Italian.

So you were the only Austrian?

Oh, we were a couple of girls.

Were there others who were Jewish besides you?

Oh ja.

Italians as well as Austrians?

Well, Italians I cannot tell. We never talked about religion. That was never brought up, never.

It was all acting, art.

Italians never ask you any questions. We had to go to the police every six months to renew the working permit. They never ask any questions.

Do you recall some of the places where you toured? Did you perform say for troops?

We did perform for hospitals, for veterans' hospitals.

Italian veteran hospitals

Italian, yeah. Not for the Germans, never.

You didn't perform for Germans. After all the German troops...

No, we never performed for German troops, no.

By this time you have very little contacts with your parents, your father?

Well, as soon as the war started in Austria they had no contact with anyone outside because you could not write to America. I didn't know where my father was in France because he left Paris - he came to Nizza [Nice] and then he was in hiding for the rest of the war.

But you knew your family was - your mother and your brother - were safe?

I know that they were in America.

So your father was the only member of your family that you worried about?

Yes I was because France was occupied by the Germans.

How did you feel about Italy being on the same side as Hitler?

Well we always had the feeling that the Italians didn't like it too much - being on the side - but they had very little choice because the German troops were already in Brenner and Mussolini was not too happy either I think.

Do you remember any specific instances of Italian actor or actresses voicing their opinions against Germany or against Mussolini?

No. You did not voice against Mussolini too openly but we never talked about politics really. We were glad we could stay there and we worked - politics was never a big thing with us.

Politics came to you now. Suddenly in 1943 Italy surrendered and the Germans occupy all of Italy. Do you remember any changes in your life then?

Yes. Of course, first of all the theaters were closed. When the Americans landed I think in Sicily it was and in Naples the Germans destroyed all their papers in the consulate so they did not know who was in Italy of German descendants or aryan or Jewish or nothing. They knew nothing. They only could go to the police stations, to the Questura, and there they found out where German people were living. But the Italians would not give the information about religion, never did. To them everybody was an aryan.

The Germans knew that you were where?

In Rome and we were called in the German consulate and had the choice to return to the Reich or work as interpreters. Of course we worked as interpreters because nobody wanted to return to the Reich.

So you worked as an interpreter for the Germans?

For three, four months and there were a lot of German girls who spoke Italian and after the war I remember the UNRRA came and we could get some food packages from the UNRRA and all the interpreters I met there were Jews who had worked for the Germans just like we, Mimi and I and several others.

Did you change your name at any time?

No because for the German Grünbaum is not a Jewish name. We had an officer who was called Grünbaum and he certainly was not a Jew. For the Austrians this was a Jewish name.

That's an interesting difference.

Oh yes, Rosenbach in Austria was Jewish.

And one of the leading Nazis was a Rosenbach. So Grunbaum was a German Jewish name in Austria.

In Austria it was Jewish.

In Germany it was a non-Jewish name.

Both. There were Jews who were called Grunbaum but not necessarily.

And did you look Jewish or aryan?

I don't know. Apparently aryan enough because nobody ever asked me anything.

What color eyes did you have?

I have blue eyes.

You still do, blue eyes and your hair was....?

Red at the time. But anyway the Italians didn't give out any information. They saved a lot of people, I must say.

Do you know of people who were saved.

Oh yes, at least all of them who worked with me there. I know of a lot of people who were in Italy and everybody will tell you the same. The Italians did not give out information to the Germans.

Now in Rome as you know in late 1943 there were some deportations. The Germans attempted to deport Italian Jews to Auschwitz. Did you witness any of these incidents?

No, but I know where it happened in Largo Argentina but I didn't see it myself, thank goodness.

Did you know of anybody who was sent away?

I didn't know anybody, no.

How about incidents of armed resistance. For example in March 1944 there was a major partisan attack on the SS and then there was the retaliation.

The retaliation. Three hundred in the catacombs. I remember that because I lived very near where this attack took place.

Did you ever have occasion to see or meet Colonel Kappler, the commandant.

No, I never saw him but I know who he was. Who didn't know?

Was it a name that inspired trust and love or..?

No, hate. He was terrible. Every day, this was in '44 just before the war ended, they had some American and English prisoners and they would parade them and the Americans would go with the V sign and the Italians applauded.

The Italians applauded the American prisoners that were paraded by the Germans in Rome. Were you ever in danger?

Well, I don't think so. I was not really in danger.

\And you didn't have to hide?

Yes, in the last few weeks, I did hide because I was afraid that they would take me with them when the Germans left Rome.

So you were an interpreter for three or four months and then what did you do after? You kind of drew away?

No, I was pregnant at the time and could quit work in May, 1944 and then I had a very nice boss I must say and he called me up and said go in hiding because they are coming to get you. Because they wanted gentile persons, everybody, to go with them up north and of course I didn't want to go.

That was the original choice as I recall. Either return to the Reich or work as an interpreter?

But there they wanted us to go, all interpreters, to go north with the troops and I didn't want to do that.

And why was this sudden renewed interest in going north. Was anything happening near Rome?

Oh ja, the Americans.

The Americans entered. You probably remembered the date that they entered?

Yes, June 4, 1944.

So you hid just before June 4, 1944.

Yes, about ten days before.

And then what happened after the Americans came? Did you have work?

Oh ja, at first I returned to the theater and then I worked as an interpreter for the Americans until '48.

By then you must have known quite a few languages. You started out being German speaking..

Yes, I spoke Italian and English. I learned English in school.

You learned English when you were in Vienna before going to Italy?

In school, ja.

So you would be interpreting between the Americans and the Italians or between the Americans and German prisoner?

No, between Americans and Italians.

And they paid you?

They paid me, sure. And then we went to Argentina, my husband and I.

So you had married in Italy.

Yes.

Had a child?

This one. [Daughter was present at interview]

Born as an Italian citizen.

No, as an Austrian citizen.

Male, female?

Female, name Irene.

Your husband was also Austrian?

No my husband was German.

Jewish, non-Jewish?

Non-Jewish.

He was in Italy at the time?

He was in Italy at the time. Was a prisoner and we left for Argentina in 1948 because we didn't have a visa for the States. There was a long waiting period.

He was a prisoner of the Americans but he had been there a German military?

Military, yes.

Any word from your brother, meanwhile?. Your brother was in the United States.

My brother was in the United States and of course I didn't hear from him during the war because you could not write but as soon as the war was over, no, not as soon, because you couldn't write for quite some time. But one day he came to visit me. In '45 he came in September. He was then stationed in the Third Army in Schongau, Germany.

He visited you in Italy.

In Italy, in Rome.

And you hadn't seen him since when?

Since 1937, eight years. A lot of time.

Can you recollect what he was doing between 1939 and 1945 when you finally saw him?

Yes, he was in New York. He studied with Schnabel, Arthur Schnabel, the pianist. He gave concerts. He taught. He worked with a Russian singer, studied with her, accompanied her. And then he was drafted in the army. Well he was not drafted, he was a student here so they gave him a choice.

What was the choice?

The choice was to join the army or have to leave the country.

And return where?

That is the question.

What kind of citizenship did he have at that point?. He obviously was not an American citizen.

No, he was German, I guess.

German, so were they threatening to return him to Germany?.

Well, they would not return him anywhere. He just has to leave the country and try to find another country which would take him. But he has a choice to join the army which he did. First he was in North Carolina, I think was his boot camp and several others.

Did he serve in Europe before he saw you?

Ja, because he came in '44 to Europe and he came to visit me in '45. And just a month before he died, he was killed, an accident, we don't know.

He was killed a month after you last saw him?

Yes

Do you recall him telling any stories, any dramatic experiences as a soldier?. Did he describe the fighting? Did he describe what he saw in Germany, perhaps concentration camps?

Yes he told me he saw concentration camps. He said everyone they interviewed never heard of Nazis. Nobody was ever a Nazi.

He served in the US army. Was he attached to a particular unit?

Yes, intelligence. And he was an interpreter.

So in some ways you had similar jobs. And his experience was that no German...?

Ever was Nazi.

Did he believe? What were his feelings towards the Germans?

No. Well was not enthusiastic about the Germans. He didn't feel any hatred, I think. That was not in his character. All he wanted was to go back to America, resume his career as a musician. He didn't think he could be a pianist anymore because three years of not practicing the piano daily makes your fingers stiff but he wanted to go into conducting because he had the qualification to be a conductor. But music was his life. He was supposed to go home on November 19, 1945. On the eighteenth of November he told one of his friends that he was going to see Richard Strauss in Garmisch-Partnkirchen and he left early in the morning and was never seen alive again.

Do you know what happened to him?

We only know what the army told us, that he had an accident. That's what they said at the time. But not right away. He was listed as missing because nobody knew where he was and it was November and it started snowing and they could not search anymore for him and after the snow melted, my sister-in-law got a letter that he was found in Mittenwald with a fractured skull. And that is all we know. And at first he was buried in Metz and then I think the French wanted this cemetery to be eliminated so my sister-in-law got a letter where she wanted him buried and she said in New York and that's where he is, in Farmingdale, the military cemetery.

Do you have any opinions as to how and why he might have died and why the military was so secretive?

I don't know. I only know that my brother told me when he was in Rome that the Germans always thought when he interviewed somebody that he was also the one who passes judgment which was not the case. He was only the interpreter. And he said the Germans if you have a uniform think you're a general. You have so much to say, which he didn't. But I always thought it had something to do with the Germans, that it was not an accident. He was not a mountain climber. He liked to take a walk in the woods but not in the mountains. He never did that before, why should he have done it the day before he had to leave?

And then you eventually came to the United States?

I came to the United States much later because my mother was our sponsor, but the Austrian quota was impossible, very, very small. I could go on the German quota with my husband, because he was born in Germany. So we're in Argentina and we finally got the visa in 1950. We were supposed to leave on September 13. On September 12 came the McCarren Act and we already had the luggage aboard and we were called to come to the consulate, which we did and the consulate asked to see our passport. We gave him the passport and he put in "canceled."

Why?

Because my husband was born in a totalitarian country. And at this time there was the McCarren Act that nobody in a country which had at one time a totalitarian regime could go to the United States. So we had to stay in Argentina. I remembered that Truman vetoed this and so I went to the consulate once aw eek. The poor consulate when he saw me already, "No, no visa yet." And we got our visa on May of 1951 and left and we came to the United States on May 28, 1951.

Looking back on your experiences and thinking of your career in the theater and acting..

It was not much of a career

If you had to select the most dramatic moment of your life at least during the time of the war what would you..

The most dramatic I think was when we were in Rhodes
and I still had my Austrian passport. While I was in Rhodes I met two Viennese men who told me their story that they came over the border into Italy because they had an American visa and wanted to go to the States but the Germans wouldn't give them an exit visa so they went somewhere over the border and came to Italy without the visa and registered in a hotel. But the clerk brought the passport to the police and they saw they had no visa and they were not allowed to traverse Italy anymore and you cannot go to America from Venice. So they went on the first boat to Egypt and thought they could go from there and then they told me the story that Egypt wouldn't let them go ashore and they came back to Italy and they wouldn't let them go ashore and they traveled back and forth.

You're in Rhodes and these people are traveling back and forth without the visa?

They're also in Rhodes and once the Governor of Rhodes was on the boat and he was a Jew himself and he let them stay for awhile in Rhodes. He gave them permission to get off the boat and they were trying to get a visa to Egypt which they finally got. They told me the story and when we came back to Italy in Bari and we wanted to go ashore because (actually we traveled to Venice but we stood a day in Bari and I was with this English ballet and all the girls got their passport back except me so I said, "Where's my passport?" So I went in and this Italian said I'm sorry you cannot get to shore because you are Jewish and Jews cannot enter Italy anymore.

This is an Italian official.

An Italian official.

In which year. Do you remember the year?

'39. No excuse me, '38. After the Anschluss. I still had the Austrian passport hadn't expired. I said I'm not Jewish and my passport is still okay till the end of the year. And he said but if you were not Jewish you would have already changed it like all the others did. And so I remember that I voted and this was stamped into the passport. And first I did not remember it. I was so nervous I saw myself going back and forth on this boat like the people told me. Oh, God, what am I going to do? And then I remembered. I voted and I have that in the passport. And as soon as he saw that he said oh I'm sorry and he gave me the visa. So I remembered the man at the consulate. He was right.

So your decision to vote for the Nazis saved you. This would have been after Mussolini enacted the anti-Jewish laws. This was why they gave you a hard time. But these are the Italians that are giving you trouble.

Yes, Italian. But it didn't last very long. As soon as they saw this stamp, I could go in and in Rome they never gave me trouble.

And then you got the German passport without a J.

I got it without a J. That I think was my most dramatic moment because I really saw myself on the boat going back and forth to Rhodes.

And no amount of acting could have saved you, just quick thinking.

Yes

If your brother were here and had to answer the same question what do you think his answer would be based on his experiences.

I don't know. He had a lot of dramatic experiences in Germany when he was a soldier because he told me that one day there was a terrible bombardment. He said I was hungry, I was going into the kitchen and everybody said don't be crazy. You're not going out when the bombs are firing and he said, "Yes, I'm going out." And he went out of the barracks where they were staying and into the next one where the kitchen is and the barracks where they were staying was bombed and he was the only survivor.

By American aircraft.

No, by the Germans.

Germany still had an air force. Y

Yes they still had an air force.

How about before he left Vienna. You say that he left after the Anschluss. Do you remember him having any bad experiences with the Nazis in Vienna?

Yes. In the conservatory he was then nineteen years old so he was thirteen years a student in the conservatory. This professor Nielius who was a teacher for the conducting classes. And he was always a star pupil and he always talked about him. As soon as the Nazis came in he wouldn't let him into the building anymore.

So he was expelled from the Vienna conservatory?

Oh yes.

No more concerts.

No more. Nothing.

Did he have his own piano.

Oh yes.

So when your family left Vienna?

They left everything.

You owned your own home?

No, they rented.

And when you went to Italy in 1937 did you have any idea that you would never return?

No, of course not.

Did you have anything from your childhood?

No, nothing. Just my clothes, some clothes, not even everything. But I sometimes had the feeling that I would never come back because I was convinced that Hitler would come to Austria and many people did not believe me.

What made you think that?

I don't know.

Just a wild hunch.

I don't think it was such a wild hunch. I think it was in the stars that he would come but people didn't want to believe it. The Austrian Jews did not want to believe that it couldn't happen in Vienna. I don't know why they don't believe it. There was a lot of anti-semitism there and Austria was very poor at the time. They had a lot of unemployed people. Austria was very poor and they thought that an Anschluss to Germany would - because everybody heard that since Hitler is the Germans have more work and everything is going better --

So there was economic hope in Germany. Was he popular? Did people admire Hitler?

None of my friends admired him but certainly a lot of people did.

And you recall the reasons that why they admired him. What was there about him that they liked?

They thought that when Hitler will come they will all work, everything will be better. This did not last very long because I don't think he treated the Austrians too well. He wa san Austrian, but he didn't like Austria.

Now you, being in Italy must have been interesting vantage port in that Italy had been the ally of Austria.

Yes, for a long time Dollfus' widow as a matter of fact was in Italy at the time and Schuschnigg was in Italy.

You remember what the Italian reaction was to the Anschluss?

The Italians didn't like it at all. They had very little choice because Hitler's army was on the Brenner pass already at that time. As a matter of fact Hitler came to Italy, I think, in '38 right after the Anschluss. I remember because I was living in a hotel with another Viennese who was also Jewish and we were called to the police and held there the whole day. They were very friendly to us but they were afraid that people would do something to Hitler. But I remember that Mussolini did not come to greet him. Just the king greeted him and Mussolini never came because he didn't care too much for Hitler but he had very little choice. On the other hand the king cared even less.

The king cared even less but the king was not a very strong personality, it seemed.

Do you have any other recollections that you would like to tell us. Anything that we've forgotten?

Right offhand I don't remember anything. Maybe later on I will think of something then I will let you know.

Well, thank you.

Thoughts About My Life

written by Otto's close friend, Kurt Elias when he was in his nineties

My memories of my own life are in part vague and in part very clear - not necessarily correct. I don't recall any of the details of the domestic troubles except by hearsay - undoubtedly subjective. I do remember being outraged when stopped by a policeman outside my school at age 8-9 from "fighting." I complained to my father at the dinner table that "I am not permitted to fight at home, I am not permitted to fight in school - now not in the street either?" The fact that I was not supposed to fight at all did not occur to me.

At that age I also apparently had a good memory for texts, could memorize well (without necessarily understanding). The result was that I was asked by my teacher to recite a poem (mind you, 8-9 years old) about alcoholism, while dressed as a painter with broadrimmed hat, a palette and brushes, white sailor suit etc. It was a raging success but I had no idea what I was saying.

My relationship to my sister, 15 months older, are vague at that stage but she claims to remember protecting me - e.g. taking the blame for a urinary stain on the floor for me.

At the age of 12-13 we were in Carinthia or Tirol (Iselsberg) for a summer vacation and at the end of the summer a Viennese guest (later known as journalist) named Hans Weigl [*I believe it was Hans Weigel*] wrote a poem about each Hotel guest. The only one I remember was mine: "*Der Bube boxt mit Kraft und Freude, liebt gleich was ihm wohl gefällt, liebt sich selbst, liebt alle Leute, liebt kurzum die ganze Welt!*" Roughly translated, "the boy boxes with vim and joy, loves at once what he likes, loves himself, loves all the people, in one word, loves the whole world.

My interest in the early teens were diverse, including music, Greek mythology (Grandfather was Greecist [*classicist*] at the University, art and philosophy.

At 10 years I started piano lessons (my father, upon request for permission, called it "headless art.") My sister was in line to do something with music (piano?) a year or two later but rejected it. My guess is that she wanted not to feel inferior when I showed some aptitude and also: she was repelled by my mother's excessive (truly!) enthusiasm about "my music." It has been a life-long aversion from music for her. It came to the point when she - going to a concert with her husband, given by a pianist friend - she waited in the entrance outside the music hall until the concert was over. (A rejection with genuine conviction - she was proud of her honesty and consistency).

I also joined the boy scouts about age 10, a rather (only our troop) left-wing bunch who had great influence on me. My first scoutmaster was a medical student who later became a psychiatrist in the USA. Then he was in the twenties of age. The group had diverse kids - a barber's son who worked in his father's shop, a violinist, a chemist (later famous enzyme researcher Otto Hofman-Gerstenhof who visited us decades later in USA. His son is now a major journalist in Vienna), a law student, two boys involved in learning tailoring, and one of my best friends, a non-Jewish son of the big-wheel agriculture (woodsman) official. He didn't know that he had a Jewish grandparent, which I knew.

Before Hitler's invasion of Austria 12 March 1938 Fritz Klimesch - my friend and schoolmate - who defended me in school against attack, joined illegally the Nazi party - but after the annexation - when he generously offered me protection - he was thrown out of the party, joined the transportation Corps of the German Army (Austria existed no more) and was killed, shot in the back while trying to escape into Yugoslavia (or Italy?).

I had two other good friends: OTTO GRÜNBAUM, a budding promising pianist who once even composed a song for me. By Nazi law he was Jewish even though his parents had converted Catholicism. He was a loving, soft-hearted gentle soul, left Vienna after I did and came to the USA. Still training to become a professional pianist (recitals etc) he was inducted into the US Army after marrying another pianist (Susi Hohenberg). After a short time overseas, he attempted to visit Richard Strauss and was killed (the war was over - he was occupation) His body was only found in the spring after the snow melted. The friendship with his widow continued until many years later. She had by that time moved to Seattle, became voice coach at the Seattle Opera, developed lymphoma and several years later died. She was so popular in the Orchestra that they gave a performance just for her, to defray the costs of her medical treatment.

My third good friend was Frank Bellac, who at the time in school was a Swiss citizen. His father was a big-wheel in Radio (RAV/AG) It took me over a year of courting him before we became friends. He was and emailed an avid hiker and mountain climber. He also did not know that after Nazi law he was totally Jewish (the Nazis expressed it in 100%, 75% etc. - which is of course nonsense). We once were at the Habsburg Schönbrunn castle with him when - walking backwards with my camera - I fell into the pond in the shallow water, with the camera, on the cement edge of the pool. My mother, Frank Bellac and I dried out at home and kept the embarrassing event from my father. Two days later - at lunch - he told us that he knew. It reinforced my impression that he was omniscient and omnipotent.

My first year in *Realgymnasium [Stubenbastei],* (age 10-18) with Latin (not Greek, which I took for a year privately), and French (English privately), was traumatic for me. In the first place, my mother, under the pretext of having to go to the market (daily?) crosstown, walked me to school in the morning, making me a bit of a laughing stock among school mates. That lasted for several years, making it difficult to form friendships, isolating me and increasing my excessive closeness to my mother. It also led (age 10) to difficulties in writing German essays so that I flunked German the first quarter (1928). When my mother went to a parent-teacher conference with Dr. Norma Linker (orig. name Nuchem Lev) and burst into speechless tears when the teacher told her to take me out of school because *"Der ist ja blöd"* i.e. he clearly is stupid. My father took a day off from the Clinic (Wenchelbad) where he worked and told the teacher that he - now medical Professor - was also a slow developer - to be patient with me. By the end of the year, I was doing well. In between, my mother (without my father's knowledge) took me for psychological counseling with Dr. Fritz Rede - then a high school teacher, later a leading child psychologist (He wrote the well known book "Children Who Hate") I shall never forget the meeting 80 years ago, when he asked me the simple question "Do you daydream a lot?" I said that I did and he said "What about?" And I answered "BAD THINGS." I have no idea what I meant by that, but protested that he only asked me about what subject, while I answered with a value judgment. He indicated that he thought I was constantly sitting in judgment on myself and suggested I do handiwork, drawing etc. to redirect my preoccupation to the outside world.

It worked for me, and in retrospect makes me realize how early children start trying to figure out who they really are. That search still goes on. It involved wondering whether I was Jewish or Christian, whether I was German or Austrian, whether I was an artist or a scientist, whether I was American or Austrian refugee etc.

In 1933 the Christian Socialist (Dr Dollfuss) [Dollfuss was actually a Christian Fascist] became Austrian chancellor and a law was passed to have every schoolroom have a crucifix on the wall. We had religion class and there were separate Catholic (10) Protestant (5) and Jewish (3) students. Our Rabbi had the nice name of Taglicht (daylight).

In 1934 there was a revolution from the left - general strike - all streetcars stopped in their tracks.(The story goes that one absent-minded professor was still sitting along in a streetcar hours into the strike, reading.) The government called out the troops to shoot with howitzers at the "red" community homes of the labor people. My later scoutmaster, Curt Ponger, was one of the workers in those buildings being shot at. Labor was suppressed. Even though strong in the city (Vienna), they were weak in the countryside.

Later the same year, the Nazis tried a *Putsch* (take over of the government) and assassinated Dr. Dollfuss. The strongly Catholic *Heimwher* (home defense) defeated that attempt and postponed the inevitable for 4 years.

To say that these events made all of us very insecure is an understatement. The summer of 1935, my sister and I spent in England for 8 weeks to learn the language. It was interesting to learn about another culture. In 1933, I spent one week in Gödöllö in Hungary at an international Jamboree, where we lived in tents and met scouts from all over the world (my first meeting with a black person!). It was exhilarating to feel that there is friendship and brotherhood around the world - a dream!!

During gym class (1935?) I was knocked down and fell on my head with a short period of unconsciousness (concussion). I was sent home by ambulance and the janitor called my mother to tell her that I was coming by ambulance. When she

frantically wanted to know what happened, he blandly told her "You'll see, he will be there soon!". For one week I stayed in bed with liquid diet (that was "therapy").
During the late 1934 -1936 period there was a lot of political activity in Vienna from all parties - gluing stickers unto walls and doors. Frank Bellac and I collected them. I had a whole album scraped off walls etc. On our way home from school a man stopped us and asked what school we went to and later reported us to the authorities for "distributing political maters" which we did not do.
I got a "C" in deportment and was quite upset, especially when my father sided with the authorities even though he knew I was innocent. He stated that that was a permanent blot on my record that could taint my name and my future!
In 1936 I graduated from High School (*Matura*) after strenuous final exams. During the years around then (2-3?) I had a girlfriend (Pia). Totally platonic but very intense with lots of moves and dancing some parties. She later married a photographer and moved to Geneva [??] and had one daughter, Barbara. Pia died some years ago. Incidentally, my dancing for Vienna concepts was good enough for me to be invited to take a Government employee's daughter to the Ball of the City of Vienna, making me be in the movie news report about dancing in the [??] - a friend from Paris called to say he saw me!
Two important lessons were drummed into me as I grew up. One was, that one can take everything away from me, but my knowledge! Also, that money - while necessary - is not the prime goal in life - not physical possessions. These two "rules" were somewhat of a handicap coming to America - but called for warm, close friendships for the rest of my life.
The conflict between my artistic, emotional mother and my rational, scientific father was so blatant and as dutiful son, I had to love them both - it made it necessary to find a coping mechanism with both and their inevitable conflict. Over the decades I decided (and succeeded to some degree) to combine the artistic emotional in me with the rational scientific and become eventual the kind of physician who is competent, knowledgeable but also warm and caring. Needless to say, permitting yourself to be emotionally involved with a parent (caring for her/him, liking her/him) can be psychologically painful, seductive and dangerous - often misinterpreted. That's the kind of difficult to himself Doctor I decided to be. An old saying from Greek Literature (Kreon) states "Not to join in hate, but to join in love, is what I am here for."

In 1936 - fresh out of HS graduation - I joined the Austrian Army as a volunteer for one year (light artillery Regiment!). I was so poor at the mounted Artillery (horseback riding), that they transferred me to the motorized division. In my outfit was a Prince Hohenlohe who was not very bright but quite posh And fat. A Jewish friend Otto Marmonk was there among others. He had a motorcycle with a small side-wagon in which I rode often (scared as hell!). Late in Spring 1936, we were on a maneuver and 28 of us soldiers on an open truck which, on a sudden swerve to avoid a policemen on a motorcycle, tipped the truck over and we were thrown headfirst at 30 miles speed into the gravelly tarred Landstrasse-Hauptstrasse. My second concussion, to the point that I did not feel it when they sewed up a 1-1/2" laceration on the left cheek and the forehead. I just want to be left alone, no anesthesia. When I awoke the next morning my father and mother were peacefully standing at my bedside - bandages covering 2/3 of my face. Since my parents had had an angry contentious divorce in 1935, my first and only thought was that I had to almost die for my parents to be at peace with each other. Later that week my father (professor of medicine) came to visit when the policeman from the motorcycle that caused the accident and broke 10 ribs on one side - was going on the bedpan, begging to be taken off. My father (since none of the male Catholic nurses responded) went across the ward, expertly taking him off the commode, including wiping his behind clean. When he returned to my bedside he said "This should show and teach you that it is never below your dignity to help somebody in distress "- and he was an outstanding teacher. In September 1937 I inscribed at the Vienna University to study medicine (starting with physics, chemistry, anatomy and Patriotism(!)). We (4 of us) shared dissecting a cadaver and we studied hard. During that time, my father's father died. I went to a lecture by the famous author Sholem Asch (whose son had just converted to Christianity and Sholem had written a book about it - later, "The Nazarene". The meeting took place at the Bnai Brith Lodge - my father presiding. The talk was about father-son relationships but hit too close to home for me to have a reaction or even a memory.

The year before, while still in Army uniform, I had the sweet duty to pick up Pablo Casals at the railroad station to take him to his hotel. My mother - who arranged for him (by mail) to play a whole concert program at her friend's (Frau Lederer) house and my mother stayed friends with Casals for life - even was invited to

Budapest for a premiere performance there (later, when I was already in the USA).

On the night of 12 March 1938 - while I was at a scout meeting in the first district (Inner City) Hitler's Army had crossed the border to occupy Austria. 10 days before, the Austrian chancellor flew to Berchtesgaden to void the "Annexation", was treated by Hitler like dirt, he returned to Vienna and announced a Plebiscite, a vote for Sunday, March 15th. HItler by 13 March, sent 700 planes over Vienna, successfully scaring everybody and taking over the election Sunday with 95% of Austrians allegedly voting for Hitler. That night my aunt Melitta and uncle Gabor - on the second floor of our house (owned by my father) - committed suicide. I was not permitted to enter the University to get my medical tools out - had to send a non-Jewish friend in.

It took a long while before I really understood about all that would change in my life! A friend of Maria Lederer of Casals fame had an American friend who would give me an affidavit for the USA, promising I would not become a financial burden to the state. My mother's sister (Herta) had a friend in England who could put me up in Cambridge, England on Kings Parade on an English visitors visa - waiting from July to November for the visa to USA and a trip across on the old Normandie. It was all an adventure and still I didn't realize the gravity of it all (healthy? denial?)

My father reported (when asked) to Adolf Eichman as my father was a high functionary in the Jewish Community of Vienna (Kultusgemeinde). I could never overcome a negative reaction to my father quoting Eichman as calling him a "*Ein ganzer Kerl*" (great guy) and my father being proud of that praise.! I would not be! The day after Hitler marched into Austria, I walked around Vienna and it was a glorious spring day (14 March '38). I walked across Hero Square (Heldenplatz) with the Habsburg Palace and the two equestrian statues (Prince Eugen of Savoy, Prince Charles of Lorraine) and the lilac was in full bloom. For one moment I felt outraged about this magnificence in the face of my life being in stumbling state. But within seconds I had the thought that the lilac is telling me something! There is a rebirth every year of <u>bloom</u> and <u>aroma</u> - hence there IS A FUTURE and hope. Lilac has ever since been my reminder of survival and hope! Arriving in the USA after a few months in Cambridge with lovely Mrs. Boston started the new life. The Wolf family who gave me the affidavit were childless. He was a good physician with common sense but his wife was socially very ambitious - with "upper class" yearnings and - like many luxuries she amassed - collected ME and wanted to run my life even though I was nineteen - after 1 year in the Austrian Army etc. Max Wolf would take a bus, a subway, go to a 5 and 10c store while she went by taxi. She often gave me money for a taxi and I would take a bus and save the money. This saving let me later survive going back to school (see later).

Through my stupidity, the relationship of the Wolfs and my father and his second wife Ada was destroyed and so eventually was mine, and I became independent from the Wolfs. They had put me up in the Hotel Carlisle (76th and Madison) where I could order food on room service and invite some of my poor refugee friends for a meal. Edith Wolf was furious and suggested I should drop all my Austrian friends, stop trying to get my mother over from Vienna and NEVER wear a red tie ("they'll think you are a Commie").

I joined the Austro-American Youth (the founder of which was my Vienna scoutmaster and had been in jail in Vienna for being a Communist) but had to interrupt attending there when I received a scholarship to Southwestern College in Memphis, Tennessee (I had to look it up on a map. The only Memphis I knew was in Egypt). I started there in early February 1939 for the second semester and graduated in summer 1940 with a BS degree in Anatomy. My 1-1/2 years in Memphis were very helpful. Arriving with only some knowledge of English (months in England and 2 months in New York) the warm and hospitable environment of the South enabled me to adapt to life in a new country much easier. In retrospect, I was a curiosity there in a student body of only 300+ - a Viennese (identified with waltzes , many Strausses, Haydn, Mozart and Beethoven) and not with Hitler). I got along very well with the students - both female and male - and the teachers. One advice given me the first month there by a Rhode Scholar not much older than me (Clarence Pendleton Lee) was "there are two courses about American History - Before the Civil War and After the Civil War. Nothing happened here before or after - Don't take either!" I am forever sorry I followed his advice. The president and founder of the College - Southwestern, now Rhodes College, "Papa Diehl" treated me like a son. Peyton Rhodes was my physics teacher. Mr Davis my biology teacher who - on the side did research on Malaria. Professor Kelse in "The Philosophy of Religion" (in a

Presbyterian College) welcomed lively stimulating ecumenical discussions that I remember to this day. While there the first year I lived in a dormitory with the football players, which was fun. Their language was not necessarily appropriate for a drawing room, which I found out in several embarrassing instances. One local family stands out. Prof. Robert Pond (Mathematics) lived one block off the campus with his wife Ethel and their four children. Mary, the older daughter, was working at the College (later with her husband). Harriet was a student with me and I was much enamored with her and saw a lot of her. She and her younger brother were much into music and we did a lot singing together - both with the College Glee Club and the Memphis Symphony - but also among ourselves. I may have introduced Schubert and Brahms songs to them all. Once the Polish-born tenor Jan Kiepura came to town for a concert. His accompanist was a friend of Susi Hoheberg (see above) and called and introduced me - and the Pond clan. This is how it came about that the Ponds and I took Kiepura to the Memphis Airport (1940). On the way - Christmas Eve,- we all sang Christmas carols together in the car! It was an unforgettable experience! John - the younger son (Robert Jr I did not know well) graduated with me and joined the Navy during WWII. He later settled outside Washington D.C. with Nancy, another graduate and had delightful children and grandchildren. Some (several) of John's kids joined the Peace Corps and they were all bright, sound and caring people. I am still in contact with him by phone - albeit in a nursing home. One illuminating story about him - an elder in the Presbyterian Church - he initiated a joint cultural program of his church with a local synagogue. There is an example of ecumenical activism! We saw in the local Evergreen Presbyterian Church choir together and I was so impressed by him and his whole family that I joined that church. This was the first (and only?) time in my life that I saw and felt people truly living the spirit of the Bible ("love thy neighbor") My experience at home had been lip-service - while acting with racial hatred and resentment on *both* sides of my family. What a contrast! That's why I (who had been Bar Mitzvah in Vienna) joined <u>that</u> church. Today I consider myself a Jewish Citizen of the World. I was going to remain in Memphis for life until the U of Tennessee Medical school broke their word to me. They promised to take me into Medical School if I took a Master's degree in Anatomy. I took the degree (1940-41) and wrote a thesis on "cyclic changes in neuronal Nissl bodies in the cervical ganglion of rats. It was frustrating work and exciting, but they broke their promise and I returned to New York with a BS and MS after my name and acceptance to the Flower Fifth Avenue Hospital Medical School as of Sept. 1941.

Arriving in NYC in 1941 with two suitcases, a Master's thesis and very little money, I took a small room to live in on the corner of Madison and 106th Street. The room was so small I used to say that I had to take the doorknobs into bed with me. Down the hall was another Viennese student, Leo Bellac (Bellak) who already had a Master's or PhD in Psychology, knew the Freud family and took medicine - as far as I gathered - for the MD degree. This earned my contempt for not taking medicine seriously enough. In addition, he irked me by having frequent and varied overnight companions. Another memory of that time was the noise that emanated from the third room on that floor which indicated a life-and-death fight between a woman and a man. Not much later, they emerged arm-in-arm, lovey-dovey. The tumult was apparently their idea of a sex life and happiness.

My meals were mostly in the corner "café" of one building where the man behind the counter had such an obvious abnormal pulsation in the side of the neck (indicative of an aortic aneurysm, usually syphylitic) that we named the place "Charcot Joint", a reference to the syphylitic joint destruction described by Charcot.

My best friend in school was John Kazaijian, later called himself Martin. We agreed in our rebellion against authority (passive) and long discussions on ethics, etc. One such was "what would our choice be when we needed surgery? A brilliant but morally defective surgeon or a competent but ethical one." I have not solved that conundrum yet, but lean to the ethical one.

During my medical school days I developed a rapidly growing tendon mass in my buttock. My typical medical school fear was a rapidly growing malignancy. The chief of surgery, Dr René Kaufman 5ft1in, with a blatant Napoleon complex, operated and found a benign fatty tumor into which a hemorrhage had caused the "growth".

With a Master's degree in anatomy, the first year was fairly easy. One of the anatomy teachers was Dr Clifford Haynor, who was a real gentleman. Many years later I made a middle of the night house call to his wife. She had dementia and an abdominal aortic aneurysm- and he only wanted his own diagnosis confirmed. The chief of surgery, Dr Harald Tharaldsen, was less of a gentleman.

The first week of school he walked across the front of the classroom saying "At the end of this year some of you will be bus drivers! So work hard!" I found this less than inspiring. My subsistence was earned by running the elevator of Flower Hospital, 106th and 5th, now the Cardinal Spellman Center, from 6 to 8 in the morning before classes. For a while I also gave anatomy lessons to a middle-aged plastic surgeon who wanted to pass his Boards. Later, in school, I had a job at the [???] Hospital (6 blocks south) as morgue keeper - nights and weekends. I got that job with permission to eat and sleep there through the good offices of Dr Paul Klemper (of "lupus" and ground substance fame.). When there was a question of $5.00 monthly, less salary than I need to survive, this old Viennese friend of my father, Paul K, paid the difference out of his own pocket. Where will you find people with such generosity? I have been blessed to always find such people in strenuous, difficult times who helped - not just with money!

When I graduated with my MD degree in June 1944, the ceremony was held at the Academy of Medicine and - to my surprise - I was number <u>one</u> in my class and received a welcome $100 price for that. Added to my happiness was that my father (a teacher of medicine at Flower) was in the audience.

During that whole time I didn't have enough money for "dating", going to movies (except the local [???] On Madison and 103rd street) and steady relationships were impossible. I had social contact with OTTO GRÜNBAUM, the pianist, Peter Lynn, the later Jungian Sr Analyst, with Susi Hohenberg, who later married Otto. In between I did attend some Austro-American Youth meetings (103rd off Columbus) and even went on some excursions with them, especially to the "left wing" Nature Friends Camp in Midvale, N.J.

The founder of that outfit was Curt Ponger (4-5- years my senior), who had been an avowed Communist in the past, jailed by the Nazi regime in Buchenwald. He had been my scoutmaster in my teens and a thoroughly reasonable person. The program included weekend outings, lectures, and on one memorable occasion, a concert in which a performance of the - to me previously unknown - "Alte Rhapsodie" by Brahms absolutely SENT ME!

I was never approached to join the Communist Party but gather that some others were - especially by Otto Verber, who was my assistant in the Vienna Boy Scouts [and later Ponger's brother-in-law]. As I understand it, after many conversations with Ponger early and late, he was hired by the US Government for a job of helping with his knowledge (inside) of concentration camps. His left-leaning was known well enough to US authorities, so that they did not give him a Commission, nor had him wear a uniform while meeting with all manner of high functionaries. This was the time when Russia was our friend and ally and we (the group) were singing "Peat Bog Soldiers" and Russian songs too, the Ballad of America, Robeson etc. According to Curt Ponger, he came back to base in Germany after two weeks of vacation and felt "there was "a different wind blowing" with obvious hostility to Russia, like a change of policy. He resigned his job (Army?), gave up his US citizenship and returned to Vienna with his wife in the meantime with him, they opened a hardware store in Vienna. We visited there briefly. About 1953 he was arrested in Vienna and spent - after being sentenced - 10 years in American prison. He had all kinds of trades from jeweler to goldsmith and claimed he learned dentistry, among other things, in prison. He also claimed that he had NOT given any secrets to the Russians (as accused) but he thought it might have been his brother-in-law, Otto V. I will never know. In my second marriage, on a trip to Vienna, he drove Gloria and me to the *Wiener Wald* (Vienna Woods) and was generally very helpful. He had remarried. His wife had committed suicide (or died from a neglected ruptured appendix ?) while he was in prison. I gather their son is a well-known jazz musician in Vienna now. The reason for this much detail is that Ponger was a major influence on my life - bridging for me the barrier of social prejudice and introducing me into "worldwide brotherhood", help me overcome class consciousness and see the world in more realistic but humanitarian way.

The social group mentioned earlier (OTTO, Susi, Peter Lynn etc) were a regular - occasional- enjoyment, most often with Susi accompanying, or all of us singing *Lieder* and parts of Opera (usually Mozart). Peter Lynn is and was a veritable encyclopedia of especially operatic music.

While all this was going on, my father and his second wife Ada (Dr. Hirsch, Pediatrician, with early publication about Erythroblastosis Fetalis <u>before</u> blood groups were discovered by Landsteiner, the famous or infamous Rh factor as cause) lived their lives in the city and my sister had married a Viennese Ann Arbor graduated dentist and moved to Detroit.

My internship at Mt Sinai (1941-44) was grueling, with roughly 3-4 hours of nightly sleep - working every other night through and two weekends out of three.

I still have friends from those days - such as a 94 (?) year old Otolaryngologist Dr Leon Arnold - still in practice and with it. We used to have midnight meals on one of the hospital floors, often talking about everything.

The next year, I was resident in internal medicine at Metropolitan Hospital (then on Welfare Island) where I met my wife Nina Rutcher and fell in love with her and married her in 1946. The attraction for me was that she was politically and philosophically in agreement with me (in retrospect, possibly her Dutch American background, identification with my also chronically depressed mother ?) And rather beautiful in a shy sort of way. This was to become a problem later when my attempts (or so I believe) to pull her out of her depression were unsuccessful and made her withdraw more and get more depressed. Yet, we had a lot of interesting and fun times together including raising three children. During the time on Welfare Island I initiated and ran a Clinical Pathological weekly conference with the New England Journal in hand. I thought it was useful and I enjoyed it.

From 1946 to 1948 I was in the US Army (my second Amy) - this time as a physician - first at Ft. Sam Houston and then the better part at Ft. Bragg. Without any training (except 3 months on the psychiatric ward A at Mt Sinai) I was assigned to the Psychiatric section (and the prison ward). The local Army Chaplain and the regimental surgeon taught me some budget. I learned how and why to inspect and judge mess halls and respect for authority (some?) I learned that I knew nothing about alcoholism, when a Major N. Had an acute delirium. It was news to me since I had known and liked him and knew nothing about his drinking. Everybody else did.

Another interesting episode I remember is the MPs bringing in a very drunk young lieutenant of the 82nd Airborne Division. Shortly after Major (or General?) Westmoreland, of later fame, rode up telling me he was with the lieutenant all evening and he had not had too much to drink. I was amazed to find myself saying to him that this was MY expertise, not his - and the man was drunk.

Nina had been afraid of consequences of my recurrent conflicts with authorities and possible consequences. I had had a "fight" with several of my chiefs at Mt. Sinai! The Chief Resident in Psychiatry (Dr George Nambey) once responded to my "eruption" with a comment: "Kurt, I am not your father!"

Peter was born in Ft Bragg and we lived in a small house off the post and enjoyed the generally secure life. I had to relearn how to drive with Nina's help after having learned in the Austrian Army first (1936).

After my discharge from the Army as Captain, I had a fellowship in Pathology at Mt Sinai, then a Cancer Society fellowship also at Mt Sinai - learning, learning and running the tumor Clinic there for one year, making a living working part-time in the Butcher's Union Health Center and one other center. I was all over the place at that point, from 14th Street to 56th Street to Mt Sinai, covering night calls for some of the Mt Sinai Medical Staff. I was busy, when I met at a social occasion Drs Charles and Ann Bolstein- chief of Radiotherapy and the wife a pediatrician - she became our pediatrician. Charley told me that Montefiore and its medical group was looking for an internist and in January 1953, I started in the Bronx. We bought a house in Yonkers after having lived in Queens for a while (since out of the Army). Joan was born while we had been living in Queens. For a while we were staying on in Queens while I worked in the Bronx. When on call at night (covering the entire Bronx and lower Westchester for the HIP group) I would stay overnight in the hospital and at times having supper at the Botstein house at their cordial invitation. Among their children I met Leon, later to become president of Bard College, conductor of the American Symphony, and generally a leading light of culture and knowledge in NYC. He was a teenager then.

Just before moving to Yonkers in 1953, Margaret was born - with her we moved into the new just built house - the builder and his slightly aberrant son and his wife across the street. Having a house of my own, the really first time in my life was all new and scary. Nina's uncle, who had been an electrical engineer in the Canal Zone, came to visit and "rewired the house" which he found unsafe.

Our house (2 story and basement) was on a dead end street and some of the neighbors became my patients. The children enjoyed the local public school and I was proud when my older daughter later briefly dated a black classmate, evincing an absence of prejudice not so common in those days. All three children joined the youth group at the local Methodist Church and Peter even (at 17) was president of the senior youth. He invited me to speak to the young people about "Your body, a Tabernacle" during the height of the drug period. He uttered some doubts afterwards that anybody really listened. At that time I was also invited with Peter's scout troop. Peter became Eagle Scout and the Mayor (Flynn) honored him in Eastchester Town Hall. I was also given an honorary something after an overnight in the Berkshires.

Our house had a magnificent peach tree when we moved in, but it only lasted a couple of years. A lovely back porch looked on a small yard with a little block house hat we assembled ourselves.

After the war was over, my mother came to visit in Yonkers and I remember fondly the bond she established with Margaret, then about 5 years old.

At the hospital I was attending physician in oncology and on medicine for 4 months each for years (1953-1993) which was fairly strenuous with house calls. We (twenty some physicians) were having our offices on the hospital grounds in a separate building and were paid through the hospital by check. My salary for the first year was $8,500 and I had over 5000 services - including home and hospital visits. My service on the Cancer Department came about on my first interview with the Oncology Chief Dr Daniel Laszlo (first medical oncology, with all prior ones part of and run by surgeons) He was a Hungarian true gentleman who had been a lowly resident under my father in Vienna in the 1920s (Clinic K. Wenchelbad of [???] fame) He remembered me from Vienna and my sister sitting on his lap in our apartment in Liechtensteinstrasse 2. He was a most wonderful teacher. When he became ill with a brain tumor, which made him mute and "absent" to sensory input, sitting at his bedside was some of the most painful experiences of my life. This was later repeated when my father died of Alzheimers at age 90. The sensation of losing contact in devastating. That must have been the sensation my mother had when she visited us - not feeling any relevance in our own lives - and being needed - not able to reconnect.

Medicine and oncology were fascinating to me. On the Oncology service I was dismayed by the fact that nurses and doctors didn't communicate well. The doctors worked on a different level just wrote the orders, with the nurses spending much more (10 times?) time with patients, had essential knowledge of patients that the doctors missed totally. I decided to make weekly rounds with the nurses who often had a grasp of the patients' fears, fantasies and family interactions that could be essential in making medical, therapeutic and general decisions. Gradually, the interns and residents joined, realizing they would benefit. Last, but not least, some attendings joined and it became known as Dr

Elias' rounds - spread to other services. Even the Chief of Medicine from Mt Sinai once came to check out what we were doing.

One of my warmest memories is being invited to a small luncheon by three former oncology nurses and one resident for my 90th birthday! We tried to publish our experiences but medical journal rejected our paper, calling it "voyeuristic" since we did indeed write about some of the feelings nurses and doctors about death, futility, impotence and healing. I arranged for Dr. Rene Dubos to speak to the whole hospital staff (nurses and doctors, young and old) about the topic "Curing sometimes, helping often, consoling always" (written on Trudeau's Statue in Saran [T6????]

In addition, I was actively involved (not the initiator) in a visiting lecture by Dr Elizabeth Kübler-Ross and another by Dr. Bruno Bettelheim. (I sat next to him at the dinner and found him excessively pleased with himself).

I thoroughly enjoyed teaching interns and residents and also learning plenty from them. Being asked to discuss a Clinicians Pathological Conference was a thrill also.

I had one bad experience being publicly (in the hospital) criticized for ordering barium enema on a young color cancer patient with partial obstruction, whose past history of colitis as a child neither the surgeon or I was aware of. Upon investigating my office charts as a consequence of the Chief of Gastroenterology , my notes were found to be inadequate - too short and often meaningless. That was actually true! Even though I spent more time with my patients than most - just did not write it down.

 In retrospect, after losing my life environment as a teenager in the flight from Hitler, I had built a new life and the Medical Group was my new FAMILY. Being rejected and abandoned by most of these colleagues reawakened the Hitler memory. The rejection at that time had no real (conscious) emotional reaction, but the "rejection" at Montefiore led to a real and severe depression for a whole year (insomnia, weight loss and the works). In 1993 I finally left Montefiorr and opened an office in Manhattan. Private practice in Manhattan was more unpleasant to me because money was involved. All my life, I had little sense or prepared for money - but I learned. Being a devoted helper does not mean you should not be paid properly.

In my second marriage (to Gloria Karshaw Clare - a psychiatrist) I learned a lot about the reality of life. That went with an increased (appropriate) self-respect and self-confidence.

Most of my life I was in one way or another an outsider - a Jew amount Protestant or "partial" Christian among Jews; a Jew among Nazis; an Austrian among Americans, Southerners, New Yorkers. There was no end to my search to where I belong. I know now - to myself! And my ideals.

One thread that has run through my life has been the presence of depression and suicide. My mother had attempted suicide twice with my being totally at a loss to understand - but engendering a strong obligation to love and support her more. When Hitler marched into Vienna in 1938, my father's sister and her chronically depressed husband committed suicide the next day. Their son, a lawyer who moved to Israel with his family, had chronic depression. While I was transiently in Cambridge, England, waiting for my visa to the States, I read in the British Paper that one of my high school classmates had committed suicide. It so happened that I ran into him two days before and only said hello without speaking to him. For years afterwards I tortured myself, thinking I could have saved or done something to prevent the tragedy. My first wife Nina had a tragic background. Her father abandoned his wife and two girls when Nina was 7 years old. Her mother - in a frustrating new relationship (as far as I gather) drowned herself in the ocean in San Diego and the two girls were raised largely by two elderly half-sisters in Westchester. It was not surprising that Nina had (as did her sister) severe depression and at least one suicide attempt. The obligation I had always (unconsciously) felt to help, to save, to cheer, was surely part of my genuine love for my wife. The fact that I could not help and cause "cheerful change" was very hard on both of us and eventually led to divorce.

After the divorce I met - through my sister - Dr. Clare and we got married a year later. Her joie-de-vivre and ability to enjoy - introducing me to the [???], to accept that it is OK to buy new clothes, opened mental and real doors for me.

There surely are things I remember incorrectly and other that have slipped my memory even though they might be significant. For this I apologize.

The trials and tribulations of my life were bearable because of the memory of the glorious spring day 13 March 1938 on Hero Square in Vienna, when the blooming lilac in the face of apocalyptic events (Hitler) reminded me of spring - and with it hope will always return.

Otto and Kurt attended the STUBENBASTEI Gymnasium where Kurt seemed more aware or more affected by anti-Semitism

This Wikipedia article tells the history of the school from 1938-1955

As early as March 17, 1938, shortly after the annexation of Austria (and before the so-called referendum on April 10, 1938!), director Jungwirth and four professors were relieved of their posts by decree (line: 2213/1-IIa-1938) . three other teachers were transferred and a provisional new head (Tschernach - teacher for M, geometry) was appointed. [12]On March 19, the faculty was sworn in to the Führer and Reich Chancellor. On March 25th, a decree regulated the introduction of the "German salute" at the beginning and end of each lesson! By Pentecost 1938, eight willing teachers had completed Nazi leadership training courses in the sense of re-education. The foreword of the 1938 annual report (the school had 16 classes at the time) is a contemporary document: the newly appointed director wrote there "... all Jewish teachers were initially fired, which put an end to the shameful and unnatural situation in which Jews teach Aryan children was, the separation of the Aryan from the Jewish pupils followed in a very short time; With that, pure, fresh air flowed into our institution, which was probably free of Jews for the first time in its existence. Already on the 29th On April 1st we were able to receive the newly assigned Aryan pupils from the 2nd district, the way was cleared for those major tasks that the school has to fulfill in the National Socialist state. ... Our new school must also familiarize the young people entrusted to it with the problems arising from the special situation in Germany, which are caused by the lack of space and raw materials, and keep reminding the young people of the difficult tasks will approach them later. The times when many young people only studied in order to acquire a so-called general education and then believed that they could look down on all those who worked with educational arrogance are finally over!" the path was clear for those major tasks that schools have to fulfill in the National Socialist state. ... Our new school must also familiarize the young people entrusted to it with the problems arising from the special situation in Germany, which are caused by the lack of space and raw materials, and keep reminding the young people of the difficult tasks will approach them later. The times when many young people only studied in order to acquire a so-called general education and then believed that they could look down on all those who worked with educational arrogance are finally over!" the path was clear for those major tasks that schools have to fulfill in the National Socialist state. ... Our new school must also familiarize the young people entrusted to it with the problems arising from the special situation in Germany, which are caused by the lack of space and raw materials, and keep reminding the young people of the difficult tasks will approach them later. The times when many young people only studied in order to acquire a so-called general education and then believed that they could look down on all those who worked with educational arrogance are finally over!" ... Our new school must also familiarize the young people entrusted to it with the problems arising from the special situation in Germany, which are caused by the lack of space and raw materials, and keep reminding the young people of the difficult tasks will approach them later. The times when many young people only studied in order to acquire a so-called general education and then believed that they could look down on all those who worked with educational arrogance are finally over!" ... Our new school must also familiarize the young people entrusted to it with the problems arising from the special situation in Germany, which are caused by the lack of space and raw materials, and keep reminding the young people of the difficult tasks will approach them later. The times when many young people only studied in order to acquire a so-called general education and then believed that they could look down on all those who worked with educational arrogance are finally over!"

The matriculation examination held in the summer of 1938 is also interesting: So-called "homework" (written for the Matura – as it appears again in 2015 as VWA) came from the school reform period: "The Danube, a major waterway" (Gg); "Prince Eugene's Relations to Art and Science" (H = history); "The Human Eye" (Ng); "Fuels" (Ch); "Tyrol from 1805–1815" (H); "Production of an anti-scatter lens" (Ph); "model dispersion filter" (Ph); "The hair of man" (Ng). The (new) topics for the written Matura from May 30th are also informative: In German to choose from: "1. Easter 1938, the end of the German Passion; 2. Technology and chemistry, the great German powers; 3. Agnes Bernauer, Common good comes before self". There were also written exams in Latin and French – only in 8b the 3rd optional topic stood out: *"L'Connection (le rattachement)"*. Conversely, only one example of the Matura in mathematics - this time at the 8a - had a relevant question: "Two artillery observers A and B, whose mutual distance is a, see the muzzle flash of an enemy battery C at the angle BAC = Alpha and ABC = Beta, while they see their own battery D lying backwards at the angle BAD = gamma and ABD = delta. How far is your own battery from the enemy battery and which side? of the auxiliary target A receives its own battery when shooting at the enemy? (a= 1950 m, Alpha = 22.30; Beta = 12.36, Gamma = 49.30, Delta = 73.48)". Of the 12 and 32 pupils who had been declared mature in the two classes of 1938, two in 8a and 12 in 8b indicated that they wanted to be an officer.

At the end of April 1938, as a result of the German invasion and the seizure of power by the National Socialists, 274 of 634 pupils who were classified as "racially inferior" under the racial laws of the Third Reich, almost all of them of Jewish descent, were forced to leave the school. [13] They were first brought together in RG II, the present-day Sigmund-Freud-Gymnasium, which was then still located in Kleine Sperlgasse.

Addendum: In June 1986, on the initiative of teachers at the grammar school, the Federal Minister for Education, Herbert Moritz, gave a late honorary Matura to the following former pupils of years 6a and 6b, born in 1937/38: Arthur Cooper, Henry Grunwald, Herbert Lamm, Paul Lynton, Egon Schwarz, [14] Georg Temmer, Eric Kruh, [15] John K. Kautsky. [16]

Second World War
During the Second World War, the school building was confiscated several times for Wehrmacht purposes, classes were housed elsewhere (about 1941 in the high school for boys, Radetzkystraße in the 3rd district, 1942 8th classes in the academic grammar school, 1944 in the high school, Schottenbastei in the 1st district). During this time, all the young people at the school were called up again and again for auxiliary services or for

the Reich Labor Service . In the winter of 1942/43, classes started at 9 a.m. due to blackout measures, and the lessons were reduced to 35–40 minutes. In 1944, lower school students were taken to the children's deportation home in Klamm am Semming. High school students were drafted as Luftwaffe helpers.

The pupils Franz Putschi, Ernst Krivanec, Friedrich Leibnitz and Anton Sieberer, who were drafted as Luftwaffe helpers in the 7th class in 1943/44 , were sentenced by a court martial on April 22, 1944 for undermining the armed forces after an accusation by their superior lieutenant on April 5, 1944 (Among other things, they expressed their opinion that "the war will soon come to an end, since Germany has already lost it....") [17], and they had tried to set up a resistance group. They were sentenced to three months in the Kaiser-Ebersdorf juvenile prison and were expelled from all higher schools by decree of the Reich Ministry for Education and Public Education. On November 5, 1944, the school building was hit and damaged in an air raid. It shouldn't be the only war damage. [18] Numerous students and teachers were increasingly called up for military service in the Wehrmacht and the Volkssturm . In the catalog for the 8th grades, around February 1944, 17 out of 34 students left school early as Luftwaffe helpers at the Johannesberg battery (= on the south-eastern slope of the Laaer Berg). [19] The so-called "War Matura" took place in February!

A decree of February 22, 1944 decreed that due to the lack of raw materials, all brass door handles were to be replaced by wooden ones. The last decree that reached the school decreed that the school's teachers had to come together to do entrenchment work for the defense of Vienna. In March 1945 , Adolf Prochaska, for many years, removed the explosive charges that were still attached when a German Luftwaffe staff was withdrawn in the final days of the war [20]. In the days that followed, too, he tried to protect the school building and inventory from the advancing Red Army. Between April 6 [21] and April 9 [22] the front of the XXI. Guards Rifle Corps of the 3rd Ukrainian Front of the Red Army across the inner city. [23] On April 10, the German front was withdrawn behind the Danube Canal.

2nd Republic

When the fighting ended in Vienna at the end of April 1945, the Soviet military occupied the school and first set up an emergency hospital and then a telephone switchboard in the school building. Lessons could only be provisionally resumed on August 16, 1945. Classes of the RG for girls II. Schützengasse were also housed in the school building until 1948. On September 1, 1946, Radnitzky was brought back as director. As late as March 25, 1947, it was determined that 1,359 window panes were still missing as a result of the effects of the war.

In their book "Children of the Return" by Ernst Berger and Ruth Wodak, students describe "the Stubenbastei" as an interesting new "biotope" in which the different currents of the post-war period could develop freely. [24]

At the middle school competitions on June 25, 1949, students of the institution won the national competition in the 1000 meter run with a new Austrian best time of 2.38.7. From 1954/55, under the direction of the then director Franz Häußler, attempts to redesign the upper school were started. In doing so, the possibility of tying the diversified lessons a little closer together was tested. A topic could be treated from different points of view (German, history, geography, natural history, art, ...) at the same time, some teachers could also teach integrated lessons in one hour block with this goal. The matriculation examination was also based on such attempts. So-called "educational trips" were a culminating point. [25]

Stubenbastei's philosophy today

The Stubenbastei stands for democratic values, solidarity and peaceful co-existence. We condemn all forms of violence and aggression and stand for an open, pluralistic society. We see school as a place where diversity is lived—even day.
We are proud that people of different origins and nationalities come together here. It is the people who shape this place of lived diversity—the Stubenbastei—in everyday life. Political events must not lead to the exclusion of individuals because of their origin or their nationality.
The Stubenbastei is a place of peaceful cohesion where war and any form of violence have no place.

ALBERTGASSE Gymnasium was attended by Otto's sister Trude as well as Kurt's sister Hanna

This Wikipedia article tells the history of the school

The school was founded in 1905 as "K und K. [*Kaiser und König*] Staatsrealschule" at Josefstädterstraße 95, as a boys' school. [3] In 1909 the move to the current location at Albertgasse 18-22 took place, and from 1919 girls were also admitted. In 1935 the school was renamed "Robert Hamerling-Realgymnasium". [1]

After the annexation of Austria , the school was renamed "State High School for Boys" on May 2, 1938, non - Aryan students were housed and taught separately in parallel classes (Jewish classes). In addition, almost 190 Jewish pupils from other Viennese schools were assigned to this "collective school". [1]

After the end of the Second World War in 1945, the school was called the "Bundesrealgymnasium für Knaben". From the autumn of the same year, the Vienna Boys ' Choir completed their external examinations here every six months until June 2000 . [4]

In 1963 the school was renamed to its current name: Bundesgymnasium and Bundesrealgymnasium Wien 8. Girls were only accepted again in 1977 in the now co -educational grammar school.

In 2013, the school community of the Bundesrealgymnasium Albertgasse donated a stone of remembrance to commemorate the Jewish collection classes during the National Socialist era . [5] The association "Stones of remembrance Josefstadt" was responsible for the transfer. [6]

No social philosophy is expressed on the school's website.

Susanne, Otto's widow, remarried and had two children. Later, she moved from New York to Seattle. Below is her obituary published by the Seattle Times. Sadly there is no mention of her marriage to Otto.

Suzanne Szekely, Opera, Piano, Voice Coach, Founder Of School

Jun 24, 1991

Melinda Bargreen, Marla Williams

Suzanne Szekely, one of the region's most respected opera and vocal coaches, died June 19 after a nine-year struggle with lymphoma. She was 72.

Over the past 20 years, Mrs. Szekely was an invaluable mainstay of Seattle's music community, working with a list of singers and accompanists that includes virtually all the Northwest's best and busiest.

She was so widely respected that when musicians gathered to perform a benefit to help with her medical expenses in 1983, when she first contracted lymphoma, concert organizers had to turn away some volunteers because the program grew too long.

That benefit concert was a spontaneous expression of regard for Mrs. Szekely, exceeding all goals and paying off the bills in full.

"I am just overwhelmed that all my friends would do this," Mrs. Szekely said then. "I can't describe what it means to me."

Born in Vienna, Mrs. Szekely grew up in a musical atmosphere. Her grandfather was a friend of famed composer Alban Berg. Before World War II, she studied at the Vienna Conservatory. When war began, she moved to England, and later to the United States.

Mrs. Szekely's daughter, Christina Reimer, says the war caused tremendous upheaval in her mother's life but she remained determined to pursue her musical studies.

"My mother always had faith, a great sense of hope," Reimer says. "And a love of life. As one friend says, Suzanne laughed with more abandonment that anyone else. She really did have a wonderful laugh."

Settling in New York City, she continued her studies at the Juilliard School. Later, she joined the faculty of the widely respected Manhattan School of Music, where she taught piano and was operatic coach.

It was not until 1973 that Mrs. Szekely visited Seattle. After short visits, she decided she liked the area so well she would stay.

Mrs. Szekely served on the faculties of Cornish Institute and the University of Washington for five years before opening her own studio.

Seeming to possess limitless energy, Mrs. Szekely lectured and gave previews for Seattle Opera, and was active in the Ladies Musical Club and the National Association of Teachers of Singing. She also founded the independent Seattle Waldorf School and served on its board.

Fluent in every major operatic language, Mrs. Szekely was known as a first-rate accompanist who understood how to support and enhance the singer's performance. She knew the operatic repertoire thoroughly and helped countless aspiring singers learn the appropriate styles.

Known as a stickler for detail who demanded the highest standards, Mrs. Szekely usually got them. In return, she gave the best of herself.

"Since her death, so many of her friends have been calling to say Suzanne provided them with a vision and inspiration they'll never forget," Reimer says. "And I really can believe that. She delighted in teaching, in sharing ideas and music, oh, and food.

"She was always feeding somebody, always welcoming someone to her table, into her home."

With the help of the Eastside Hospice program, Reimer says, her mother was able to die with dignity and grace at home. "It made a tremendous difference to all of us," Reimer says. "It made it possible for us to be by her side every moment."

Mrs. Szekely is survived by her daughter, Christina Reimer, of Seattle, and a son, Daniel Szekely, and his wife Deborah, of Woodinville. She is also survived by seven grandchildren, Marcie Swift, of Seattle; Gabriel, Genevieve, and Tom Szekeley; Briana, Erin, and Devon Summers, all of Woodinville.

Peter Lynn - with whom Otto, Susanne and Kurt spent musical evenings was born in Vienna 1919 and died in 2012.

Dr. Lynn emigrated to New York in 1940 and co-founded the C.C. Young Institute and practiced Jungian analysis until shortly before his death. He wrote this short piece for *Narrative Magazine.*

MAY 1937

I was tall and handsome, raised motherless in an upper-middle-class home, baptized at birth as a Roman Catholic. I'd met Daphne, who was a half-year older, at a French conversation class and was instantly struck by her incandescent beauty. I was also entranced by her unusual name—Daphne, chased by Apollo and turned into a laurel tree sacred to the god of song. My Daphne lived close to the Vienna woods with her parents in the outlying district of Grinzing, famous for vineyards that attracted revelers in search of young wine. It was, and still is, a dreamy place with cobbled streets and baroque villas bordered by masses of lilac bushes. At the time, Daphne was being courted not just by a bevy of young men but also by a budding Austrian film company that had offered her a starring role in *Musik für Dich*, merely because of her looks. Meanwhile, she was escorted to every ball of the season and referred to herself smilingly as Queen of the Waltz. All this I discovered while walking her from our first French lesson to the home of a friend.

In the months that followed, I wooed Daphne with daily letters and flowers until I obtained two tickets to the Opera Ball. It was an event of the sweetest pain, since I could not match Daphne's expertise on the dance floor and had to give her up to other partners. Still, she favored me with a few turns on the crowded floor of the Opera House.

Our dates in Vienna and Grinzing became frequent and more passionate, with kissing and caressing. One wintry night as we moved from bench to bench in a locked embrace along serpentine paths in the park of a former imperial palace, she consented to my plea to make love with her. It would be her first time. Kneeling on the stony path, I swore to be protective and careful.

A few days later, on the night of my nineteenth birthday, I lifted the veil of the goddess in a small hotel in Vienna's fourth district, and gazed with awe at her creamy skin. With tears in her eyes, golden hair on crested pillow, Daphne surrendered. Like the romantic opera fans we were, we drank water from the same crystal goblet, then smashed it, so no one else could drink from the fountain of our love. It was the final scene from Strauss's *Arabella*.

A few months later, on the day Hitler's hordes marched past the Opera House, my father informed me that I had three Jewish grandparents and was, like him, a target for persecution. The news left me, a political know-nothing, stunned. That same afternoon, I had a date with Daphne at our favorite coffeehouse. As I waited, *kaffee mit schlag* untouched, jubilant throngs ran by, waving swastikas and screaming Nazi welcomes. Daphne was late. When suddenly she stood before me, she was wearing an elegant spring suit.

"Isn't it a great day," she exclaimed, kissed me, and ordered coffee.

The waiter responded with a shout: "Heil Hitler!"

I looked at Daphne's beloved face but saw only one thing: in the lapel of her beautiful jacket, there gleamed a gold pin in the shape of a swastika. My world had come to an end.

Now, both age ninety, Daphne and I talk on the phone from New York to Vienna every Sunday about what might have been.

APPENDIX F

Relevant historical information on Austria

THE MOSCOW DECLARATIONS OF 1943 include:

DECLARATION ON AUSTRIA

"The governments of the United Kingdom, the Soviet Union and the United States of America are agreed that Austria, the first free country to fall a victim to Hitlerite aggression, shall be liberated from German domination.

They regard the annexation imposed on Austria by Germany on March 15, 1938, as null and void. They consider themselves as in no way bound by any charges effected in Austria since that date. They declare that they wish to see re-established a free and independent Austria and thereby to open the way for the Austrian people themselves, as well as those neighboring States which will be face with similar problems, to find that political and economic security which is the only basis for lasting peace. Austria is reminded, however that she has a responsibility, which she cannot evade, for participation in the war at the side of Hitlerite Germany, and that in the final settlement account will inevitably be taken of her own contribution to her liberation."

This led to Austria's Second Republic being founded on the idea that the 1938 *Anschluss* was a result of military aggression by the Third Reich, and that Austrian statehood had been interrupted and thus the newly revived Austria of 1945 could not and should not be held responsible for Nazi crimes. This myth of innocence allowed many former Nazis to seamlessly reenter Austrian society. Jews and other victims of Nazism, on the other hand, found their struggles for justice often, and for a long time, unanswered.

A deeply researched book on Viennese Jews trying to reestablish their lives in Vienna in the post-war period is Elizabeth Anthony's THE COMPROMISE OF RETURN.

From the BBC Archives: By Dr Robert Knight
Last updated 2011-02-17

Historical Commission

In 1998 the Austrian *Historikerkommission* (Historical Commission) was set up to examine Austria's role in the expropriation of Jewish assets during the period of Nazi rule in World War Two, and in returning those assets afterwards. On 24 February 2003 it presented its findings to the public. The Commission has spent nearly five million pounds, and employed over 150 researchers, in its mission to comb archives inside and outside the country, concerning events that happened over 50 years ago.

The precise remit given by the government in 1998 was to investigate 'the expropriation of property in the period of Nazi rule (1938-1945), restitution and compensation in the Second Austrian republic and attendant welfare issues'. This may seem narrow in its focus on property issues, but in fact it affected nearly all aspects of Nazi rule and Austrian society. Last but not least, it was also concerned with the image and legitimacy of post-war Austria itself, as a collective victim of a foreign (German-Nazi) occupation.

When the Wehrmacht marched into Austria in 1938 (and Austrian Nazis took over the country 'from below') they fulfilled one of Hitler's life-long ambitions, the 'return' of German-Austria to the Greater German Reich. The pictures of an ecstatic Führer announcing the event in Vienna, and the equally ecstatic crowds who were listening to him, went all round the world at the time. The contemporary impression that the vast majority of Austrians supported the *Anschluss* (the union of Austria and Germany in 1938) was reinforced by the overwhelming endorsement it got in the plebiscite held in April 1938.

How much support the Nazi regime actually enjoyed at the time, and over the following seven years, has been much debated by historians, politicians and journalists ever since. Some suggest that the newsreels were misleading - who, after all, had filmed the people who were silently weeping at home? - and also that the plebiscite result was distorted, due to the attendant propaganda, intimidation and manipulation.

Targets of aggression

What is not in dispute is the intensity of the anti-Semitic aggression that was soon unleashed on Austria's Jews. The German writer Carl Zuckmayer famously described this as the opening of the 'gates of the underworld'. Mobs roved the streets inflicting physical abuse and ritual humiliation (like forced washing of pavements) on anyone suspected of hostility to the new regime.

Austria's Jews, numbering over 200,000 (perhaps as many as 214,000) were a particular object of this outburst. They ranged from those who were very wealthy and highly assimilated into Austrian society, to poor migrants from Eastern Europe. All of them were now actual or potential targets of aggression. Those who did not manage to navigate their way through the thicket of emigration regulations, as they tried to escape from the country, faced an escalation of oppression (especially after the November pogrom of 1938). When flight was no longer possible those remaining in Austria (an estimated 60,000) were deported to concentration camps and murdered. Only a handful survived underground.

As well as the Jews, nearly 10,000 Roma and Sinti (most of whom lived in the province of Burgenland, near the Hungarian border) were deported, and murdered by the Nazis; a range of other ethnic groups (among them Slovenes) and political opponents - from Catholics and conservatives to Communists - were also persecuted, albeit with less perfectionism.Top

Austria as victim?

In Moscow, in October 1943, the Allies decided that Austria should be reestablished as an independent state, once the war was won. At the same time they described Austria as the 'first victim of Hitlerite aggression'. Many of Austria's post-war leaders, after some initial hesitation, took this as a lifeline to help them in the foundation of a post-war project, in which Austria claimed it was not guilty for what had happened in the country during the Nazi years.

An investigation by the Austrian government in 1946 described Austrian suffering under German rule, and Austrian resistance to that rule. It also claimed that only a handful of traitors had collaborated with the Nazis. At the end it demanded 'justice for Austria', by which it meant the speedy end of the Four-Power occupation (in fact this occupation was to last until the State Treaty of 1955).

Using this logic, they suggested that justice - including compensation or reparation - for the victims of Nazi rule was a matter for Germany. The Austrian state could not be held liable. Under pressure from the west (the US in particular) post-war Austrian governments did, however, set up a legal administrative framework for returning some of the property taken from victims of Nazi rule in the course of their persecution.

Seven laws were passed, and the most important of them (the third) established restitution commissions for deciding on the return of expropriated property. Over 40,000 cases, many of which were extremely complex, came before these commissions. Many of them ended in out-of-court settlements, often involving the payment of an additional amount on top of the derisory amount paid after the Anschluss. Further measures followed the signature of the State Treaty, including the collection and realisation of assets for which no owner or heirs had been found.Top

The Waldheim controversy

Throughout this period the charge of 'too little too late' was occasionally levelled at Austria, but it made little impact. Austria was either too small - in international terms - to matter, or it was seen as an enclave of tranquillity and good order (and 'permanent neutrality' between east and west), which ought to be cultivated.

Things began to change in the 1970s, but perhaps the most dramatic turning-point was at the time of the controversy over Kurt Waldheim, the former UN secretary general, who was an Austrian presidential candidate in 1986. Throughout his post-war career Waldheim had concealed or 'forgotten' important details of his military service in World War Two. As his past came to be known, through journalistic investigations and leaks, during his campaign, he spoke of having only 'done his duty' in the German Wehrmacht. It was hardly the comment of a victim of the Nazi regime, and caused a furore within Austria as well as outside it. Nevertheless Waldheim was elected president, and Austria's international standing plummeted.

Domestic reaction to the affair consisted partly of a defiant, partly patriotic, assertion of Austria's right to ignore outside opinion. Other elements almost (or actually) offered an apologia for the 'good side' of the Nazi regime; many of these people were found in the Freedom Party (FPO), along with its rising star Jörg Haider. But the Waldheim affair also prompted heart-searching and self-criticism, especially from the post-war generation. And there was by now a more self-confident Jewish community in Austria, whose members were not prepared to keep quiet, or be intimidated by actual or threatened anti-Semitism.Top

The 'politics of sensibility'

The international climate was also changing through the 1980s and 90s, as a new 'politics of sensibility' developed. A number of disputes over paintings (such as those by Gustav Klimt) revealed their dubious provenance, and thus brought the issue of the expropriation of the property of Jews to a wider public, and the war record of neighbouring Switzerland also came under scrutiny. In response - after some inept initial reactions - the Swiss set up the independent Bergier Commission to investigate their own country's approach to the Third Reich.

And last but not least, 'class actions' on behalf of holocaust victims and forced labourers were started in the US, with the aim of getting compensation and wage payments. So far these have been brought mainly against German companies and banks, achieving, if not massive damages for the claimants, at least legal costs, embarrassment and image problems for those claimed against.

This complex of domestic and foreign factors seems to have persuaded the Austrian government (then a coalition of Social Democrat and People's Party) to set up its *Historikerkommission* in November 1998. From the start there were criticisms that it was a delaying tactic, or state-sponsored whitewash, like the 1946 report referred to above had been.

On the other hand, unlike the latter, its independence was laid down in black and white. Its chairman, Clemens Jabloner, was President of Austria's *Verwaltungsgerichtshof* (Administrative Court), and a leading legal and academic authority. And its other members (including the present writer) were not nominated by the government, but by outside bodies, in a transparent process.

A year after the *Historikerkommission* was set up, Austria hit the international headlines again, when, in 2000, a new coalition government under Wolfgang Schüssel (of the People's Party) brought Jörg Haider's FPO into the corridors of power. The headlines were in reaction to the acceptance or even approval of aspects of national socialism by Haider, and by some of the party's members. An international outcry against the FPO followed, and reactions included French-led 'sanctions', which included the suspending of bilateral cooperation.

As far as Austria's Nazi legacy was concerned, the new government was more than anxious to show itself willing to confront it, and talks over the two main problems - compensation for forced labourers, and outstanding compensation issues for Jewish victims - proceeded at breakneck speed. It was agreed that redress for the loss of rental property (59,000 Vienna flats) should be paid out of the Austrian National Fund.Top

Settling claims

An important agreement was reached in Washington in January 2001, in the closing days of the Clinton administration, in which the Austrian government agreed to pay into a General Settlement Fund, which would be used for settling outstanding claims. The quid pro quo (not yet achieved) was that no more legal claims would be outstanding in the US (thus reaching 'legal peace').

In the light of these events, if at first some had seen the *Historikerkommission* as a delaying tactic, it could now be argued that politics had overtaken research. In fact the commission had helped the progress of negotiations by publishing four interim reports on key issues, made available to all parties and to the public.

The commission's findings run to 14,000 pages, including 53 individual reports and one volume of conclusions. This amount of research cannot be easily summarised. But broadly speaking it shows the involvement of Austrian individuals, groups and institutions in all facets of expropriation of assets from the Jewish community in the Nazi years; from daylight robbery to more subtle forms of expropriation in the name of economic rationality. It also shows how numerous individual Austrians and institutions - from Vienna's Dorotheum auction house to the state (federal, regional and local) - gained as a result of these activities.

The commission described how a machinery was established in Austria in the first post war decade, to provide restitution to the economic victims of the Nazis. And how some survivors had had some success in getting it. For example the owners of businesses that had not been liquidated (these were in the minority, and were generally the larger firms) had quite a good chance. It also helped if the claim involved real estate. Most moveable property simply disappeared and - apart from identifiable works of art - will presumably never be found.Top

The interests of the victims

From the late 1950s funds were set up by the Austrian government, and payments from these offset a proportion of the losses suffered by some victims of the Nazi expropriations. The *Historikerkommission*, however, gave up the idea of providing a balance sheet showing how these figures tallied against what had been taken.

Valuing Jewish assets before the Anschluss, subtracting what was destroyed or removed, calculating what had been returned, and presenting the sum of the outstanding debt was a nice idea, but simply impossible - due to the complexity of the issues, the many price shifts, and the limited reliable source materials (many relevant documents had been shredded).

Even estimating the total pre-Anschluss wealth of Austrian Jews was very difficult - the researchers sponsored by the commission attempted to do this, but their answers ranged between 1,800 and 2,900 million Reichsmark.

Finally, what of the idea that Austria was a victim of Germany? The report does not throw the idea overboard completely. In international law, the Anschluss was an illegal occupation, and many Austrians - not only Jews - suffered under the regime. But the post-war Austrian state extended this legal argument to arrive at a morally dubious and historically untenable denial of liability for what went on in Austria during Nazi rule, for all of Austrian society. Whether this denial was 'functionally necessary' is debatable. At any rate it was not until the 1980s that the state began to put its weight behind the interests of the victims of Nazi rule.

The *Historikerkommission* has now completed its work, but has hardly ended the many controversies about these and related issues. Exactly what political consequences may follow from its publication is unclear - the commission made no explicit recommendations. But the data unearthed by this - for Austria - unprecedented collective historical investigation seems sure to reverberate for some time to come.

The views expressed here are the personal opinions of the writer. The publications of the Historikerkommission *can be found on their* **website** *and are being published in book form by Oldenbourg Verlag (Munich).*

About the author

Robert Knight is a lecturer in European and International Studies at Loughborough University. After a BA in history at Cambridge he wrote a PhD at the London School of Economics on post-war British policy towards occupied Austria. He has published on post-war Austria, denazification, antisemitism, Austria's Slovene minority and aspects of the Cold War. He was a member of the Austrian Historikerkommission (1998-2003).

2020 Amendment regarding Restoration of lost Austrian Citizenship

Beginning 1 September 2020, Austrian Jews and any other Austrian citizens, as well as stateless people and citizens of successor states of Austria-Hungary resident in Austria, who left Austria before 15 May 1955 because they had either suffered persecution by the Nazi regime or had reason to fear such persecution, as well as those who had suffered persecution because of their support of democracy in Austria, or had reason to fear such persecution, have been able to have their citizenship restored, while retaining any other citizenship they have since acquired. In addition, any direct descendants of those persons, including those adopted as minors, are able to claim Austrian citizenship without giving up any existing citizenship, and whether or not their ancestors have regained or claimed Austrian citizenship.

POST-WAR COVERAGE

From NEWSWEEK

Queen of the Danube
The Nazis Killed Vienna's Spirit; Now They Doom Its Beauty to Ruin

'Hunger, Ruins, and Ashes': In the Inner City, beneath the shadow of the 448-foot tower of bomb-damaged St. Stephen's Cathedral, where the bodies of Hapsburg emperors once rested in the underground vaults, there could be heard the wham of Russian guns less than a mile away. The narrow streets of the Inner City, the 150-foot-wide Ringstrasse which surrounds it, and the spacious plazas of the Hofburg were all nearly deserted. The Viennese had fled to the Tyrol or were spending their days in air-raid shelters.

April 16, 1945

2
Queen of the Danube

In Alt Wien: The political and cultural atmosphere of Vienna was the antithesis of Nazism. The Hapsburgs, whatever their faults, had been Hapsburgs first and Germans second. The country they ruled was a conglomeration of many races and Vienna was perhaps the most representatively European of all cities. The shades of Empress Maria Theresa and old Franz Josef still walked in the Hofburg and the Schönbrunn palace. And over the whole city hung the great tra- tough SS generals and onetime head of Hitler's personal bodyguard (Moscow said he had been assassinated). The gauleiter was Baldur von Schirach, once Nazi youth leader. On March 16, Dr. Hans Blaschke, Lord Mayor, announced the Nazi creed: "The greater the destruction of our cities, the more invincible do we become . . . Hunger, ruins, and ashes are the guarantors of our greatness." The Russians called on the city to revolt rather than suffer this fate, and Moscow said it had no territorial claims on Austria.

Thus the final chapter for a great city seemed to have opened. Probably Vienna's fate was first sealed on March 14, 1938, when the Germans marched in. Then the ditions of a universal music—Mozart, Haydn, Beethoven, Schubert, and a host of lesser lights. Even the waltzes from "Der Rosenkavalier" sounded less German when played under the trees of the Prater, Europe's most delightful park.

The way had been paved for the Nazis to end all that by Engelbert Dollfuss, the midget dictator who overthrew the Socialist republic. Dollfuss himself died under Nazi guns; the Jews fled the city; "Heil Hitlers" resounded in the coffee houses, and the Ringstrasse was renamed Josef Bürckel Strasse (after a current gauleiter). Austria officially became the Ostmark—the eastern outpost of the Reich. Now that bastion began to crumble under Russian attack. Vienna, the city the Nazis had already killed spiritually, seemed doomed to be the first part of the bastion to go.

For the Nazis had proclaimed their intention of defending Vienna to the last. The military commander was Col. Gen. Sepp Dietrich, toughest of the tough SS generals and onetime head of Hitler's personal bodyguard (Moscow said he had been assassinated). The gauleiter was Baldur von Schirach, once Nazi youth leader. On March 16, Dr. Hans Blaschke, Lord Mayor, announced the Nazi creed: "The greater the destruction of our cities, the more invincible do we become . . . Hunger, ruins, and ashes are the guarantors of our greatness." The Russians called on the city to revolt rather than suffer this fate, and Moscow said it had no territorial claims on Austria.

Thus the final chapter for a great city seemed to have opened. Probably Vienna's fate was first sealed on March 14, 1938, when the Germans marched in. Then the Nazis immediately set about destroying the spirit of the old Vienna. It jarred them at every turn. Prussians to whom roast goose and potato dumplings represented gastronomical perfection scorned the famous cakes from Sacher's restaurant. The Viennese wines—the Gumboldskirchner, the Nussdorfer, the Ruster—tasted insipid to palates sharpened by the raw-alcohol flavor of schnapps. The dumpy figure of Hitler was dwarfed in the vast rooms of the Imperial Hotel—formerly the palace of the Dukes of Württemberg—where he stayed after his first triumphal entry.

The following YANK MAGAZINE article was published six months after the German surrender and gives an account of post-war Vienna, Austria: the people, the shortages and the black-market. Originally liberated by the Red Army, the Americans occupied the city three months afterward; this is an eyewitness record as to what Vienna was like in the immediate wake of World War II.

Reading between the lines, one gets a sense that the Viennese were simply delighted to see an American occupying force swap places with the Soviet Army, although the Soviets

From YANK
October 5, 1945

YANK
(British Edition): October 5, 1945
p. 8

This Is Vienna

Clearing the wreckage from the streets is a slow job: There is not enough transport to haul it all away.

By Cpl. IRA H. FREEMAN
YANK Staff Correspondent

VIENNA—When advance elements of our occupation troops entered this sadly battered city, once famous as a gay capital of wine, women and song, people poured out into the great boulevards to greet us, not as conquerors but as their own heroes and friends.

"They climbed all over our jeeps and trucks," GIs in that first convoy said. "They hugged us and girls kissed us, just as in Rome and Paris. Whenever we stopped a crowd immediately gathered around each man to welcome him. They would tell you how glad they were to see you, how much they loved America, and how they had always hated Nazis."

The Viennese couldn't shower the GIs with wine, flowers and fruit, as the French did, because the city is out of almost everything. But *frauleins* gave the Americans what they could.

"I never saw anything like it," said a sergeant who had been among those men selected from the de-activated 15th Army Group Headquarters to make up the new United States Forces for Austria. "There's none of that *quanto costa* stuff we had in Italy. These Austrian girls are nice to you out of friendliness. You take them to a cafe to buy them a cup of tea or lemonade and they're happy. If, after you take them home, you like to give them a bar of candy, cake of soap or cigarettes, why, you're a big-time Joe."

Naturally, Americans are taking advantage of their popularity with the natives. But they are a bit wary of this enthusiastic welcome. Of the city's prewar population of 2,000,000, Nazi party membership is said to have totaled 700,000. "Some of them cheered Hitler like this when he marched into Vienna in 1938," a headquarters clerk, previously with the 91st Division, pointed out.

Above all, the Viennese would like us to take over from the Russians, who won the city three months ago. This is part of an open conspiracy among Viennese, particularly the middle and upper classes, to emphasize to American troops that we have "liberated" the city. About the time of the British-French-American entry into Vienna, Russian and American commands were swapping some occupation territory on both banks of the Danube, and the Viennese were disappointed to learn that their city—which they regard even now, as in the past centuries, as a great bulwark of Western Christian culture against Infidel barbarians from the East—wasn't in the exchange. They are downcast when our soldiers tell them that, apart from a small slice administered by the French, Vienna has been divided into approximately equal thirds among the Big Three.

It is not impossible that there was some private looting—similar to GI "liberating"—during the first day or two after the Russian seizure of Vienna, for Red Army patrols searched every house, room by room, for enemy soldiers and Nazis.

In any case, the Russian command soon ended the searches and the Red Army has been supplying food for the Austrian population since. Now, far from robbing the Viennese, the Soviet soldiers are buying what they need, and paying probably the most extravagant prices paid in any country in Europe except Greece.

In the *Karlsplatz* near the Opera House there is a bustling black market. Every day several thousand Viennese can be seen milling about the big square, offering their personal possessions for sale to Russian soldiers and Russian Wacs. The market is illegal, but local Austrian police and Red Army MPs seem to look the other way.

Any article small enough to be carried in the pocket or a shopping bag is likely to change hands. The Russians pay $250 to $800 for a wrist watch, $20 for a cigarette lighter, $30 for a fountain pen, $1,500 for a Leica camera. They buy up cheap jewelry, pen-knives, handkerchiefs, sun glasses. Russian girls go for cotton underwear and stockings, also cloth by the yard.

Some of our guys found a windfall in *Tovarich*.

too, when we entered Vienna. Many of the Russians in town had just been paid off after five years of missing pay days, so their wads of money were so much lettuce to them.

"They jumped all over us," one GI said, "begging us to sell them our watches, cigarette cases, flashlights, anything we had. They dumped hundreds of dollars on us. One Russian ran up to one of our fellows yelling, 'Hey, *Kamerad*,' and forced $300 on him just for nothing."

Our GIs get on okay with the Russkis despite the language barrier. The Red Army soldiers are eager to make friends and often stop us to talk in broken German or sign language. Russian is so difficult that few GIs get beyond *zdrastvuitie* (good day) in that tongue. Red Army men salute our soldiers regardless of grade; apparently they've been briefed, as we were, on this courtesy. The appearance of Soviet troops in Vienna is smarter than that of their units out in the country. Every Russian in the city always goes about armed, while only our sentries and vehicle drivers carry guns.

WHEN our troops entered Vienna they saw that one of the most beautiful cities in the world had been shattered by 22,000 tons of bombs which our planes had dropped on it, by street fighting in which Red Army men captured the place in April, and by fires the *SS* set in retreating.

Of the few people on the street, most were women and old men; the prewar population of 2,000,000 had been much reduced. Most of the buildings had been hit, but the people were still living in the usable parts of the wrecked structures. The wide streets were lined with rubble piles and the only traffic was military.

The scene of the most terrible desolation is the *Prater*, famous amusement and sports park, where *SS* troops made a last-stand defense for the city against the Russians who forced crossings of the Danube. There is scarcely one stone left on another in the *biergarten*, carousels and dance halls. A blackened and twisted ferris wheel rears starkly over the ruins like a fantastic war memento. In this and all the other parks and squares in Vienna today are the graves of Red Army men killed in the battle for the city, mounds topped not by crosses but by Soviet stars carved in wood or chiseled in marble. A huge bronze-and-marble monument to the Red Army is going up in *Schwarzenberg Garten*; it looks mighty permanent.

were not nearly as brutal to this capital as they were to Berlin.

Our men found no souvenirs to buy. In any case, the command forbade all troops to purchase anything except drinks—and there were scarcely any drinks. Outside of the black market there is little business of any kind in Vienna today. On boarded-up shop fronts are pinned handwritten notices of things people want to barter. Only a few shops are open, and those only for perhaps three days a week.

The Viennese have been undernourished for years, and they look it. Now they are close to starvation. The shelves of butcher shops and bakeries are empty. Delicatessens may have only a few bags of ersatz coffee. Full daily rations for a worker are 10½ ounces of bread, 1¼ ounces of meat, ¼ ounce of cooking oil, 2 ounces of beans and 1 ounce of sugar. Non-workers get even less.

The schools have been shut for at least a month because of malnutrition and disease among the pupils. Viennese get an average of 900 calories contrasted with the 2,000 required daily for health. The reasons for the food shortage are lack of transportation to bring the food in from the country, damage to agriculture by the fighting, and military requisitions. The lack of transport is so acute that some people hike 20 miles into the country once a week to buy potatoes and vegetables from farmers. Added to the shortage of food and transport is a lack of coal, which also means no cooking gas. So every day in the beautiful Vienna woods, celebrated in Strauss waltzes, thousands of aged people are collecting wood for stoves and painfully trudging the miles back home with towering loads on their backs. People also may be seen rummaging through rubbish piles in the streets for useful junk.

On empty stomachs the Viennese are trying to carry on their traditional gay night life. Although Special Services produced nothing in the first few weeks and the Red Cross had not even appeared, there was some entertainment for a few of the first American troops to reach here.

ON a representative week day there are now 53 movies (Russian, old American and German films, with German sound tracks and titles), 16 plays and musical shows, 3 cabarets, one opera and one concert running in the city. Admission prices are reasonable, and even though every place is

3

GIs are popular with civilians, but the capital of Austria is a far cry today from its storied past of gaiety, love and song.

This is one of the surviving cafes, once the centers of Viennese culture.

always sold out, proprietors will always make room for one of their favorite soldiers.

The Cafe Victoria on *Schottenring*, not far from the headquarters-company billet and a typical Vienna coffee house of today, became a favorite GI hangout right away. The clientele is quite cosmopolitan. In one hour there you meet not only American, British and Russian soldiers but Czechs, Yugoslavs, Poles, Greeks and Dutch civilians, in addition to the Viennese. All the foreign civilians there are displaced persons of some kind, awaiting shipment home. The place is full of people sitting at small tables. Admission is five *schillings*, or about 50 cents. Corny vaudeville goes on first for about an hour and a half—singers and dancers and native comedians GIs can't understand.

Then the older folk in the audience leave, and the remaining customers take over for dancing. The floor is so jam-packed with couples that it is impossible to do much more than wiggle in rhythm. The air is as hot and smoky as any jive joint in Chicago or Memphis.

AND the music is almost as groovy as American jazz, although it's funny to hear hot licks sung in German. "St. Louis Blues" gets the crowd jumping, and everybody joins in "Hold that tiger!" Our GIs wonder what's become of the "Blue Danube" and "Merry Widow" waltzes. In their first weeks in Vienna they heard plenty of American jazz, but never *Wienerwalzer*.

About the Viennese *frauleins* there are two schools of GI thought. Some prefer them to Italian girls because "they keep themselves cleaner, are better dressed and can speak English," while others say there are more pretty chicks in Italy and the *signorina* is a hotter number, too. The typical Viennese girl is fair skinned and blonde. She looks a little worn, and a scarcity of make-up doesn't help. Lipstick or even face powder on the girls is a rare sight.

Regulations allow American troops to fraternize only in public places, which means you can't go home with a girl. But during the first few weeks there were scarcely any of our MPs in town, so nobody knew the difference.

All the cafes and theaters close in the shank of the evening, 8:30 Vienna time or 10:30 Allied time, which is curfew for civilians. Military personnel may stay out until midnight our time. So far every place is on limits to everybody. Enlisted men are free to go anywhere in the city without a pass whenever they're not on duty.

During the first weeks we were in Vienna there wasn't much else to do except hang around the cafes and date *frauleins*. The Army took over a fine swimming pool in Bad Neuwaldegg in the hills a short way out of town, but August is the rainy season and you can't swim every day. The Army also plans to have some night clubs later, like those in Rome. Vienna after dark isn't romantic today. The rubbled streets are dim and deserted, and our men are cautioned against wandering about at night. The air is not filled as formerly with the melodies of Mozart, Schubert, Haydn, Beethoven and Lehar. From the Russian billet you may hear an accordion playing—of all things—"Beer Barrel Polka."

www.ingramcontent.com/pod-product-compliance
Lightning Source LLC
LaVergne TN
LVHW081316060526
838201LV00006B/182